WITHDRAWN

The Utopian Nexus
in *Don Quixote*

The Utopian Nexus
in *Don Quixote*

Myriam Yvonne Jehenson
& Peter N. Dunn

Vanderbilt University Press

Nashville

10 09 08 07 06   1 2 3 4 5

Printed on acid-free paper.
Manufactured in the United States of America

Publication of this book has been supported by a generous subsidy
from the Program for Cultural Cooperation between Spain's Ministry
of Culture and United States Universities.

Library of Congress Cataloging-in-Publication Data

Jehenson, Myriam Yvonne.
The utopian nexus in Don Quixote /
Myriam Yvonne Jehenson and Peter N. Dunn.—1st ed.
p. cm.
Includes bibliographical references and index.
ISBN 0-8265-1517-7 (cloth : alk. paper)
ISBN 0-8265-1518-5 (pbk. : alk. paper)
1. Cervantes Saavedra, Miguel de, 1547–1616. Don Quixote.
2. Utopias in literature.   I. Dunn, Peter N. II. Title.
PQ6353.J45 2006
863'.6—dc22   2005023119

Contents

Acknowledgments

In the course of the years that it has taken us to write this book, many friends and colleagues have asked us to explain what we were doing. As we strove to present our project in brief terms, they enabled us to clarify our ideas, to note lacunae, and to sharpen our arguments. We are grateful to them, though they may be unaware of how they helped and encouraged us. Various themes and sections of our project have been presented to academic audiences, including the Modern Language Association of America and Oxford, Hartford, and Vanderbilt universities, and we have benefited from the discussions that ensued on those occasions.

We owe a deep debt of gratitude to Hertford College, Oxford, for a Visiting Fellowship; to the University of Hartford, Connecticut, for facilitating the fellowship and to the Rockefeller Foundation for a residency at the Villa Serbelloni Research Center in Bellagio, Italy, where we presented our preliminary draft.

Our research has been greatly assisted by the eagerness and dedication of the staffs of the libraries where we have worked: the Bodleian and the Taylorian Libraries in Oxford; the Hispanic Society of America in New York; and the library of Wesleyan University in Middletown, Connecticut, whose interlibrary loan staff came to our rescue more than once.

Our thanks go to Anthony Close of Cambridge University for his detailed critical comments on an early draft. As a result, we present a more nuanced argument. In the same vein, we are particularly grateful to the two anonymous readers of Vanderbilt University Press for their extensive comments, one of whom raised important questions of organization for our consideration. And we acknowledge the continued support and friendly encouragement of Edward Friedman, Donna Randall, and Marcia Welles.

We have enjoyed an especially cooperative relationship with the Vanderbilt University Press, in particular with Betsy Phillips and Dariel Mayer. Special thanks go to the copyeditor David Ramsey for his meticulous combing of the text.

Finally, we would be remiss if we failed to mention Kaitlin Walsh, a graduate student at the University of Hartford, who has cheerfully handled all of our technical difficulties in word processing on different machines with her usual intelligence, alacrity, and skill.

Note on the Cited Texts

All citations in Spanish from Cervantes's *Don Quixote*, unless otherwise noted, are taken from Miguel de Cervantes Saavedra, *El ingenioso hidalgo Don Quijote de la Mancha,* in the edition by Francisco Rico and Joaquín Foradellas, 2 vols. Barcelona: Crítica, 1998. The English translations, unless otherwise noted, are taken from *Miguel de Cervantes: Don Quixote*, translated by Edith Grossman, New York: Harper Collins, 2003. Citations from *Don Quixote* are noted by part, chapter, and page. For example, Part II, chapter 51, page 795 would be cited: II:51, 795. Page references are to the English version first, followed by the Spanish. In most cases, the quotation in Spanish, in brackets, follows the English. When only one page reference is given, we refer to the English translation. Translations from other works are our own unless stated otherwise.

Preface

The idea for this book came about after many readings of *Don Quixote*, in the course of which we were always fascinated and intrigued by one particular episode: Camacho's wedding in Part II, chapter 20. The source of our fascination was not the course of events that take place there, but rather the lavish material circumstances and the truly gargantuan scale of Camacho's wedding feast. Out of proportion with the everyday details that appear in the rest of the novel, it also goes far beyond any verisimilar representation. This book is the result of our asking about the significance of the sudden and temporary change of scale.

We were also intrigued by the fact that the wedding is the one occasion in which Sancho Panza finds his creaturely desires satisfied to the full, an anticipation of the style of living in which he would like to be installed on his promised *ínsula*. Our curiosity turned to serious investigative inquiry as we placed Sancho's evident delight in, and subsequent nostalgia for, this landscape of abundance in counterpoise to Don Quixote's evocation of an age of virtuous frugality. So we condensed into two opposing and complementary traditional myths the two protagonists' desire for satiety: for Sancho the myth of abundance, for Don Quixote one of simple wants. Both desires nevertheless are based on mythic worlds where satisfaction is guaranteed. For Don Quixote it is the illusion of a world of limited appetites, of sober satisfactions, and of nostalgia for a pre-social golden age of communitarian freedom from rule. For Sancho it is a world of easy money and leisure. Their desires evoke, respectively, Arcadia and Cockaigne.

Each of these myths has a history which we have attempted to trace;

each occupies a definable ideological and discursive field; and each represents aspirations at different social levels. Together, the myths are as bonded within the society's structure of desires as are Don Quixote and Sancho Panza within their shared textual space. We have set ourselves the task of exploring these fields, mapping their incidence in Cervantes's novel, and uncovering their resonances by situating them within the intellectual, legal, and political currents and cross-currents of Spain in the late sixteenth and early seventeenth centuries.

In a book titled *The Utopian Nexus,* it will perhaps be helpful to explain what we mean by "utopian." Our use does not restrict the adjective to nostalgia for the mythic pasts the protagonists experience, although it does include that nostalgia. It encompasses the notion of contemporary social realities that find resonances in the fictional work, but have been altered, as Luis Murillo showed many years ago in *The Golden Dial* (1974), due to the springtime/summer cycle of the chivalric romance which *Don Quixote* purports to be.[1] The result of this alteration, especially in Part I, renders contemporary realities conventional, stylized, and "utopian" in the sense that they become devoid of overtly political nuances.

In the rural setting of Part I, Don Quixote can *perform* as a knight-errant. When he cannot control the vicissitudes of external reality, he can simply refuse to test the "magical" transformations he has brought about (I:1; I:21). And when nothing else works he can always blame his fictional enchanters. Critics have consistently spoken of the reality of the Spanish inns, mountains, and roads in *Don Quixote* that are where one would expect to find them. The action itself unfolds among places whose names are readily found on our maps—Puerto Lápice, Argamasilla, Campo de Montiel, Toboso, Sierra Morena, Toledo, and Barcelona. The characters encounter real institutions of contemporary Spain in the officers of the Santa Hermandad. We are reminded of the oppressive heat of Spanish summers (I:2) and of the social tensions that exist between different strata of society: laborers like Sancho Panza complain about the hunger experienced as part of their lot and insist continually on prosaic realities that are wholly irrelevant to the hidalgo. The fulling-mills that frighten Sancho in Part I are appropriately located beside running water and could conceivably scare any stranger who, like him,

---

1. We were recently reminded of this by Anthony Close.

becomes lost in the dark. Both protagonists are routinely pummeled as a result of their anomalous behavior: Sancho is tossed in a blanket; Don Quixote loses an ear and most of his teeth; prostitutes, thieves, and violent men exist among the lowlife that the pair encounter in the inns; there is vindictive cruelty in the Andrés-Juan Haldudo incident (I:4); there is a "real" suicide in the Arcadian bower (I:11–15); there is bitter ingratitude displayed by the liberated galley slaves (I:22); there are, for current and contemporary readers, reminders in the captive's tale of a painful historical reality the author himself experienced (I:39–41); and there are real class differences that jeopardize the happiness of young Clara and Don Luis, and of which all who hear their tale are fully aware (I:43). But such "realities," and their more serious consequences, are palliated through humor. During some of the most violent pummeling of Don Quixote in Part I, the narrator tells us that the "canon and the priest doubled over with laughter, the officers of the Brotherhood jumped up and down with glee, and everyone sicced them on as if they were dogs involved in a fight" (I:52, 439–40) ["Reventaban de risa el conónigo y el cura, saltaban los cuadrilleros de gozo, zuzaban los unos y los otros, como hacen a los perros cuando en pendencia están trabados" (584)]; the knight's supposed friend, the barber, even "helped the goatherd to hold Don Quixote down and rain down on him so many blows that the poor knight's face bled as heavily as his adversary's" (I:52, 439) ["el barbero hizo de suerte que el cabrero cogió debajo de sí a don Quijote, sobre el cual llovió tanto número de mojicones, que del rostro del pobre caballero llovía tanta sangre como del suyo" (584)]. Such "realities" seem to be part of comic decorum and function as part of the knight's distorted view of the world. The narrator tells us, for example, that in all these instances, Don Quixote "considered himself fortunate, for it seemed to him that this was the kind of mishap that befell knights errant" (I:4, 41). It is in this restricted sense, then, that we refer to Part I as "eutopian." This will not be the case in Part II, in which both protagonists will be made to face severe crises in the urban world that is there mirrored.

Once Cervantes changes his protagonists' direction from Saragossa to Barcelona in Part II, the text describes a "real" world of urban power and institutional violence in Barcelona and at the ducal palace. In such a world Don Quixote's functional mechanisms of disavowal are impotent. He swings from moments of euphoric validation at the ducal palace to perplexed frustration as his "enchanters" wound him ever more deeply. Not content with merely walling up his library, or turning armies into flocks of sheep, they now strike at the heart of his knightly identity by "enchanting" his lady. And he is forced to become dependent on an illiterate and devious peasant who will deceive him, exploit him, and finally humiliate him.

This is the reason why in studying Part II we use neither the terms "eu-topian" nor "u-topian"—terms that we have used for sections of Part I—for social realities function differently here. In Part II (although limited examples can also be found in Part I), the text uses social realities in order to juxtapose what Louis Marin calls, in another context, the utopian *discourse* to the utopian *fantasy*. It is this theory that enables our study. Marin distinguishes between utopian fantasy and utopian discourse or practice. He describes the former, utopian fantasy, as a finished product with its own spatial and temporal coordinates.[2] The latter, the utopian discourse, on the other hand, he sees as a kind of *processual* practice, not as a mode of representation. The text seeks to alter or transform the real world in the literary work, thereby "neutralizing" it in the process of setting up the utopian fantasy. But, at the same time, the utopian discourse's "obsessive references to actuality" (*Utopics* 7), that is, to the real world outside the text, expose not only "the historical and ideological contradiction" that lies behind the fantasy constructed (62), but the "absent term," that is, the figure of that real world that the text has sought to alter (196). A text, then, may seem to elide everyday reality through a utopic or mythical fantasy conjured by its characters, alluded to by its author through the narrator, or evoked by the romantic description of its setting. The utopian discourse, on the other hand, which may also be composed of the narrative, the narratorial interventions, the characters' sayings, or/and the actions in a novel, ironizes and interrogates the fantasy that has been textually constructed. To paraphrase the use Cervantes's friend makes of an old saying in the

---

2. Edward Baker concurs in seeing utopias as mental constructs independent of functional implementation: "Like God and abstract painting, utopias are metatextual by definition, since they are constituted by a body of signs that, lacking a strictly denotative function, create a self-sufficient reality." ["Las utopías, lo mismo que Dios y la pintura abstracta, son por definición metatextuales, puesto que las constituye un conjunto de signos que, al carecer de funciones estrictamente denotativas, crean una realidad autotélica" (Baker 135)].

Prologue, under cover of its cloak, the utopian discourse can actually subvert the fantasy ("under cover of my cloak I can kill the king" (3–4) ["debajo de mi manto, al rey mato" (10)].

In a fine analysis of the work of Jules Verne, Pierre Macherey has shown how figuration, as he explains below, can actually be incompatible with a text's manifest representation (191): "Figuration is something rather more than representation," Macherey explains, "since it is a question of devising, or at least collecting, the visible signs in which this important adventure can be read: the *reading* of these signs will give a certain representation of the project but it is necessary first to *discover the signs*" (175: emphasis added). The signs need not have been intended by a given author. They may have "intruded without his knowledge from his direct grasp" (Macherey 199). In this study, the term utopian *discourse* will be used in this way—to indicate a polyvalent and critical discourse whose recurrent topical allusion to the real world, implicitly or explicitly, consciously or unconsciously, keeps the absent term (the real) ever present in the utopian *fantasy.* Its effect is to cast doubt on the fantasy as a self-sufficient reality.[3]

As we have said, this is especially the case in Part II of *Don Quixote,* where the utopian discourse functions as a stratagem—at times deliberate, at times unconscious—to question the utopian fantasy that has been set up either in the text, by the narrator, or by the characters. As a result, the utopian discourse fractures the smooth utopian surface of the narrative. Though it is prevalent in Part II, Cervantes also uses this stratagem in Part I of the novel. We are speaking here of something more subtle than the narrator's mirthful noting of the madness of the knight as he prepares for adventure in chapter 1, and as he attempts to transform reality through the lens of his chivalric books throughout the novel. To give but one example: Don Quixote speaks in Part I of the values of the Arcadian golden world. It is an important speech for in it he spells out the values of that lost age which, for the knight, the original

---

3. This is similar to, though not identical with, Roger Chartier's reminder that though a book "always aims at installing an order, a distance exists in the dialectic between imposition and appropriation." Consequently, "[w]orks—even the greatest works, especially the greatest works—have no stable, universal, fixed meaning. They are invested with plural and mobile significations that are constructed in the encounter between a proposal and a reception" (*The Order of Books* preface, pp. viii-ix).

order of chivalry was instituted to resurrect. These are the values Don Quixote claims enable his own chivalric exploits. The utopian discourse, however, is made to question the utopian fantasy. It allows the reader to see what lies beneath Don Quixote's expressed desire to resurrect the golden age of Chivalry in compensation for the loss of the Age of Gold. That is, a return to hierarchical values (not his avowed egalitarian values), and to the overt power and fame the old hidalgo seeks in his more covert need to restore the values of an aristocratic chivalric order that the historical decline of his class has denied him. The text thus puts in question both the selflessness of the egalitarian pre-historical golden world whose values Don Quixote sets up as exemplary, and the altruism of the subsequent historical chivalric age in which he intends to "right wrongs" ["desfacer agravios"].

As contemporary realities, though altered, are recognizable beneath the utopian façade of *Don Quixote*, so juridical issues of the time resonate in Don Quixote's nostalgic speech on the Golden Age. That is, issues which are focused upon by reformers and legists of the times— the necessity of egalitarian values in a society now divided between the haves and the have-nots, and the return to a model of humanity's primordial condition supposedly marked by natural justice and freedom from judgment and authority. These resonances add historical depth to Don Quixote's operating reasons. They do not attenuate the insanity of his acts.

For us, unlike José Antonio Maravall (*Utopía y contrautopía en el "Quijote"*), the irony (or lack of irony) in the utopian discourse's treatment of these issues is more difficult to determine. Maravall argues that Cervantes debunks the idealism of contemporary reformers. We would not subscribe to such a view. It is not that we deem his argument without substance, but that the irony of Cervantes's book precludes any such affirmation of Cervantes's intentions. Our analysis is less simple and has as its premise that any text, because it is written at a specific historical moment, necessarily resonates with the crises and contradictions of the historical moment that has produced it.

We discuss Sancho's utopian fantasy in terms contrapuntal to Don Quixote's classical Golden Age and to his aristocratic chivalric order. Sancho's fantasy in following the hidalgo includes experiencing a world wider than his peasant existence has heretofore allowed, stuffing his belly, eventually lining his pockets, living undisturbed in leisure, and having himself and his family titled. These are, after all, what his master has promised him. Some of these delusions, especially that of eating well, begin as merely a fuzzy chivalric promise of an *ínsula*, but take substantial shape for Sancho in six instances in Part II: in the home of Don Diego de Miranda (II:18), at Camacho's Wedding (II:20–21), in Basilio and Quiteria's home (II:22), in the ducal palace (II:30–57), in the island of Barataria (II:45–53), and in the home of Don Antonio Moreno (II:62, 1133). The myth to which we resort in addressing Sancho's fantasy, unlike the hidalgo's, is implied rather than explicitly stated in *Don Quixote*. It is the fantasy of the plebeian Cockaigne, a pan-European myth which was given enhanced currency at the time as a result of the marvelous tales circulating in Spain of the "golden worlds" of the Americas—especially of the *Tierra de Jauja* that the Spaniards had actually found in Peru. As Eugenio Asensio affirms when writing about Lope de Rueda's *paso* with that title:

> The land of Jauja brings up to date the medieval tale of the land of Cockaigne, transplanting it onto the American continent where the discovery of Jauja had prompted a smart rhymester to give new life to the myth. Several chapbooks evoke that dream of empty bellies always on the move: the garden where trees produce cooked delicacies, rivers overflow with wine and honey, and life is all idleness and endless feasting.

> [La tierra de Jauja moderniza la conseja medieval de la tierra de Cucaña, transplantándola al continente americano donde el descubrimiento de Jauja había espoleado a un coplero astuto a remozar el mito. En varios pliegos de cordel se nos evoca aquel sueño de vientres hambrientos, de panzas al trote: el jardín donde árboles producen manjares cocinados, los ríos desbordan de vino y miel y la vida es holganza y banquete perenne. (47)]

It will be at Camacho's Wedding Feast, as we shall see in chapter 4, that Sancho's desire for "hot food and cold drinks" (II:51, 795) ["comer caliente, beber frío" (1051)] will begin literally to be made flesh.

1

Discursive Hybridity
Don Quixote's and Sancho Panza's Utopias

It is a given of social theory that no discursive field is homogeneous. It produces different meanings and subjectivities, exposes conflicts and contradictions, and thereby enables new forms of knowledge and practice to emerge. Nowhere does this truism become more apparent than in the sixteenth century, when new realities exposed ancient discourses that were once held to be indisputable and not open to contradiction. Nicolaus Copernicus seemed literally to turn the Ptolemaic world upside down by moving the sun to the center of the universe: "In the middle of all sits the sun enthroned" (quoted in Boas 81); and Andreas Vesalius's dissection of human bodies revealed systemic inaccuracies in Galen, the most respected of medical authorities. Already in the fourteenth and fifteenth centuries the views of ancient writers had begun to be challenged, but by the middle of the sixteenth century Vesalius could write, in 1542, that "those who are now dedicated to the ancient study of medicine, almost restored to its pristine splendour in many schools, are beginning to learn to their satisfaction how little and how feebly men have laboured in the field of Anatomy from the time of Galen to the present day" (quoted in Boas 129). The Jesuit José de Acosta, on passing the Torrid Zone and finding it cold and not, as Aristotle had said, scorching, would exclaim, "[w]hat could I do then but laugh at Aristotle's *Meteorology* and his philosophy?" (quoted in Grafton 1).

The Reformation had already shaken the roots of the Church's certainties. And no less unsettling was the fact that many of these new realities had been discovered not by traditional Scholastics, nor by the hermeneutical tools of the Humanists, but often through empirical

1

evidence. The invention of the printing press, which had furthered the acquisition of ancient knowledge, now became crucial in promulgating awareness of the contradictions between the old and the new. It also made available to a wider audience the early modern age's challenges to ancient theories in mathematical geography and astronomical methods. The authority of revered books, then, seemed to be sharply challenged everywhere. And it is from this world of change that Don Quixote emerges still holding on to the same—the absolute truth of his treasured books.

It would be incorrect to say, however, that the century's "new" learning wholly supplanted the "old." In fact, as Anthony Grafton points out, these scientific thinkers were "no intellectual radicals." They "used classical precedents as well as modern evidence to support their iconoclastic enterprises" (Grafton 115). The same can be said of legists and reformists of the century. As we shall see below, Spanish theologians, philosophers, and lawyers will blend Biblical narratives, the tradition of the Church Fathers, pagan myths, and historical precedent in dealing with questions of legal theory, ethics, and history in the century.

One of the issues that would be heavily impacted in this heady intellectual age was the ongoing question of the originary condition of humankind, which the discoveries of the Indies (as the Americas were then referred to) had intensified. Since the "barbari" were not civilized, how was their condition to be categorized? Were "barbari" natural slaves, as Aristotle had maintained, or were they "educable?" As such, could they be Christianized? This question spawned others. Since the "barbari" had never been exposed to civilization, could they be said to be living in a state analogous to the original condition of our first parents? Could the lost Eden itself, which scholars, theologians, and folklore never affirmed to have disappeared altogether, be found in this New World, as Columbus believed? Traces of these contemporary conflicts will be discernible in *Don Quixote*. The fact that they are often refracted and distorted in the discourse of a madman does not make them less relevant to our study.

Don Quixote, then, is a product of an age of hybridity,[1] in which the

---

1. We use the term "hybridity" as it is formulated by Homi K. Bhabha in *The Location of Culture*. For Bhabha, the notion of "hybridity" constitutes the process of "remaking the boundaries" of a culture, of "exposing the limits of any claim to a singular or autonomous sign of difference" (219). It is the "hybrid gap" (58),

experience of practical men enlarged and challenged knowledge once restricted to scholars. It was an age in which feudalism yielded to capitalism, in which the wealth of merchants created possibilities of acquiring titles once reserved to aristocrats, a period in which the views of the ancients were both challenged and employed in explaining the new and the experimental. This cultural polyphony resonates throughout Cervantes's novel.

When Don Quixote loses his wits (I:1), he decides to "become a knight errant and travel the world with his armor and his horse to seek adventures and engage in everything he had read that knights errant engaged in . . ." (I:1, 21) ["hacerse caballero andante y irse por todo el mundo con sus armas y caballo a buscar las aventuras y a ejercitarse en todo aquello que él había leído que los caballeros se ejercitaban" (40–41)]. But what does this notion of *adventure*, so inclusive for Don Quixote and for Sancho Panza, convey?

In *Ideology of Adventure*, Michael Nerlich has sketched a history of the transformations of the idea of adventure as a program for living. Following Mikhail Bakhtin, Nerlich points out that in the literature of classical antiquity, the hero's adventures are ordeals prescribed by the gods (4). In the middle ages, on the other hand, a new conception arises. The "essential hallmark" is that "adventures are undertaken on a *voluntary* basis . . . (*la quête de l'aventure*, 'the quest for adventure*') thereby glorifying both the quest and the adventurer himself (5: emphasis his). Nerlich marks the contrast between the classical and the medieval heroic adventure thus: "*Aventure*, which in its literary ocurrences before the courtly romance means fate, chance, has become, in the knightly-courtly system of relations, an event that the knight must seek out and endure, although this event does continue to be unpredictable, a surprise of fate" (5).

The knight, then, *seeks* adventure. He is not a pawn in the hands of a god, nor merely instrumental in fulfilling the god's plan. The element of obligation nevertheless remains, now internalized as part of the

---

the third or "*in-between* space that carries the burden of the meaning of culture" (38: emphasis his). It is in this Third Space that "cultural differences 'contingently' and conflictually touch" (207). For a fascinating account of how contingently and conflictually the "new" discoveries touched the methods and theories of the "old," see Grafton.

whole system of courtly values, of what it means to be a knight. Hence the medieval knight is obliged by his courtly code to seek, like Parzifal, the Holy Grail, or to fight, like Gawain, the Green Knight. In the case of Don Quixote, however, adventure consists of two phases. One is the personal, freely chosen, adventure in which Quijada, Quesada, or Quijana transforms himself, creates a new persona, leaves his village, and embarks on a new life. The other is the knight-errantry which he adopts. The latter carries with it the duty to seek the kinds of adventure that from time to time he enumerates: to rescue damsels in distress, to humble proud giants, and so forth.

We are particularly interested in the first phase in which the country hidalgo transforms himself and leaves home. To embark freely on an adventure, as Don Quixote does, is to create a new and ideal space, a compatible setting within which desire and fantasy can take shape. In exceeding the commonly accepted and limited notion of what constitutes an adventure, that is, by transforming his entire life into an adventure, Don Quixote extends an ideal space into a world lived without temporal or spatial horizons. In the relevant words of Georg Simmel's elegant phenomenological essay, "The Adventure," "the most general form of adventure is its dropping out of the continuity of life" (243). While it forms a part of our whole existence, adventure "occurs outside the usual continuity of this life" (243).

The structural relation of adventure to life, then, is homologous with that of a dream sequence because adventure is "bound to the unified, consistent life-process by fewer threads than are ordinary experiences" (Simmel 244), and when recalled later it seems dreamlike. The "more fully [the adventure] realizes its idea, the more dreamlike it becomes in our memory" (244). Unlike the ordinary incidents in our everyday lives, an adventure is independent of "before" and "after." It is literally *out of* the ordinary, and so is the adventurer. Analogues of the adventurer for Simmel include the artist and the gambler. The former because his work of art "cuts out a piece of the endlessly continuous sequences of perceived experience" (245), the latter because, in the process of gambling, he has "abandoned himself to the meaninglessness of chance" (246).

Like Bakhtin's chivalric hero, Don Quixote "can live only in this world of miraculous chance, for only it preserves his identity. And the very code by which he measures his identity is calibrated precisely to this world of miraculous chance" (Bakhtin, *Dialogic* 152). Like Simmel's gambler, Don Quixote needs "to draw chance into his teleological system by means of omens and magical aids, thus removing it from its inaccessible isolation and searching in it for a lawful order, no matter how fantastic the laws of such an order may be" (246). In *Don Quixote*, both knight and squire are made to function within such a teleological system regulated by omens and magical aids.

In a geographically imprecise setting ("in a village of La Mancha whose name I am not about to tell you" [our translation] (I:1, 13) ["un lugar de la Mancha de cuyo nombre no quiero acordarme" (35)], an hidalgo emulates his chivalric heroes in creating for himself "*a miraculous world in adventure-time* (Bakhtin, *Dialogic* 154: emphasis his). His actions are allowed to unfold largely among roads and inns that provide insular settings in which he can transform reality by means of "magical aids" into the feudal chivalric past he wishes to resurrect. In his self-created world an illiterate laborer can not only become a knight's squire, but be promised a governorship. Even in the urban setting of Part II, disillusionments can still be subjected, though less successfully, to the knight's teleological system of omens and magic: the "enchantment" of Dulcinea, the unfulfilled "adventure" of the Enchanted Boat (II:29), the humiliating *burlas* to which Don Quixote and Sancho are subjected in the ducal palace, to name three salient examples.

In Part I, traces of the social and material problems of the time in which the book is written, though present, are more nuanced and stylized since they do not occasion serious self doubt for Don Quixote the adventurer. Part I, especially in the mind of the knight (but certainly not in the world he traverses), is suggestive of the subtext that Henry Ettinghausen finds to be active throughout the novel. Ettinghausen has characterized it as the "nostalgic praise of a utopian communistic mythic past" ["la alabanza nostálgica de un mítico pasado utópico-comunista,"] of which "the most outstanding characteristic is . . . precisely the absence of the idea and the sense of private prosperity in the power of money" ["la característica más distintiva . . . es precisamente la ausencia del concepto y sentimiento de la prosperidad privada en el poder del dinero" (27)]. Thus, Don Quixote's nostalgic evocation of a golden age before the notions of "mine" and "thine" prevailed is wholly discordant with the real economic extremes between the haves and the have-nots that are subtly alluded to and which, as we shall see in chapter 6, are insistently repeated in theological and *arbitrista* treatises of the time. In Part II, on the other hand, the protagonists on the road to Barcelona, and in Barcelona itself, will be exposed to armed bandits, to corpses of hanged men, and to brutal realities of power and corruption over which they have no control.

Nostalgias for utopia are of course always indicative of crises in the contemporary context from which such nostalgias emerge. To cite Carlo Ginsburg: "Only in periods of acute social change does an image emerge, generally a mythical one, of a different and better past; a model of perfection in the light of which the present appears to be a deterioration, a degeneration . . . The struggle to transform the social order then becomes a conscious attempt to return to this mythical past" (77–78). But for most of Part I such crises are either under erasure or palliated by comic decorum. References to the natural catastrophes at the end of the sixteenth century, for example, are passed over throughout the novel: the famine, the floods of the period 1596–1602 whose aftermath augmented the century's already-dismal economic and social tensions, and the plagues that entered northern Spain in 1596 and spread southward reaching Andalucía in 1599. In Seville alone, the bubonic plague claimed 8,000 victims, and its total casualties may have reached a half million out of a Castilian population of about six million. Unmentioned are the consequent increase in the depopulation of the land, the unrest in the towns, the "[l]ittle Ice Age which resulted in years of cold and wet summers" (Geoffrey Parker 17–28), and the hardships which continued through the next decade (Lynch, *Hispanic World* 6–11; Domínguez Ortiz 68–70).

In the mind of the chivalric knight of Part I, a skinny old nag can become a knight's noble stallion through naming; forgotten rusty armor and shield knightly accoutrements through the application of cardboard and paste; and a humble village girl the lofty Princess Dulcinea through the transformed hidalgo's wishing it so.[2] In the still chivalric setting fabricated by the Duke and Duchess in the palace of Part II, a setting equally unbounded by specific temporal or spatial horizons, the aged hidalgo, in poor health (II:18, 568; Rico 772), can nevertheless see himself recognized as an energetic knight-errant, and so alluring

2. For Murillo, repeated by Rico, the humor is enhanced by the incongruous fact that this princess lives in a *pueblo* that is far from "lofty," one in which the majority of the inhabitants are Moorish.

that "girls only have to look at me and love sweeps them away!" (II:44, 745) ["no ha de haber doncella que me mire que de mí no se enamore!" (990)]. And an illiterate peasant can aspire to being a count (II:65, 890; Rico 1163), and can eventually become a wise governor, leaving constitutions named after him (II:51, 797; Rico 1053).

The transformation of Aldonza Lorenzo into Dulcinea is of course not random but necessary once the hidalgo, now Don Quixote, chooses to seek adventure. In the chivalric *vita nuova* that Don Quixote has created for himself, love must have its place. And it must be love of the courtly kind. Through it, he will perfect himself as a knight in service to his lady. Love becomes a spiritual ordeal: adventure and love "seem . . . to stand in a symbiotic relation, [with] love inspiring the adventures that make a knight worthy of love" (Bloch 141). Both adventure and love, then, serve to isolate the individual from the particular community to which he belongs, for "[l]ove conceived as an obsession with another serves to sever the individual's bond with society" (Bloch 141). By embracing adventure as a way of life, and its necessary corollary in idealised courtly love, Don Quixote has transformed himself in accordance with his fictional models. He has also separated himself from his former life in order to create a new existential space in which his utopian desires and fantasies can be played out.

As Elizabeth Eisenstein has pointed out, it is not that Don Quixote reads books of chivalry because his life is boring, but the other way around. It is the adventures he reads about in his books of chivalry that make his routinized lifestyle impossible to maintain (Iffland 25–26). The flesh and blood person remains identical with itself, and in his memory retains the links with the past—his family, his property, and his ancestry—but Quixote the adventurer now becomes discontinuous with Quijada, Quesada, or Quexana, the country hidalgo. Once he has freed himself from the trammels of the everyday, the new persona emerges and, like Simmel's adventurer, "treats the incalculable element in life in the way we ordinarily think is by definition calculable . . . The obscurities of fate are certainly no more transparent to him than to others, but he proceeds as if they were." While "to the sober person, adventurous conduct often seems insanity . . . for . . . it appears to presuppose that the unknowable is known," for Don Quixote, as for Simmel's adventurer, "the unlikely is likely," and what for the ordinary individual "is likely easily becomes unlikely" (Simmel 249–50).

Hence, the escape of the aging and intelligent country hidalgo from his cramped and tedious domestic routine is as much an adventure as it is madness.

Such fantasies fill a need, as Julio Caro Baroja confirms when he cites the indignant response of a woman who opened one of the novels, *La busca*, by his uncle, Pío Baroja. "Why would I read books about poor people and suffering? I have enough poverty at home! I want books that tell about princesses, lords, salons, and things I've never seen!" ["¡Para qué —decía—voy a leer libros en que se habla de pobres y de miserias! ¡Ya tengo bastante pobreza en casa! Lo que yo quiero son libros en que se hable de princesas, de títulos, de salones y cosas que no he visto nunca!" (318)]. Here we have, in the twentieth century, a testimonial of how satisfying Don Quixote's timeless world of romance must have been. It also allows us to correct a time-honored assertion that *Don Quixote* killed the romances of chivalry and that Cervantes wrote the last *novela de caballerías*. In eighteenth-century England, Samuel Johnson read *Don Felixmarte de Hircania*. In Spain, as late as 1900, the Imprenta Universal's "Biblioteca Moderna" was still selling abbreviated editions, in twenty or thirty pages, of such works as *Carlo Magno, o los doce pares de Francia, El caballo de madera, Pierres y Magalona, Oliveros de Castilla, Tablante de Ricamonte*, among others (Caro Baroja, *Literatura de cordel* 319–20). "What would Cervantes have said," Caro Baroja asks rhetorically, "had he known that around the year 1900 the novels of chivalry continued to be read in the inns and the fields of La Mancha and Andalucía, as they had been around 1600 or earlier?" ["Qué hubiera dicho Cervantes de comprobar que, allá por los años 1900, los libros de caballerías se seguían leyendo en las ventas y campos de La Mancha y Andalucía, como por los de 1600 o antes?" (*Literatura de cordel* 318)].

If Cervantes's project had really been to discredit the romances of chivalry, it would have been a vain pursuit. Referring to the romances that incited Don Quixote to madness, for example, Caro Baroja observes the "plain fact that a great many level-headed people enjoyed them without ill effect, just as nothing happened to the readers of the serials in newspapers and magazines, with [even the nineteenth century] General O'Donnell, who was regarded by his contemporaries as icy cool, being the greatest reader of all" ["la realidad es que gustaron de ellos cantidad de gentes sesudas, sin que les pasara nada, como tampoco les pasó más tarde a los lectores de folletines, con el general O'Donnell a la cabeza, hombre gélido según sus contemporáneos . . ." (*Literatura de cordel* 317)].

Simmel touches our argument most closely in the observation that the adventurer "is also the extreme example of the ahistorical individual, of the man who lives in the present" (245). The adventures of our Manchegan knight have an additional and more complicated twist in that the present in which he chooses to live is a virtual past. His present is a no-time, an *uchronia* in which he will install his utopian project, as well as a no-place, a *utopia*. For Don Quixote, it is not the everyday temporal dimension, but adventure, that fills his life with meaning. Fernando Savater's perspective on the function of adventure in the life of the traditional hero is certainly applicable here to Don Quixote's project. "Adventure," Savater explains, "is a *time that is full* in contrast with the empty and interchangeable time of routine" ["La aventura es un *tiempo lleno* frente al tiempo vacío e intercambiable de la rutina" (170: his emphasis)]. Adventure, then, is the essential category within which the deeds of any knight —his trials, submission to ordeals, encounters with the marvellous, with monsters and with sorcerers—is to be evaluated. If he succeeds in his adventures, it is because of his virtue and the nobility of his aims. If he fails, the opposite is true. To alter Don Quixote's celebrated phrase somewhat, in his chivalric *vita nuova*, the Knight is the architect, the sum total, of his adventures: "each man is the architect of his own fortune" (II:66, 893) ["cada uno es artífice de su [a]ventura" (1168)].

The notion of adventure as the creation of an ideal space within which desire and fantasy can take shape opens up another perspective in Cervantes's novel. By focusing on an hidalgo and a poor laborer as its adventurers, the text directs our attention to the desires emanating from two different cultures and two different value systems. The confrontation of these diverse cultures, while distilled through the medium of humor, also discloses two important elements: how the fantasies of a representative of the underclass differ from those of the dominant culture and how social positionality determines the shape of the adventures each representative plays out in the ideal space.

For Don Quixote, desire is manifested in his chivalric project to restore the traditional values that were lost in the times following the prehistoric Age of Gold, and thereby to win glory and renown. For the laborer Sancho, desire is projected onto a promised *ínsula* which will make him wealthy, titled, and free from toil. The shape their desire takes makes the protagonists' fantasies different. Constructed by his class in society, Don Quixote, the petty country gentleman and hidalgo, is conservative in the utopia he tries to revive. He turns to the hierarchized golden world of classical antiquity and to the frugality lauded in the Hesiodic and Ovidian Arcadias in which he can afford to indulge. Sancho Panza, on the other hand, knows only too well how far removed is the real world of restraint, toil, and poverty that has constructed him from Don Quixote's romanticized image of austerity. Being an illiterate laborer, he does not have access to his master's literary capital. He does have access, however, to another "golden world," one that is equally ideal and mythical, and one that had also pervaded the European imaginary for centuries and had been fashioned, unlike the classical Hesiodic myth, by the collective memory of the *pueblo*. Called by A. L. Morton "the people's utopia," it is the myth of Cockaigne, reinforced by the magical tales brought back to Spain by *indianos* made wealthy in the wondrous "tierra de Xauxa" or "isla de Jauja" the Spaniards had found in Peru. The Inca Garcilaso de la Vega, son of a Spanish nobleman and an Incan princess, describes in his *Comentarios reales/Royal Commentaries* (bk. III: ch. 24) one of the many marvels with which Peru would present the Spaniards, namely, the golden quarter Coricancha:

> That garden, which now serves to supply the monastery with vegetables, was in Inca times a garden of gold and silver such as existed in the royal palaces. It contained many herbs and flowers of various kinds, small plants, large trees, animals great and small, tame and wild, and creeping things such as snakes, lizards, and snails, butterflies and birds, each placed in an imitation of its natural surroundings.
>
> There was also a great maize field, a patch of the grain they call *quinua*, and other vegetables and fruit trees with their fruit all made of gold and silver in imitation of nature. There were also in the house billets of wood done in gold and silver, which were also to be found in the royal palace. Finally, there were figures of men, women, and children cast in gold and silver, and granaries and barns, which they call *pirua*, to the great majesty and ornamentation of the house of their god, the Sun. Each year, at the great festivals they celebrated, they presented the Sun with much gold and silver which was used to decorate his temple. New devices were continu-

ally invented for this purpose, for the silversmith assigned to the service of
the Sun did nothing else but make these figures, together with an infinite
quantity of plate as well as pots, jars, vases, and vats used in the temple. In
short, in the whole of the house there was no implement necessary for any
function that was not made of gold and silver, even the spades and hoes for
weeding the gardens. Thus with good reason, they called the temple of the
Sun and the whole building *coricancha,* "the golden quarter." (trans. Livermore vol. I:187–88)

[Aquella huerta que ahora sirve al convento de dar hortaliza era, en tiempo
de los Incas, jardín de oro y plata, como los había en las casas reales de los
Reyes, donde había muchas yerbas y flores de diversas suertes, muchas plan-
tas menores, muchos árboles mayores, muchos animales chicos y grandes,
bravos y domésticos, y sabandijas de las que van arrastrando, como culebras,
lagartos y lagartijas, y caracoles, mariposas y pájaros y otras aves mayores
del aire, cada cosa puesta en el lugar que más al propio contrahiciese a la
natural que remedaba.

Había un gran maizal y la semilla que llaman *quinua* y otras legumbres
y árboles frutales, con su fruta todo de oro y plata, contrahecha al natural.
Había también en la casa rimeros de leña contrahecha de oro y plata, como
los había en la casa real; también había grandes figuras de hombres y muje-
res y niños, vaciados de lo mismo, y muchos graneros y trojes, que llaman
pirua, todo para ornato y mayor majestad de la casa de su Dios el Sol. Que
como cada año, a todas las fiestas principales que le hacían le presentaban
tanta plata y oro, lo empleaban todo en adornar su casa inventando cada
día nuevas grandezas, porque todos los plateros que había dedicados para el
servicio del Sol no entendían en otra cosa sino hacer y contrahacer las cosas
dichas. Hacían infinita vajilla, que el templo tenía para su servicio hasta
ollas, cántaros, tinajas y tinajones. En suma, no había en aquella casa cosa
alguna de que echar mano para cualquier ministerio que todo no fuese de
oro y plata, hasta lo que servía de azadas y azadillas para limpiar los jardines.
De donde con mucha razón y propiedad llamaron al templo del Sol y a toda
la casa Coricancha, que quiere decir barrio de oro. (*Comentarios reales,* ed.
Miró Quesada, vol. I:170)]

Juan Ruiz's *Libro de buen amor* (stanza 122a; stanza 341b) had evoked
the "Cucaña" of those who aspired to the easy life. In its Spanish conflation with the Peruvian analogue we find it referred to in Rueda's *Paso*
titled *La tierra de Xauxa* and in Mateo Alemán's *Guzmán de Alfarache*
(pt. I: bk. 2, ch. 6). It is nevertheless important to keep in mind two

things at this point. First, as Alexandre Cioranescu has reminded us, the myth of a golden age and that of Cockaigne are not fundamentally different. They both constitute imaginary nostalgias for utopia:

> The nostalgic side of utopia, which consists in exorcising reality by conjuring up a perfectly happy society, is simply a repetition, made conscious and orderly, of that same series of insoluble questions and imaginary solutions that led to the creation of the myth of the golden age or that of the land of Cockaigne.

> [L'aspect nostalgique de l'utopie, qui consiste à exorciser la réalité par l'évocation d'une société parfaitement heureuse, n'est que la répétition, devenue consciente et méthodique, de la même série de curiosités insolubles et de solutions imaginaires, qui ont conduit à la création du mythe de l'âge d'or ou de celui du pays de Cocagne. (Cioranescu, *L'avenir du passé* 47)]

Second, that although Sancho Panza's utopia includes the vision of a life free from toil and one in which he can stuff his belly, as the denizens of Cockaigne do, the pragmatic squire also aspires to the easily acquired noble status his master will provide him in installing him as a governor or a count.

We now focus briefly on the culture from which the figure of a Sancho Panza, and the "people's utopia," would have emerged. Early in the nineteenth century, Juan Eugenio Hartzenbusch saw this popular culture as essentially an oral one, and he located Cervantes's novel within the context of the carnivalesque (Rico p. ccxxv). Among recent critics, Augustin Redondo has also associated many of the incidents in which Sancho Panza himself participates, or is forced to participate, with the carnivalesque world of popular culture. Maurice Molho is explicit in affirming that the mechanism that underlies Cervantes's fashioning of Sancho is folkloric, and that Sancho is a popular archetype: "even if no Sancho Panza appears in folklore," states Molho, "there exists a number of figures who, like Sancho, can be derived from the same original archetype" ["si no hay ningún Sancho Panza folklórico, sí existen varias figuras que, como la de Sancho, se dejan derivar de un mismo arquetipo original" (231)].

It is often remarked, and rightly so, that the knight and his squire are established "as traditional figures of fun in the popular mind" (Russell 318). But even before Cervantes transferred the folkloric figure of Sancho to the literary medium of *Don Quixote,* his name had already become a part of popular phraseology: "There goes Sancho with his nag" [*Allá va Sancho con su rocín*]; or alluding to his peasant cunning: "Whoever tries to cheat Sancho has a lot to learn" [*Quien a Sancho quiera engañar, mucho ha de estudiar*]; or to the figure's folkloric delusions of grandeur: "Sancho has hidalgo delusions" [*Rebienta Sancho de hidalgo* (Márquez Villanueva, 51; our translations)]. Sancho was a familiar carnivalesque presence at Salamanca, as Caro Baroja has shown, where students celebrated the feast of *Sancto Panza* ["the Holy Belly" (*Carnaval* 111–12; our translation)].

Looking beyond Sancho Panza himself, we find a popular subculture that is part and parcel of the novel. Cervantes appropriates and makes ample use of a repertory of existent popular *refranes* in *Don Quixote.* Sancho's wife Teresa, for example, is depicted in the novel and in popular sayings as the conventional rustic housewife (II:5): "Sancho's wife—spin, pray and cook" [*la mujer de Sancho, rueca, religión, y rancho*] (Molho 251), and Aldonza as loose and flighty: "Aldonza will do as well as any other girl" [*moza por moza, buena es Aldonza* (251; our translations)]. In Aldonza's case, Joaquín Casalduero believes that the name, which conjured images of easy virtue, when paired with the "spiritual" Dulcinea, would have elicited much laughter from the contemporary reading public (Molho 289 n. 23). This may well be, but the association of Aldonza with easy virtue, was not an absolute. Sebastián de Covarrubias tells us that the name Aldonza, "many noble ladies of this kingdom have borne" ["hanle tenido señoras muy principales destos Reynos" (80a)].

There exists, then, in *Don Quixote* another culture, that of the *vulgo*– Sancho, Teresa, Juan Palomeque, the *ama,* the rustics—who speak in a different register, a lower level of discourse, that is juxtaposed to the culture of such figures as Don Quixote, Cardenio, Don Fernando, the priest, Dorotea, and others. This other culture consists of a community that shares stories, jokes, naming by reference to popular sayings, and proverbs, a linguistic register that Don Quixote, in accusing Sancho of being a "corrupter of good language" (II:19, 579) ["prevaricador del buen lenguaje" (786)], would deem "incorrect." This culture is clearly distinct from that of the novel's pseudo-rustics and performers of literary pastoral who, on one occasion, are described as "so many of them that this place, so crowded with shepherds and sheepfolds, seems to have been transformed into the pastoral Arcadia" (I:51, 437) ["tantos que parece que este sitio se ha convertido en la pastoral Arcadia" (581)]. It introduces what Homi Bhabha would call a "Third Space of enunciation, which makes the structure of meaning and reference an ambivalent process, [and which] destroys . . . [the] mirror of representation in which cultural knowledge is customarily revealed as an integrated, open, expanding code" (37). In other words, it serves as utopian discourse.

The effect is to highlight, by contrast, the fantasy performance of the novel's pseudo rustics: that of the wealthy Eugenio, who admits to being "pure of blood, and in the flower of my youth, and [having] a rich estate" (I:51, 434) ["limpio en sangre, en la edad floreciente, en la hacienda muy rico" (577)] , and who plays the role of a love-sick goatherd; of the "shepherds" Anselmo, Marcela, and Grisóstomo, who play the game with serious consequences; of the frolicking pretty "pastoral" youths in the countryside, scions of wealthy families (II:58), or of respected members of their communities (Marcela's uncle is the village priest). Such contrasts between cultures subjects the fantasy of idealized country living to doubt and can highlight the sometimes serious consequences of playing literary games with the emotions, as in the case of Grisóstomo.

When Don Quixote, for example, pictures the innocence and bucolic bliss that he and Sancho's family will enjoy in a pastoral setting, Sancho reacts. More country-wise than Quixote, and with his daughter in mind, Sancho reminds his master that the countryside harbors lusty predators: "there are shepherds more wicked than simple, and I wouldn't want her to go for wool and come back shorn; love and unchaste desires are as likely in the countryside as in the cities" (II:67, 901) ["y hay pastores más maliciosos que simples, y no querría que fuese por lana y volviese trasquilada, y tan bien suelen andar los amores y los no buenos deseos por los campos como por las ciudades" (1177)]. Eugenio the goatherd tells those who are taking Don Quixote home that "[f]armers who by nature are crafty . . . become the very embodiment of craftiness when idleness gives them the opportunity . . ." (I:51, 435) ["La gente labradora, que de suyo es maliciosa y dándole el ocio lugar es la misma malicia . . ." (578)]. And the text discloses, in the case of the wealthy farmer's daughter Dorotea, part of the peasant "upper crust" of the *labradores ricos*, a story of ambition and erotic manipulation that is negotiated with extraordinary pragmatism, though couched in the guise of modesty and victimization.

The reader's attention is consistently directed to the gratuitousness and artificiality of the country dwellers' performances. The affair of Leandra, also a *labradora rica*, and Vicente de la Rosa, for example, is figured as comically implausible; the high melodrama of Marcela, highlighted as spectacle;[3] and the exquisite fancy-dress *fête champêtre* of the "shepherdesses" in Part II, chapter 58, displayed as pure divertimento. While the poised, articulate "shepherds" and the spellbinding "shepherdesses" grace the pastoral vignettes in the novel and charm their "readers," the utopian discourse produces, in contrast, images of a contemporary reality consisting of "authentic" village neighbors. There are the rustic Lorenzo Corchuelo and his daughter Aldonza—tough, sweaty, bronzed by the sun (I:25, 155–56; Rico 283, I:31, 203–4; Rico 358–60); Sancho's daughter, barefoot and disheveled (II:50, 782; Rico 1036); and Sancho's wife Teresa, either "wearing a dun-colored skirt so short it looked as if it had been cut to shame her" (II:50, 783–84) ["con una saya parda—parecía según era corta que se la habían cortado por vergonzoso lugar—(1036)" or "disheveled and half-dressed" (II:73, 930; Rico 1212).

In the same way, language exposes to irony any romanticized view of rusticity. The laborers en route to Camacho's wedding find the archaism of Don Quixote's language wholly alien to the countryside in which he

---

3. "I think it will be something worth seeing; at least, I'll be sure to go and see it, even if I knew I would not get back to the place tomorrow" (I:7; our translation) ["Y tengo para mí que ha de ser cosa muy de ver; a lo menos yo no dejaré de ir a verla si supiese no volver mañana al lugar" (129)]. "We'll all do the same, the goatherds responded" (I:7, 82) ["—Todos haremos lo mesmo—respondieron los cabreros" (129)]. "And so my advice, Señor, is that tomorrow you be sure to attend his burial, which will be something worth seeing . . . " (I:7, 85) ["Y así os aconsejo, señor, que no dejéis de hallaros mañana a su entierro, que será muy de ver . . . " (134)]. "It seems to me, Señor Vivaldo, that we must consider our lingering to see this extraordinary funeral as time well spent, for it most certainly will be extraordinary" (I:8, 86–87) ["Paréceme, señor Vivaldo, que habemos de dar por bien empleada la tardanza que hiciéremos, en ver este famoso entierro, que no podrá dejar de ser famoso . . . " (135–36)]. Marcela's theatrical entrance on the scene, atop the rock, simply climaxes the spectacle all are anxious to see.

utters it, for "all of this was like speaking to them in Greek or in gibberish . . ." (II:19, 576) ["era hablarles en griego o en jerigonza" (782)]; and the anachronism of the Don's literary utopia is ironized in the reception accorded it by the bewildered goatherds in Part I, chapter 12. Side by side with Don Quixote's eloquent harangue on the romanticized askesis of the Classical golden world, the utopian discourse figures "real" goatherds eating salted goat meat, a half cheese harder than any mortar, and a heap of dried acorns.

The novel's other culture, then, is not a mere backdrop or picturesque diversion. Though filtered through the literary medium, it nevertheless introduces the world of the "folk" or *pueblo*, thereby exposing the ideological contradiction of the myth of idealized country living and the permeability of all fixed social categories. Rooted in the people's communal practices and language, it presents, in Antonio Gramsci's terms, "a reflection of the conditions of cultural life of the people" (189–90). It is not an autonomous world that is sealed off from the novel's "high" culture, but its effect is to set up an ironizing frame around the pseudo-Arcadians who would appropriate and intellectualize country living in production and circulation (II:58), as well as around those who would turn love into tragic pastoral poetry (I:11–14). The challenge that the rustic world presents in the novel becomes three-fold: it discloses, in the interstices between the disparate cultures, fissures in the smooth surface of the novel's utopic façade; it reveals the cultural capital that has been distributed unequally in *Don Quixote*; and it subjects to humor any notion "of the inherent originality or 'purity'" of hierarchical claims (Bhabha 37).

The repertoire of *refranes* provides an example of this challenge. Proverbs are, as Don Quixote admits to Sancho, wise sayings, "brief maxims derived from the experience and speculation of wise men in the past" (II:67, 902) ["sentencias breves, sacadas de la experiencia y especulación de nuestros antiguos sabios" (1178)]. Sancho's adept and "elegant" use of such experiential wisdom is highlighted by the narrator, who says in praise of Sancho that "the area in which he displayed the most elegance and the best memory was in his use of proverbs" (II:12, 528) ["en lo que él [Sancho] se mostraba más elegante y memorioso era en traer refranes" (720)]. The Duke's page also remarks on the pleasure Sancho's proverbs bring to the Duke and Duchess (II:50, 789), and even Don Quixote tries to compete with Sancho in using them: "I am speaking in this manner, Sancho, so you may understand that, like you, I too know how to pour down rainstorms of proverbs" (II:7, 499) ["Hablo de esta manera, Sancho, por daros a entender que también como vos sé yo arrojar refranes como llovidos" (682)]. But Don Quixote displays frustration at his inability to match Sancho's facility: "Tell me, where do you find them, you ignorant man, and how do you apply them, you fool, when to say only one that is really applicable, I have to perspire and labor like a ditchdigger" (II:43, 735–36) ["¿dónde los hallas, ignorante, o cómo los aplicas, mentecato? Que para decir yo uno y aplicarle bien, sudo y trabajo como si cavase?" (977)]. Though Sancho is their primary exponent in the novel, proverbs are seen to constitute an essential part of the other culture's capital. The Priest admits: "I can't help thinking that everyone in the Panza family was born with a sack of proverbs inside" (II:50, 788) ["todos los deste linaje de los Panzas nacieron con un costal de refranes en el cuerpo" (788)]. As Sancho himself complains to Don Quixote: "Why the devil does it trouble you when I make use of my fortune, when I have no other, and no other wealth except proverbs and more proverbs?" (II:43, 736) ["¿A qué diablos se pudre de que yo me sirva de mi hacienda, que ninguna otra tengo, ni otro caudal alguno, sino refranes y más refranes" (977)]. Such cultural capital, Elias Rivers reminds us, is powerful: "Sancho's *Refranero* is his own . . . Disticha Catonis. It is his oral heritage's answer to Don Quixote's written cultural dicta" (79).

Differing modes of narration in the novel also constitute examples of a cultural register and modus operandi that provide this "social articulation of difference" (Bhabha 2). The "normal" way in which the principal storytellers and the pseudo-Arcadian denizens tell their tales, that is, with a well-defined beginning, a middle, and a foreseeable end, contrasts with the subculture's form of storytelling. We remember Sancho's hilarious mode of narrating the comings and goings of la Torralba (I:20), and we can certainly identify with the ecclesiastic's impatience in the ducal palace at Sancho's similarly interminable tale of the rich hidalgo from Medina del Campo (II:31, 662–64; Rico 885–87). To the literate mind, Sancho's narrative is disjointed, fragmented, and unfamiliar. We laugh at Sancho, as we are meant to, but we are not allowed to forget that Sancho's modus narrandi is as "normal" as is that of the principal storytellers. It is simply one with which the literate reader and the characters from the dominant culture are less familiar. As Sancho asserts, it belongs to an "other" culture, for "[t]he way I'm telling it is how tales are told in my village" (I:20, 145) ["De la misma manera se cuentan en mi tierra todas las consejas" (213)]. His telling of the story of La Torralba is also purposeful, a brilliant tactic on Sancho's part to keep Don Quixote a captive audience and not to be abandoned within sound of the terrifying fulling hammers (I:20). The tactic works, at least until Don Quixote breaks the generic contract and interrupts the narration. We may note at this point that such a mode of storytelling is presented as characteristic of the other culture in the novel. It is parodied in the rambling narration by the mock laborer from Miguel Turra in Barataria, and governor Sancho is as irritated by it as Don Quixote and the ecclesiastic at the ducal palace had been with him.

Examples of the popular culture within the literary world of *Don Quixote* occasion some of the most humorous moments in the novel. When the pseudo rustic Eugenio, for example, inscribes the tale of Leandra and Vicente de la Rosa's love in the generic conventions of romance, Sancho, reducing "humanity to its common nature," as Pierre Bourdieu would have said (*Language* 88), debunks so artificial a world. He shows that bliss in the peasant world has nothing to do with Eugenio's mastery of generic conventions, still less with Don Quixote's romantic askesis, but with somatic gratification whenever it may be available. Sancho ignores Eugenio and walks away in order to "stuff" himself:

> I'm going over to that brook with this meat pie, where I plan to eat enough for three days, because I've heard my master, Don Quijote, say that the squire of a knight errant has to eat whenever he can, and as much as he can . . . (I:50, 433)

> [yo a aquel arroyo me voy con esta empanada, donde pienso hartarme por tres días; porque he oído decir a mi señor don Quijote que el escudero de caballero andante ha de comer cuando se le ofreciere, hasta no poder más. (575)

The text nevertheless reveals its serious aspects even as it encourages us to laugh at Sancho's concern with food. Later, the Cura will feel obliged to invite the Duke's page to his home for supper because the resources of Sancho's wife Teresa are simply too humble, and she "has more desire than provisions for serving so worthy a guest" (II:50, 790) ["más tiene voluntad que alhajas para servir a tan buen huésped" (1044)].

Sancho shows the same skeptic indifference to any idealized view of country living that he has shown to Eugenio's perspective on country loving. Sancho hears the Cura say that he already knows "from experience that mountains breed learned men and shepherds' huts house philosophers" (432) ["de experiencia que los montes crían letrados y las cabañas de los pastores encierran filósofos" (575)]. But neither the kind of verbal performance at which his cultured "betters" play, nor the Cura's *experiencia* of the learned men and philosophers he claims inhabit the countryside, accords with Sancho's "real" experience of the rustic content and practice of country living and storytelling. Sancho simply walks away. At other times, Sancho does more than ignore his educated "betters" by showing up their vacuity, as in the case of the humanist Primo in Part II, chapter 22, who wastes people's time by collecting irrelevant trivia. As Sancho impatiently exclaims: "As for asking fool questions and giving nonsensical answers, I don't need to go around asking my neighbors for help" (II:22, 601s) ["para preguntar necedades y responder disparates no he menester yo andar buscando ayuda de vecinos" (813)]. The confrontation between these two cultures, then, elicits our laughter because of its incongruity, because we do not expect it. It defamiliarizes the givenness of the dominant culture's modus narrandi and operandi, discloses the permeability of hierarchical rank ["revela lo insustancioso de las escalas jerárquicas" (Molho 258)], and thereby "opens up the possibility of a cultural hybridity that entertains difference without an assumed or imposed hierarchy" (Bhabha 4).

The permeability of fixed categories/identifications also throws into relief the pretentious emulation of their "betters" on the part of the other culture. At Camacho's wedding, as students and countryfolk chatter away about classist differences, the text demonstrates the reciprocal influence of cultural products: we hear that "the fair Quiteria's [lineage] is superior to Camacho's" (II:19, 577) ["los linajes . . . [el] de la hermosa Quiteria se aventaja al de Camacho" (783)]; and we see that Sancho's wife Teresa, in La Mancha, is hurt by the supposed airs of "the gentlewomen we have in this village who think that because they're wellborn the wind shouldn't touch them, and who go to church with all the airs of queens, and seem to think it's a dishonor to look at a peasant woman" (II:50, 785)] ["por ser hidalgas no las ha de tocar el viento, y van a la iglesia con tanta fantasía" (1039)]. But the utopian discourse subjects Teresa's "oppression" to doubt when she receives the fine necklace from the duchess and believes herself to be a governor's wife. She asks the priest if he knows of anyone who can buy her a petticoat like that of these country *hidalgas*, one that is "nice and round and just the way it should be, right in fashion and the best quality" (II:50, 788) ["un verdugado redondo, hecho y derecho, y sea al uso y de los mejores que hubiere" (1042)], and is convinced she will surpass the country *hidalgas* by becoming a countess (1042). As humorous as these incidents are, they are also purposeful. The text allows neither culture to be privileged. However widely differentiated these registers may seem to be, in the interstices we see the circularity of their cultural influences.

A similar reciprocity is true of the protagonists' utopian constructs. Don Quixote sees the Hesiodic age as "golden" because it is communal, free from toil, and devoid of greed in its simple abundance. The popular image that Sancho envisions for his *ínsula* is also "golden," but because of its sumptuous abundance and its exemption from toil which his hypothetical title and black slaves will make possible (I:19). Despite differences, both worlds betray three fundamental similarities: 1) in each, the real world (or the attempt to exorcise it through the fantasy) is present, as Emmanuel Levinas would put it, "in the image as it were between parentheses" (6–7); 2) each discloses its human centeredness; and 3) in each we discern the desire for abundance which, whether couched in simplicity or sumptuousness, is its foundational concept. As Cioranescu sums it up: "A parallel fiction, the preoccupation with human destiny, and the exclusively materialistic solution are the three basic characteristics that utopia and the land of Cockaigne have in common" ["La fiction parallèle, la préoccupation envers le destin de l'homme, et la solution strictement matérialiste sont les trois traits fondamentaux qu'ont en commun l'utopie el le pays de cocagne" ("Utopie" 95)]. But, as each protagonist strives to have his fantasies actualized, he will discover the gap between aspiration and actualization. We now turn to the utopian constructs.

2

Utopia as Cultural Construct

Theorists have long grappled with definitions and processes of utopianism. Lewis Mumford, for example, distinguishes between what
he terms utopias of escape and utopias of reconstruction. "Utopias of
escape," he asserts, "are less interesting than those of reconstruction . . .
If the first utopia leads backwards into the utopian's ego, the second
leads outward—outward into the world" (21). What Mumford seems
to have overlooked is the degree to which most utopias of reconstruction do their work of construction upon the blueprint of an idealized
past like that evoked by his "utopias of escape," a static past supposedly
purified of the errors, the corruption, the greed, and the overcomplica-
tion of the present age. Lyman Tower Sargent, who first defines the
"general phenomenon of utopianism as social dreaming" (3), is more
helpful. He discusses three different strands in utopianism. The first
strand is *utopian literature,* which for him includes two separate traditions: utopias or eutopias that come about without human effort, and
utopias that are implemented through human effort. Sargent refers
to the former tradition—utopias that come about without human effort—as "body utopias or utopias of sensual gratification." And he calls
the latter tradition—those implemented through human effort—as
"city utopias or utopias of human contrivance" (13). The second strand
that he distinguishes is *communitarianism,* which he describes as "an
economic system without private property" (14). The third strand of
utopianism for Sargent is *utopian social theory,* whose roots he sees as
founded in the idea of progress and of human perfectibility (21). In this
study we are primarily interested in the first strand of utopianism, *utopian literature.* Due to the permeability of distinctions among the three

strands of utopianism, however, at times the other two will impinge on our discussion. Sargent's definitions and distinctions help to clarify aspects of utopia in which Mumford was not particularly interested but which are relevant for us.

Utopias that come about without human effort are the result of a Providence or Nature that supplies and gratifies all human needs. These myths of a now-lost perfection evoke a world of pre-lapsarian equality in which justice is not an issue. As David Hume declares in *A Treatise of Human Nature*, "if every man had a tender regard for another, or if nature supplied abundantly all our wants and desires, . . . the jealousy of interest, which justice supposes, could no longer have any place. . . . Encrease to a sufficient degree the benevolence of men, or the bounty of nature, and you render justice useless" (quoted in Welsh 68). Utopias that are implemented through human effort, on the other hand, must negotiate among such post-lapsarian realities as racial, ethnic, and economic injustice. These utopias deal, as the others do not, with questions such as: What constitutes just laws? Is individual freedom or personal happiness a primary objective of ideal societies? Or is the *social* welfare of these commonwealths more important?

In our modern usage, the idea of utopia has expanded beyond its original limited sense to include any social vision that offers an alternative and a critique of present arrangements in the writer's everyday world (Kumar 95). The concept of utopia has become generalized into "utopianism," the term we use, and it can break the time barrier by referring back to the originary projection of a Golden Age, or forward to the anticipation of an apocalypse or New Age. Hence utopia, not as an imaginary *place*, but as an idealized *time* in the past, as is the Golden Age whose lost values Don Quixote aspires to revive through the exercise of chivalry, an age when life was supposedly simpler, easier, and more virtuous. Kumar notes the uncertainty that utopian literature provokes: " . . . is this satire? Is it wish fulfillment? Is it a call to action?" (*Utopianism* 87).

Don Quixote's fantasy does not evoke an imaginary place that provides an alternative society with its own social organization and political institutions. But neither did the fictional place in *Amadís de Gaula* after which the conquering Spaniards named the real California provide such an alternative society. In other words, no one would have considered *Amadís* or *Palmerín de Inglaterra* as a call to action. Yet this is indeed the way in which Don Quixote read them. For him, chivalric texts were utopian texts, that is, exemplars for implementing in history the values lost after the pre-historic Golden Age had vanished, and which the chivalric age had been instituted to resurrect. Much of the comedy of *Don Quixote* resides precisely in this. The curious fact is that with so much truly utopian literature in his own time, as we shall see, and with so many well-reasoned reformist ideas circulating from the middle of the sixteenth century and into the seventeenth, the mad knight could still embrace a theory so at odds with the century's prevailing view, encapsulated in the judgement of Jean Bodin, that it was his age (and not Don Quixote's primitive and uncivilized past ages) that was truly golden: "These were the golden and the silver ages," Bodin sarcastically affirms, "in which men were scattered like beasts in the fields and the woods and had as much as they could keep by means of force and crime" (quoted in Grafton 124). Yet, it is precisely the values of so primitive a fantasy that the knight wishes to restore by means of chivalry, and in which to install his incongruous figure in the role of dashing hero.

We return to the concept of utopianism. Cioranescu speaks of the "fiction parallèle" ("Utopie" 95), the alternative world that utopianism sets up. Louis Marin calls it the "absent term" in utopian discourse. Both refer to the real world beyond the text as a parallel or absent referent that the fantasy within the text seeks to dissimulate, yet nevertheless exposes, consciously or unconsciously (*Utopics*).

More than twenty years ago, Juan Antonio Maravall, in his *Utopía y contrautopía en el "Quijote"* (its earliest version [1948] entitled *El humanismo de las armas en Don Quijote*) wrote of the utopian urge in *Don Quixote*. Whereas for Marin the utopian discourse opens spaces for the cultural ideologies dissimulated in the utopian fantasy to become accessible to the reader, and thereby subject to criticism, for Maravall all utopianism is fantasy. He declared the reformism in late sixteenth-century Spain to be regressive, this regressive reformism to be the backcloth in Cervantes's *Don Quixote,* and pronounced it to be seen as illusory by Cervantes as the model of the past imagined by Don Quixote.

So totalizing a position cannot be justified. Speaking of poetry in the fifteenth and sixteenth centuries, Antonio Rodríguez-Moñino cautioned us to "refrain from speaking of a collective national consciousness derived from a collective national knowledge" ["prescindir de hablar de una conciencia nacional colectiva derivada de un colectivo conocimiento nacional" (56)].[1] It is a caveat that applies equally here. It is true that all utopias are constructs of desire, that they all share as a basic premise what J.C. Davis calls "limited satisfactions exposed to unlimited wants," and that the shape that desire takes in each case is culture-specific. But it is also true that any fantasy, despite (or because of) its being illusory, is bound to disclose correspondances between the text that has constructed it (the *parole* of its author) and the nation (the collective *langue*) that has produced it at a specific historical moment.

Other utopian theories have been deployed in connection with Cervantes's *Don Quixote*, especially as a result of Bakhtin's notion of utopia in *Rabelais and His World* (1968). Bakhtin had used the term as conceptually and anthropologically akin to carnival. He argued that the clearest expression of carnival lay in the notion of a return to the past, to the model of the Roman Saturnalia "perceived as a true and full, though temporary, return of Saturn's golden age upon earth" (7–8). For Bakhtin, this return was two-fold. It was marked by "the suspension of all hierarchical rank, privileges, norms, and prohibitions"; and in the "new, purely human relations" that emerged in carnival, an experience "unique of its kind" would merge the "utopian ideal and the realistic" (10).

This Bakhtinian view of carnival as a momentary explosion of popular freedom through indulgence and the dissolution of class boundaries—a utopian vision of sorts— inspired a cluster of studies on the carnivalesque in *Don Quixote*. In the collection of essays *Cervantes and the Renaissance* (1980), Luis Murillo drew attention to the motifs from popular culture that contribute to *Don Quixote*'s "all-inclusiveness as a 'secular' epic" (62). Murillo observed that the order of the episodes in *Don Quixote* "discloses an entire evolution of motifs from popular culture, of which Carnival is one." He notes especially the "mock rituals, coarse tricks and hoaxes, disguises, masks, songs and games." Sancho is tossed in a blanket, the narrator emphasizes, "as if he were a dog at Carnival" (I:17, 122) ["como perro por carnestolendas" (184)].

The beatings and humiliations meted out to Quixote can certainly "be related to the traditions of folk humor, where it is usual to inflict

---

1. Diana de Armas Wilson has also objected to Maravall's assumed "coherence of the class values of Spain's lower nobility . . . which presupposes a monolithic culture" (146).

the cruelest physical punishment in both real and mock form on the fool figure" (Murillo 62). In the same volume of essays, Manuel Durán's "El *Quijote* a través de la prisma de Mikhail Bakhtin" emphasized the aspects of *Don Quixote* that presented, for him, a "visión carnavalesca," namely, "the world as festival, as an orgy, as an explosion and transformation of our personality, as disguise and deception, as a drunken party, but, also, as triumphant madness, as a praise of folly" ["[e]l mundo como fiesta, como orgía, como explosión y cambio de nuestra personalidad, como disfraz y engaño, como festín y borrachera, pero, también, como locura triunfante, como elogio de la locura . . ." (72)]. We take issue here with Durán's celebration of carnival because it tends to blur two distinctions we consider essential to maintain. First, carnival is a popular ritual event. It does not resemble in any way the pranks and humiliations *imposed* upon Don Quixote and Sancho Panza from above by the ducal pair. Secondly, Bakhtin did not make the claim that that is how the real world operates, simply that that is how Rabelais's fantasy presented it as operating. The carnival "king," unlike Sancho the governor, was always *aware* of the role that he was playing (see Durán 82–83).

In 1978, Augustin Redondo published his article "Tradición carnavalesca y creación literaria del personaje de Sancho Panza al episodio de la Insula Barataria en el *Quijote*." Taking as his starting point the writings of both Bakhtin and Mircea Eliade on the culture of carnival as it institutes rituals of inversion, of misrule, and of folly, Redondo focuses on Sancho's governorship. Like Bakhtin, Redondo takes for granted a conceptual affinity between carnival and utopia, but focuses on the point we are making, the *imposed* carnivalesque quality of Barataria: "The government has been conceived by the Duke and Duchess, representatives of the dominant group, in order to make fun of the peasant, manipulating him according to the traits they presuppose in him: naiveté, gluttony, cowardice" ["El gobierno, lo han concebido los duques, representantes de los grupos dominantes para burlarse del campesino, utilizando para ese fin las peculiaridades sobresalientes del personaje tal como ellos lo ven: tontería, glotonería y cobardía" (51)].

Redondo emphasizes the contrast between Sancho's judicial behavior and the Duke's frivolous and corrupt administration: "his verdicts have been swift and impeccable, whereas official justice is delayed, venial, and corrupt" ["sus sentencias han sido rápidas e intachables mientras que la justicia oficial es larga, venial y viciosa" (68)]. Far from offering a performance of misrule and revelry, Sancho's actual comportment, he points out, is one of sobriety and of shrewd government in which "the person who ends up frustrated is not Sancho but the aristocratic perpetrator of the prank" ["[e]l que sale frustrado . . . no es Sancho . . . sino el aristocrático promotor de la burla" (67)]. Echoing Maravall's claim, but in a more nuanced form, Redondo concludes with a question that leaps over the conceptual boundary between carnival and utopia: "Could Cervantes be asking himself whether the passion for rectitude and justice is no more than a dream, that can only be brought about in another world, in a longed-for Golden Age?" ["¿Pensará Cervantes que ese afán de rectitud y de justicia no es más que un sueño, que tan sólo puede hacerse efectivo en otro mundo, en una añorada Edad de Oro?" (70)]. As always with Cervantes, we ask, where does his irony direct us? Is it aimed at cynical authorities such as the Duke, or at the ritual fool (the *homme moyen sensuel*) who believes not only that we have a right to expect fair judgments, but that just public acts can actually be performed in this world, or at both?

Cervantes's irony always cuts both ways, whether he is describing the novel's characters, their values, or the hegemonic practices of imperial Spain. He will show us Don Quixote eulogizing the egalitarian views of a past era while conferring upon his squire the governorship of a colony whose inhabitants Sancho would be happy to enslave. He will allow Don Quixote to expound on his peaceful aspirations, to call himself a man of peace, while exposing him as a man who admires men of violence (Reinaldos et al.), who commits a number of violent acts himself, and who dreams of conquering empires. The knight's human values and ideals, as Heinz-Peter Endress remarks in a somewhat different context, will be validated and simultaneously exposed to ironic scrutiny (132). And, as we shall later see, the text is allowed *both* to encompass the recent imperialist history of the age *and* to critique it as founded on a naive anthropology. Given the author's delicious irony, as well as the polyvalent voice of the text's utopian discourse, unequivocal answers of any kind become neither possible nor desirable.

In the figuration of Sancho we encounter the same ironic treatment. Sancho's performances have been said to be grounded in the carnivalesque, and so they are. But in Barataria it is not a performance constituted symbolically by carnival, as the Bakhtinian model would require, nor a performance which he initiates. The events of Barataria do not constitute ritualized license deriving energy from below and issuing from a tradition of carnival, but a mockery imposed instead from above and designed to humiliate Sancho by means of "a ridiculous ceremony" (II:45, 747) ["ridículas ceremonias" (992)] invented ad hoc and ad hominem. Again, though Sancho emerges both chastened and disillusioned as he falls into the pit after the actualization of his "island," the utopian discourse ironizes the "redemptive" value of his experience. There is little change in Sancho's desire for power. The first question he asks the Enchanted Head is: "By any chance, head, will I have another governorship?" (II:62, 871) ["Por ventura, cabeza, tendré otro gobierno?" (1141)]. And the narrator ensures a little later that we understand the motivation behind Sancho's question. "Sancho, although he had despised being governor . . . still wished to give orders and be obeyed, for command, even mock command, brings this misfortune with it" (II:63, 875) ["aunque aborrecía el ser gobernador . . . todavía deseaba volver a mandar y a ser obedecido, que esta mala ventura trae consigo el mando, aunque sea de burlas" (1146)].

Part of the irony is already contained in the very notion of utopia. Ernst Bloch may claim that without the utopian fantasy one cannot strive for justice, yet the historical reader is always aware of the distance between the utopian "dream" and the reality meted out to utopian theorists. Plato's failure to implement the grand vision of the *Republic* and the *Laws* in Sicily is the most celebrated example; Tomasso Campanella's imprisonment as a result of his reformist ideals is another; the ultimate fate of Thomas More needs no reminder; and the lack of recognition or support that Francis Bacon and his *New Atlantis* met with on the part of James I is well known.

Let us now see the forms that utopianism takes for the knight. Don Quixote's fascination with pastoral literature and with the pastoral way of life in fiction is evident throughout *Don Quixote*. Although pastoral and chivalric fictions are very different in their worlds of action, their mobility, and their social representations, they participate in a similar utopian discourse that crosses the lines of their difference and can blur the distinctions in the mind of a dedicated reader of romance such as Don Quixote. The inquisitorial inventory of Don Quixote's library contains nine pastoral romances, which is a substantial body of reading and evidence of his fascination with that genre. They are presented as a block in his library. To the author and the reader it is obvious why both the chivalresque and the pastoral modes would appeal to Don Quixote, since they are avenues of escape. For Don Quixote, the chivalresque fantasy offers the lure of heroic deeds, present satisfaction, and future magnificence. In recommending the books of chivalry to the Canon, for example, he describes what the chivalresque fantasy has both effected and promised him:

> since I became a knight errant, I have been valiant, well-mannered, liberal, polite, generous, courteous, bold, gentle, patient, long-suffering in labors, imprisonments, and enchantments, and although only a short while ago I saw myself locked in a cage like a madman, I think that with the valor of my arm, and heaven favoring me, and fortune not opposing me, in a few days I shall find myself the king of some kingdom where I can display the gratitude and liberality of my heart. (I:50, 430)

> [después que soy caballero andante soy valiente, comedido, liberal, bien-criado, generoso, cortés, atrevido, blando, paciente, sufridor de trabajos, de prisiones, de encantos; y aunque ha tan poco que me vi encerrado en una jaula como loco, pienso, por el valor de mi brazo, favoreciéndome el cielo y no me siendo contraria la fortuna, en pocos días verme rey de algún reino, adonde pueda mostrar el agradecimiento y liberalidad que mi pecho encierra. (571–72)]

The chivalric enterprise provides him with two levels of excitement: one, the adventure of leaving his life as a village hidalgo in order to live as a knight; the other, the individual encounters of everyday life which he can now raise to the level of extraordinary adventures. He assures Sancho at each encounter of "the most famous adventure ever seen" (I:8, 46; our translation) ["la más famosa aventura que se haya visto . . ." (99)]. These encounters legitimize the transformation of the sedentary Quijada into the adventurous knight-errant Don Quixote. He will of course eventually come to terms with the fact that legitimacy has to be conferred, and that for him to be truly a knight-errant he must be *recognized* as such. But when that longed-for moment finally comes in Part II of the novel, it is unfortunately the beginning of Don Quixote's most painful *burla*.

The attractions of pastoral for Don Quixote are clearly less spectacular and outwardly seem to be in opposition to those of chivalry.

The lives of pastoral characters are static. They share a world of feelings—hope, despair, elation, yearning—rather than one of action and of productive individual energy. Don Quixote is an actor in the presence of windmills, merchants, armies of sheep, silent mourners, and ladies with escorts, in a series of one-to-one correspondences within a total chivalric paradigm. His encounter with the pastoral world, on the other hand, is different. The pastoral world *presents itself* to him as "other" than the chivalric world, which has become the always already of his quixotic identity. In the pastoral episodes, unlike the chivalric ones, Don Quixote is passive. He merely "reads" the signs of literary pastoral. The group of six goatherds that presents itself to him, for example, sheepskins spread on the ground, goat meat cooking in a pot, an upturned trough for a seat, and a handful of acorns, produce obvious reading codes. No transformation/imposition is necessary. He does not need to resort to magic in order to create so Theocritan a setting. By its very familiarity, pastoral simply invites Don Quixote to be an ideal spectator in a paradoxical and conflictual new world of dramatized innocence.[2]

The ideal of service and of the protection of the weak and defenseless is replaced in pastoral by a solipsistic immersion in the pain of loss, of absence, and of desire. Adventure is constituted by a glance from a beautiful maiden, a smile, or even a gesture of disdain, which can provoke a torrent of tears and of verses. While the chivalresque romance exists in a fictitious past time, pastoral literature, despite its filiation to an

---

2. The contemporary public, unlike Don Quixote, was well aware, given the discoveries of the New World and the conflicting images of noble innocence and savage barbarism there, of the conflictual nature of any pastoral projection of ideal worlds. This is clear, even fictionally, in the pastoral literature of the time. In Jorge de Montemayor's *Diana*, for example, the various lovers are beset by frustration, rejection, and jealousy. Cervantes's *Galatea* (1585) goes even further. Beyond amorous frustration, it proliferates with scenes of violence and murder. By the end of the book, even the sensitive shepherd Elicio "is determined to win Galatea with his fists if need be, as would any neighborhood bully, which belies his poetic essence" ["queda dispuesto a ganarse a Galatea a fuerza de puños, como cualquier gañán de vecindad, con lo que se aniquila su esencia poética" (quoted in Avalle-Arce 231)]. It is also not unusual for "shepherds" to turn out to be fugitives from violent quarrels and jealousies in the city of Coimbra (*Diana*) or, as in *La Galatea*, for pastoral to make multiple connections with "real" urban society beyond the rustic world.

edenic past, inhabits an idealized space in the present underwritten by the myth of primal innocence and simplicity. But notwithstanding the unrequited loves in the pastoral romances of *La Diana* and *La Galatea*, with which Don Quixote is familiar, or the fatal episode of Marcela-Grisóstomo in which he actually participates, Don Quixote still clings to the myth of pastoral's tranquil enjoyment of bliss in the *locus amoenus*. The discrepancy is no more problematic for Don Quixote than is the inadequacy of his physical strength, his weapons, and rusted armor in facing wicked giants, monsters, and entire armies.

The text produces here, in order to critique them, two literary fantasies: a utopia that escapes into an imaginary "then" (the chivalric) and one that escapes into an idealized "elsewhere" (the pastoral). The prosperous, beautiful people acting out the fantasy of Arcadia in *Don Quixote* have fashioned themselves no less than has Don Quixote; the life of the mimetic consumers and enactors of genres in which they have the leisure and luxury to participate is no less bookish than is Don Quixote's. They simply enact the pastoral, while he enacts the chivalric romance.

For some—Grisóstomo, for example, in the Marcela episode (I:11)—the fantasy of love in the pastoral genre can prove more destructive than delusive. The "love-ly" place becomes a site of alienation, not healing, of artistic escape, not transformation. Dominick Finello sees the Marcela episode as an attempt "to narrow the gap between the ideal myth of the golden age and the harsh realities of shepherd life" (70). We suggest, instead, that the utopian discourse widens the distance between the artifice and the real, thereby exposing the illusory desire of early modern, socialized humanity, to regress to so-called primordial simplicity and pastoral wholesomeness.[3]

---

3. The text fractures all such "wholesomeness," including the heteronormative assumption of idealized country living. Suggestions of alternative erotic practices hover over at least three pastoral episodes in the novel: in the Marcela incident (I:4), in which Marcela rejects men and chooses to live in "perpetual solitude" (our translation) ["perpetua soledad" (154)] with "the shepherdesses of this village" (our translation) ["las zagalas desta aldea"(155)]; in the comic pseudo-pastoral episode of Leandra and Eugenio/Anselmo/Vicente de la Rosa, in which de la Rosa is not in the least bit interested in depriving the all-too-willing and sought-after Leandra of her "jewel that, once lost, can never be recovered" (I:51, 436) ["joya que, si una vez se pierde, no deja esperanza de que jamás se cobre" (580)]; and in the strangely

The text creates a discursive bridge between the two genres dear to Don Quixote in order to pinpoint them as fantasies. Don Quixote goes out in search of chivalric adventure while pastoral topoi intrude upon the narration independently of his knightly quest. As befits a narrative that is self-consciously inscribed in the traditions of epic and romance, formulaic phrases announce the dawn that precedes significant chivalric actions.[4] The formulae are made to serve the purpose of highlighting both the pastoral and the chivalric as *performances*.

The first of these momentous instances occurs as Don Quixote sets out declaiming to himself the well-known words with which his phantom historian will assuredly set forth the chronicle of his chivalric exploits. His chivalric initiation, however, begins with almost the exact words with which Don Quixote will initiate his Arcadian Golden Age speech in the pastoral interlude of Part I, chapter 11: "Fortunate the age and fortunate the times . . ." (76) ["Dichosa edad y siglos dichosos . . ." (121)]. The dawn that rises upon his heroic events is similarly given this form of stylistic treatment: "No sooner had rubicund Apollo spread over the face of the wide and spacious earth the golden strands of his beauteous hair . . ." (I:2, 25) ["Apenas había el rubicundo Apolo tendido por la faz de la ancha y espaciosa tierra las doradas hebras de sus hermosos cabellos . . ." (46)]; later, when he awakens to do battle with the Caballero de los Espejos: "By this time a thousand different kinds of brightly colored birds began to warble in the trees, and with their varied and joyous songs they seemed to welcome and greet the new dawn . . ." (II:14, 543) [" En esto, ya comenzaban a gorjear en los árboles mil suertes de pintados pajarillos, y en sus diversos y alegres cantos parecía que daban la norabuena y saludaban a la fresca aurora . . ." (740)]. The formula is repeated, in a slightly abbreviated form, as Don Quixote and others set out to witness the funeral of Grisóstomo: "Dawn had scarcely begun to show itself on the balconies of the east when five of the six goatherds arose . . ." (I:13; our translation) ["Mas apenas comenzó a descubrirse el día por los balcones del oriente, cuando los cinco de los seis cabreros se

---

comical and passionate relationship Eugenio entertains with his beautiful nanny goat Manchada" (I:50, 432) ["hermosa cabra" Manchada (574)].

4. Cf. the famous lines in the *Poema de mio Cid*: "Now dawn was breaking and morning came / the sun rose; Lord, how beautiful it looked" ["Ya quiebran los albores e vinie la mañana, / ixie el sol ¡Dios, que fermoso apuntava!" (vv. 456–57)].

levantaron . . ." (135)]. The formulaic bridge thus created between the two narrative modes marks Don Quixote's pastoral and chivalric ideals as utopian fantasies, and the utopian discourse exposes the stylization of the "real" inns, roads, sheep-routes, highways and, above all, the barren hills of La Mancha which Quixote's chivalric and pastoral delusions seek to transform.

Just as Don Quixote chooses to ignore the problematic bliss of the *locus amoenus* in the pastoral romances he has read, he is similarly oblivious to the topical allusions to post-lapsarian melancholy inherent in the genre itself. The fact that pastoral romances are predominantly sentimental tales of woe, of loss, of separation, of the failure of Nature to underwrite our pathetic fallacies, does not prevent Don Quixote from extrapolating his utopian fantasy from them. Pastoral may constitute a generic lament for the lost innocence and perfection implied in the harmonious interaction between animate and inanimate nature, doubtless the source of its allure, but this is not how Don Quixote chooses to read pastoral romance. As with the romances of chivalry, he is never reconciled to myths of loss. His moral imperative is precisely to restore, as knight-errant, the primordial simplicity and innocence of the golden world of myth whose loss pastoral is supposed to bemoan.

It is well to remember that the golden world, whose values Don Quixote eulogizes, is one that originally emerged without human effort. Work was non-existent: "no one, for his daily sustenance, needed to do more than lift his hand and pluck it from the sturdy oaks that so liberally invited him to share their sweet and flavorsome fruit" (I:11, 76) ["a nadie le era necesario para alcanzar su ordinario sustento tomar otro trabajo que alzar la mano y alcanzarle de las robustas encinas que liberalmente les estaban convidando con su dulce y sazonado fruto" (121)]. Shelter, like food, was provided by nature, and justice reigned supreme: "[j]ustice stood on her own ground" (77) ["La justicia se estaba en sus proprios términos" (123)]. As a result, "there was nothing to judge, and no one to be judged" (77) ["entonces no había que juzgar ni quien fuese juzgado" (123)]. Chastity was a given as "maidens in their modesty wandered . . . wherever they wished . . . without fear that another's boldness or lascivious intent would dishonor them . . ." (77) ["andaban, como tengo dicho, por dondequiera . . . sin temor que la ajena desenvoltura y lascivo intento le menoscabasen" (123)]. This myth, as is well known, has its most familiar embodiment in the Golden Age of Ovid's

Metamorphoses, Book I, in which no one worked, no one judged and no one was judged. The section from the *Metamorphoses* bears citing at length, for as Geoffrey Stagg points out, "[n]o other author's treatment is as close to Cervantes's as Ovid's" (82):

> In the beginning was the Golden Age, when men of their own accord, without threat of punishment, without laws . . . did what was right. There were no penalties to be afraid of, no bronze tablets were erected, carrying threats of legal action . . . there were no judges. . . . The peoples of the world, untroubled by any fears, enjoyed a leisurely and peaceful existence, and had no use for soldiers. The earth itself, without compulsion, untouched by the hoe, unfurrowed by any share, produced all things spontaneously, and men were content with foods that grew without cultivation. They gathered arbute berries and mountain strawberries, wild cherries and blackberries that cling to thorny bramble bushes; or acorns, fallen from Jupiter's spreading oak. . . . In time the earth, though untilled, produced corn too, and fields that never lay fallow whitened with heavy ears of grain. Then there flowed rivers of milk and rivers of nectar, and golden honey dripped from the green holm-oak. (31–32)

In his exhaustive study of the knight's oration on the Golden Age, the late Geoffrey Stagg showed how conventional and derivative Don Quixote's evocation is. There is, Stagg demonstrates, "[v]irtually no element of Don Quixote's discourse [that] is original" (81). The knight's grasp of the ancient topos in its variations in Classical antiquity is clear, whether these be the Hesiodic acorns, water in Horace's version, wine and oil in Claudian's, or the Italian humanists' preference for milk, nectar, and wine in the Renaissance (84). Don Quixote's utopia is certainly nostalgic when taken at face value. His introduction of a property-less existence, however, where "the two words *thine* and *mine*" were not known (I:11, 76), is not prevalent in Classical treatments of the theme. It is of course the basis of Plato's ideal city in which private property is abolished (for the Guardians at least), it is part of Seneca's vision in his *Epistulae Morales*, 90, and it resonates in both the medieval *De consolatione philosophiae* of Boethius and in the Renaissance where it becomes a *locus classicus* of contestation and negotiation. So concerned, for example, is John Calvin about the Anabaptists' and Libertines' position on the issue of individual property that he reinterprets the Biblical claim that Christians in the Early Church had held nothing in common. Acts

4:32 expressly states: "Now the company of those who believed were of one heart and soul, and no one said that any of the things which he possessed was his own, but they had everything in common" (Revised Standard Version). Calvin "explains," however, that the passage must mean that the early Christian "retained his household goods and governed them by himself. But they had such fellowship that none suffered indigence" (*Against the Libertines*, translated by Farley 287; quoted in Doody 229). Like Thomas Aquinas before him, Calvin stresses the "pile of confusion" such "communitarianism," (to use Sargent's term) would occasion; following Cicero, he insists that a man must have power over his own possessions in order to contribute to the *res publica*.

In a fine analysis of the work to which we owe the form that defines the genre, More's *Utopia* (1516), and within the context of the period's ongoing discussions as to what constitutes true *nobilitas*, Quentin Skinner addresses himself to the importance of the issue of private property among humanists of the time.[5] The Aristotelian and Scholastic argument on "the indispensability of private property in any well-ordered commonwealth," he shows, was simply taken for granted (Skinner 138). As the protestant Calvin would later insist, and as the Catholic Thomas Aquinas had already warned in *De furto et rapina* in the *Summa*, a state of disorder would result in any commonwealth where the distinction between "yours" and "mine" was not maintained: work would be avoided, and so poverty, quarrelling, and instability could be predicted (Skinner 138). We have already cited Jean Bodin's description of the thievery and disorder he too predicts of an age when primitive humankind was deprived of the right to private property. All "had as much as they could keep by means of force and crime" (quoted in Grafton 124). On the other hand, Antonio de Guevara, bishop of Guadix and later of Mondoñedo (to whom Cervantes sardonically refers in the Prologue to *Don Quixote* Part I), refers in his *Relox de príncipes* (vol. I: ch. 31) to the conditions of that mythic Golden Age as orderly precisely because of the possession of private property. Guevara postulates that work is essential to any ideal commonwealth, and that what made the primordial age golden is that "*each individual cultivated his lands*, planted his olives,

---

5. There was no Spanish translation of *Utopia* until 1637, but the 1516 edition in Latin was widely circulated among Spanish humanists until it was put on the Inquisitorial List of Forbidden Books in 1583. See Wilson 143.

gathered his fruit, harvested his vines, reaped his grain, raised his children; finally, *since they ate by the sweat of their brow*, they lived without causing any harm to others" ["*cada uno curava sus tierras*, plantava sus olivos, cogía sus frutos, vendimiava sus viñas, segava sus panes y criava sus hijos; *finalmente, como no comían sino de sudor proprio*, vivían sin perjuysio ageno" (vol. I: ch. 31, 215: emphasis added)].

The counter view, one that both resonates with Don Quixote's Golden Age speech and simultaneously echoes Bodin's, shows how contestatorial the issue was. The widely read sixteenth-century scholar Ioannes Boemus admits that the denizens of the Golden Age must have lacked private property, but seems to breathe with relief as he considers the progress of his age, in Anthony Grafton's words, the fact that "the human race had moved from the Golden Age of its earliest history, in which people lived under trees and had no desire for possessions, to modern civilization" (Grafton 100). In the final passage of More's *Utopia*, More describes the "communitarianism" of the city of Utopia, and Utopia's abolition of private property. To this More adds the Utopian prohibition of trafficking in gold. While More the character lauds these aspects of the utopian fantasy that More the author has set up, he is careful to frame his objection to the city in the same terms, and for the same reason, that the theorists we have cited had done. That is, Utopia's foundational concepts, he claims, are alien to the accepted Aristotelian connection between wealth and virtue. And we cite More: " . . . my chief objection was to the basis of their [the Utopians'] whole system, that is, their communal living and their moneyless economy." More adds to his objection what Frederic Jameson in *The Political Unconscious* and subsequent essays will describe as the revolutionary praxis entailed in all utopian theories and works. That is, that in the process of setting up the ideal commonwealth, the utopian author nevertheless makes the reader aware of the impossibility of her/his task—that of transforming a society in which powerful cultural ideologies will always resist the utopian impulse (Bossert 140). And so More's utopian discourse shatters the utopian construct: "This one thing alone" [communal living and the utopians' moneyless economy], the character is made to say, "utterly subverts all the nobility, magnificence, splendour and majesty which (in the popular view) are the true ornaments and glory of any commonwealth" (More, 247).

Whether this statement is ironic or not has been the basis of much critical discussion (see White 135–50 and Skinner 152–53). It nevertheless makes accessible to the reader of *Utopia*, More the character's awareness of More the author's skepticism about the ease with which cultural transformation can be brought about. A century after More, as we shall see, the Aristotelian view on private property, and the issue of work as a naturalizing of hierarchy in society, will still present unresolved ideals and challenges to Spanish legists and theologians.

It is time to return to Don Quixote's eloquent oration on communal ownership to see how the utopian discourse wedges in between utopian fantasy and the absented real. Class relations are a structuring absence in Don Quixote's implicit denial of how power operates in the everyday world of the novel. But the text exposes these absent relations as well as the contradictions and conflicts passed over in the fantasy. The niece had pointed out to Don Quixote that "[a]lthough hidalgos can be *caballeros*, poor knights [like Don Quixote] cannot" (II:6; our translation) ["aunque [caballeros] lo puedan ser los hidalgos, no lo son los pobres" (674)]. In the real historical moment of rising prices and agrarian crises in which Don Quixote finds himself, as Javier Salazar Rincón points out, rich farmers (*villanos ricos*) and new-titled bourgeois have superseded old and impoverished hidalgos like Don Quixote who are devoid of their erstwhile class function as warriors (150). Don Quixote's chivalric adventures restore him to the status of the *bellatores,* and offer him "in the chivalric past a liberating dream and hope of [personal] redemption" ["en el pasado caballeresco un sueño liberador y una esperanza de redención" (87)]. It is the values and privileges of this past hierarchical order that Don Quixote seeks to revive, an age in which the nobles, "la clase nobiliaria," would have been entitled, and "in which merchants were not present nor [was] money important" ["en que no aparece el mercader ni [tenía] importancia el dinero . . ." (Salazar Rincón 150)]. This, while the knight simultaneously avows the abolition of that very hierarchy in his Golden Age fantasy. It is of these contradictions that the text reminds us as the hidalgo, reinstituting the past values and privileges to which members of his class belonged, orders Sancho the *labrador* to sit and to eat with him in the *locus amoenus*, despite Sancho's resistance (I:11).

This incident leads us to a foundational flaw in utopia to which its opponents point. Karl Popper (*The Open Society*) may be one of its earliest exponents, but Aldous Huxley's *Brave New World* puts it more memorably: "that is the secret [in ideal societies] of happiness and virtue—liking what you've *got* to do" (17: emphasis his). If utopia is supposedly free from the disorder of the contemporary world, so the argument of its skeptics goes, it is because all citizens of utopia are made to conform to a norm that has been set up for them. From their perspective, utopia leads to totalitarianism at its best, to violence at its worst. George Sand would write of the French revolution that "during the terror, the men who spilt the most blood were those who had the strongest desire to lead their fellow-man to the dreamed-of Golden Age, and who had the greatest sympathy for human misery" (quoted in Sargent 22). Utopia and freedom, then, are issues that beg discussion even though we know beforehand that any definitive conclusion will prove unsatisfactory to proponents of both sides of the debate.

Isaiah Berlin's Inaugural Lecture delivered at Oxford in 1958 on the "Two Concepts of Liberty," namely, that of "negative" and that of "positive" freedom, is pertinent in this regard. Negative freedom, according to Berlin, raises the question: "What is the area within which the subject—a person or group of persons—is or should be left to do or be what he [or she] is able to do or be, without interference by other persons?" (194). Positive freedom addresses a different question: "What, or who, is the source of control or interference that can determine someone to do, or be, this rather than that?" In each case, the good of the individual supposedly derives from the good of the whole.

In dissecting the notion of negative freedom, Berlin exposes a paradox that is inherent in all utopian fantasies, whether in terms of Mumford's utopias of escape or of restoration. Their success lies in "coercing others for their [the others'] own sake" (204). But as Berlin reiterates: "to manipulate men, to propel them towards goals which you—the social reformer—see, but they may not, is to deny their human essence, to treat them as objects without wills of their own, and therefore to degrade them" (209).

In another context (a review of Louis Marin's *Utopiques: Jeux D'Espaces* in *Diacritics*), Fredric Jameson is equally strong in his view that in utopias, "to the degree to which the Utopian citizens take on individual specificity, their exemplary value as abstract citizens is undermined and they come to stand as figures for discord, for what is unassimilable to a Utopian harmony which has itself correlatively undergone a dialectical reversal into tyrannical unanimity" (17). Even Karl

Mannheim who, like Bloch, sees utopia as essential for social change, advocates that utopia's planners institute "a new form of social control" (*Ideology* 165). It can be argued that when Don Quixote's fantasy of chivalry is recreated in the ducal palace, and Sancho Panza's in Barataria, their subsequent degradation by the Duke and the Duchess should not cause surprise. They may have simply paid the price exacted in all attempts to actualize utopian fantasies, namely, submission to norms set up by someone else, and therefore, in Isaiah Berlin's words, to becoming "objects without wills of their own" (209).[6]

---

6. See Sargent 22–26, for arguments for and against the judgment that utopia is totalitarian. As Sargent shows, for Fredrick Polak "utopia means choice, freedom, and creativity"; for Ernst Bloch utopia actually leads us *away* from totalitarianism because it gives us alternatives upon which we can act and a dream upon which to build a future. In fact, Sargent explains, for Bloch "freedom is not possible without utopias" (25–26).

3

Parallel Worlds
Myth into History and Performance

How did the concept of "utopianism," as we have used it, develop? The notion of a primitive age of equality among ancient Greek and Latin writers has been extensively documented by Arthur O. Lovejoy and George Boas and, more recently, by Jean Delumeau. They have noted the different ideas of history that frame such imaginative speculation (e.g., meliorative, pejorative, cyclical). The Christian doctrine of "the Fall" eliminated all but the pejorative, investing with post-lapsarian nostalgia a vision of a world forever lost, of what Eden might have become had "[m]an's first disobedience," in the language of Milton, not provoked the wrath of God.[1] And so in this tradition the originary state of humankind becomes imaged as a life of leisure, of abundant fruit and grain, and of universal harmony. It is this topos, marked by different socio-cultural emphases, that we will see informing the vision of primordial bliss when it is represented.

Christianity had fixed the originary place of unspoiled happiness and blissful innocence in Eden's garden. Whereas the pagan myth of the different ages—gold, silver, brass, iron—presented an orderly sequence of decline, the Christian story presented an abrupt and traumatic ejection from paradisal leisure and abundance into a hostile world marked

---

1. Lovejoy's and Boas's distinction between the "soft" primitivism which we have seen privileged in Ovid, characterized by a bountiful Nature and life without labor, and its difference from the "hard" kind with its heat and cold and meager diet of acorns (which is partly the one Don Quijote conjures up in Part I, chapter 11, and which scholars from Lucretius to Hobbes make even more barbaric), can be made for the pagan view of the originary state of humankind but not, of course, for the Judeo-Christian Eden.

by the compulsory labor that had become the human lot: "by the sweat of your face / you shall eat bread" (Gen. 3 RSV). Humankind's fate was irrevocable. Not only was it determined by divine decree, but it was moreover a matter of faith. Saint Augustine had urged Christians to "believe in the actual truth of the story of Eden" in *De civitate dei* (bk. XIII: ch. 21, 288). The expulsion, then, unlike the Stoics' concept of a recurrent history, postulated an irreversible loss.

But faith and doctrine, as has so often happened, left a residue of obstinate practical questions. Where, for example, was Eden located? Was it washed away in the Flood, as some maintained, or did it still exist in some remote and inaccessible part of the world? (Delumeau, *History* ch. 2). Origen had assumed that paradise did exist somewhere, and he placed it as a way station for the souls of saints on their journey to heaven (Boas 156–57; Delumeau, *History* 31). Delumeau cites numerous medieval writers on geography who claimed to situate the earthly Paradise and he reproduces twelve maps showing its supposed location (ch. 3). The anonymous *Hortus sanitatis* of 1491, which describes more than five hundred plants, actually includes the Tree of the Knowledge of Good and Evil and the Tree of Life, and declares their provenance and existence in the Garden of Eden (Grafton 162). Imaginative descriptions of the earthly Paradise also include features derived from pagan writers. The treatise on the phoenix (*De Phoenice*), long attributed to Lactantius, describes a place without frost or burning sun, without hunger or disease, where trees are forever green (Boas 157–58). Antonio de Torquemada's *Jardín de flores curiosas* (1560; frequently reprinted), Book II, records a lengthy discussion among three speakers on the location of the earthly Paradise (208–22) in which one of the speakers repeats the pseudo-Lactantius's description, but leaves unresolved the question of whether the original Paradise of Genesis still exists somewhere.[2] Covarrubias in his dictionary also leaves the

----

2. One of the speakers, Antonio, explains:

There is a wood there, dense with trees that are perpetually green and in leaf . . . when the flood engulfed the world, it rose above the waters of Deucalion, which did not reach it. There is no sickness there, nor difficult old age, nor death, nor harsh, cruel fear of any thing. There is no wickedness, no greed for riches. There are no pangs of hunger; no storms, no force in the winds that

question open: "The Fathers of the Church have written treatises on this place, as to its location and duration. Whether it is still extant or was destroyed in the Flood is a large and contentious subject, and I will not get into it" ["Los doctores hazen tratados particulares deste lugar, assí de su sitio como de su duración. Si está todavía en su ser o si se destruyó con el diluvio, esto es cosa larga y de opiniones; no me toca el averiguarlas" (Covarrubias 852b).

Medieval travellers and chroniclers had no doubt that an earthly paradise existed, with a legendary ancient personage in residence there. St. Brendan (or Brandan) allegedly voyaged to an island where he was admitted to a city with walls of precious stones, set upon a mountain topped with gold, defended by dragons, having trees continually in fruit, and enjoying the familiar paradisal climate (Boas 158–59; [*Navigatio Sancti Brendani* vol. I:15]). St. Brendan's island also figures on numerous late medieval and renaissance maps, along with other "Fortunate Isles."[3]

The greatest fascination, however, was exercised by the fabulous legend of Prester John's opulent land described by Sir John Mandeville in the account of his travels through marvellous places, and who solemnly declared to his readers that "All that I have said I have seen with my own eyes" ["todo esto q[ue] es dicho yo lo he visto de mis ojos" (*Libro*; Libro 2, [cap.xlvi, fol.xlii recto, a-b]). *Mandeville's Travels* circulated in nearly

---

arise, and the frost does not touch this land; . . . in the middle is a spring . . . clear and gentle with plentiful sweet water: each month, and in all seasons, it waters the whole wood . . . .

[Allí hay un bosque entrejido de muchos árboles, los cuales perpetuamente están verdes y con sus hojas; . . . y cuando el diluvio somorgujó el mundo, sobrepujó también a todas las aguas de Deucalión que no llegaron a él. Allí no hay enfermedades ni vejez trabajosa, muerte, ni cruel ni áspero miedo de cosa ninguna; no hay maldades ni codicia de riquezas . . . No se siente hambre violenta; allí no hay tempestad, ni hay fuerza ninguna en los erizados vientos, y el rocío helado no toca a esta tierra; . . . está en el medio una fuente . . . muy clara y blanda, abundante de muy dulces aguas, y cada mes, en todos tiempos, riega abundantemente todo el bosque . . . . (212)]

3. See, for example, the illustration of Martin Behaim's globe of 1492 in Morison, *Discovery* 32–33, and Flint.

two hundred and fifty manuscripts, and it was one of the first books to be printed (1470). The longevity of *Mandeville's Travels*, and its many editions, served to proliferate the marvels of Prester John's land. Reports of such marvels were widely distributed from the twelfth century onwards and by the sixteenth century had become axiomatic.

As early as the twelfth century, news of the spiritual power of this Christian Prince had been disseminated by Nestorian Christians (Delumeau, *History* ch. 4). Prester John's original "letters" to the Emperor, the King of France, the Pope, and the Byzantine Emperor can be said to be utopian in a two-fold sense. First, as the late Jacqueline Pirenne has shown, they fed the urgent desire for a truly spiritual Christendom. They called attention "to what ought to be [. . .] a campaign inspired by the desire to move away from a Christianity marked by rivalries, ambitions, betrayals, fratricidal struggles, wars, massacres, and misery among the people," and "they sketched a picture of a truly Christian empire" (Pirenne 81, 86, quoted in Delumeau 75). Second, the picture of Prester John's domain was utopian in a more vulgar sense as well. His power was immense. Kings waited upon him, the rivers in his kingdom flowed with the proverbial milk and honey, the land was richer than any place on earth, abounding in precious stones and metals: "in the land of Prester John there are many pearls and precious stones as well as other things it would take too long for me to account for" ["[e]n la tierra del preste juan ay muchas perlas y piedras preciosas y muchas otras cosas que seria largo de contar"] (Mandeville, *Libro* Libro 2, cap. lxiii, fol. lvi recto a.), and it harbored no dangerous or poisonous creatures. The sumptuousness of Prester John's realm could easily be conflated with the description of Eden and its land of Havila, where "gold," "bdellium and onyx stone" abounded (Gen. 2 RSV), and with the promised reward of the New Jerusalem of Revelation adorned with jewels of all kinds (21:15–21 RSV). Its fountain of youth would be familiar from the restorative properties of the New Jerusalem's rivers of life "yielding its fruit each month; and the leaves . . . for the healing of the nations" (22:2 RSV).

Prester John's realm is also given a location on fifteenth-century maps and its truth simply taken for granted by, among others, Duarte Pacheco Pereira, who situated paradise in the newly discovered Western Indies (*Esmeraldo de situ orbis*, ca. 1508, bk. I: ch. 4); by Antonio de León Pinelo (*El paraíso en el nuevo mundo*, 1650–1656), who claimed that it had already been discovered (Lecoq and Schaer 43); by Peter Martyr (Petrus Martyr d'Anghiera); and by the latter's translator Richard Eden (Brandon 20).

Many European travellers searched for this fabled ruler and his land of marvels. In 1481 Joos van Ghistele and his companions left Ghent with jewels and assorted treasures to bring to Prester John. Already his country was widely known for rivers that flowed with milk and honey, its fountain of youth and its abundant food with "fish [who] willingly offered themselves for consumption" (Pleij 250, 258). In the early sixteenth century, Gómez de Santisteban would describe the entirely fabulous journeys of Dom Pedro de Portugal, brother of Henry the Navigator, to the "seven parts of the world," including his supposed reception by Prester John in his city of "Alves" (Delumeau 88–89). Dom Pedro's book had more than one hundred printings (Rogers vii; 273–76). A Portuguese embassy was sent to Ethiopia in 1520–1527, and as late as 1610 a Dominican, Luis de Urreta, published a "history" of Prester John: *Historia . . . de la Etiopía, monarchia del emperador llamado Preste Juan de las Indias* (Delumeau 93). By the time Cervantes writes his novel, the Canon of Toledo simply takes Prester John's existence for granted in *Don Quixote* (I:47; and Prologue, 5).[4]

---

4. When the Canon refers in *Don Quixote* to *Preste Juan de las Indias*, "las Indias" has already become ambiguous enough to suggest that this magical kingdom was to be sought in the New World (I:47, 412). We see this again in a letter to Antonio Perrenot, Bishop of Arras, dated 5 May 1551, in which Don Diego Hurtado de Mendoza reports:

A monk came from Prester John of the Indies, and it is said that in those parts the land is irrigated, and it never rains. He asked Cardinal Francisco Ximenez how wheat harvesting was done in Spain, and the Cardinal explained how it would rain, and there would be sun, and it would rain again, and it would snow and freeze and there would be sun again, and the north wind would blow, and then we would harvest. The Indian began to ponder, and after a great while he spoke, shaking his head: 'Spain cannot last,' for it seemed to him that Spain's world would come to an end, since we could not eat bread without all that trouble

[Vino a Madrid vn fraile del Preste Juan de las Indias, y en aquellas partes diz que es la tierra de regadío y nunca llueue. Pregunto al cardenal fray Francisco Ximenez como hazian en el coger del trigo en España, y el cardenal diole

In this respect, the two highly imaginative protagonists of Cervantes's novel are the cultural products of an Early Modern Europe in which the utopian fantasies of their contemporaries were simply projected upon each journey of exploration and discovery. As Harry Levin pointed out several decades ago, whereas the Middle Ages had buried the vision of a golden age "under the conception of Eden: the Renaissance not only revived the original conception, but ventured forth on a quest to objectify it" (59). The notion of Paradise, and its location somewhere in the world, pervaded the cultural imaginary of the age. Valerie Flint notes "[f]rom the passages in Pierre d'Ailly's *Imago Mundi* and Sir John Mandeville's *Book*, from the *Chronicle* of John of Marignolli, and from those writings of the Fathers and Doctors of the Church which d'Ailly, especially, so carefully cites (thus obviating the need actually to read them), we can see that the Terrestrial Paradise was a matter deserving of the most serious attention on the part of medieval exegetes, theologians, scientists, story tellers and eye witnesses" (174–75; see ch. 5, "The Terrestrial Paradise"). We have the well-known example of Christopher Columbus's conviction as he sailed in the Gulf of Paria on his third voyage that he was in the vicinity of the Earthly Paradise. The navigational quandary, the strange variations in the apparent position of Polaris, and the unexpected currents of fresh water that led him to this belief are explained by Samuel Eliot Morison (*Admiral* 556–58) and Felipe Fernández-Armesto (129–32).[5] Columbus even thought at one point "that he was hot on the trail of Prester John in Cuba" (Morison, *European* 5), and inscribed

---

quenta como llouia y hazia sol y tornaua a llouer, y neuaua y elaua y tornaua a hazer sol, y hazia tramontana, y despues segauamos. Pusose el indio a penssar y dende a vn gran rato, meneando la cabeça, dixo 'España no puede durar,' paresçiendole que en España se hauía de acabar el mundo, porque no podiamos comer pan sin estas diligencias. (Hurtado de Mendoza 234–35)]

Prester John's historical existence is taken for granted by Margaret Anne Doody in *The True Story of the Novel*: ". . . and in 1450 Prester John sent an Ehiopian envoy to Naples" (210).

5. Columbus believed that he was sailing uphill on a protuberance of the world's surface where Eden would be located, and that the fresh water must issue from one of the four rivers of Eden.

his first encounters with the inhabitants of the Caribbean islands in a golden age discourse. They were simple people, he said, without malice, subject to no ruler, living in a temperate climate with plentiful vegetation and their simple wants abundantly supplied. The Indians of the Antilles supposedly sowed and harvested their grain in common and without discord, satisfied their need for food with a plentiful supply of readily available fruit and vegetables, walked naked, and lived in modest dwellings.

Peter Martyr, who had interviewed Columbus, perpetuated the paradigm. He described the islands as a paradise of eternal springtime (Decade III: bk. 5, 335; III:7, 350; III:7, 353); with rivers filled with gold (III:5, 337; III:7, 354; III:8,363) which the New World inhabitants nevertheless used only for their decorative arts (I:3,.131); and with an abundance of flora and fauna that fulfilled the inhabitants' needs (I:3, 152; I:8, 180). In short, it was a golden age. "They wear no clothes," Peter Martyr announced, "have no weights or deadly money in a genuine golden age without lying judges" [" . . . viven desnudos, sin pesas, sin medidas , sobre todo, sin el mortífero dinero en una verdadera edad de oro sin jueces calumniosos . . ." (I:2, 12)]. The words 'mine' and 'thine,' he stressed, had no place in the language of these docile and humble people (III:4, 318): "they had lived without quarrels over 'mine' and 'yours'; 'give me' and 'I won't give you'—the two things that draw men and compel them not to live in reality, while they live" ["habían vivido sin las disputas del 'mío' y 'tuyo,' del 'dame' y 'no te doy,' que son las dos cosas que arrastran, fuerzan y obligan a los hombres a que, viviendo, no vivan en realidad" (II:52, 231], and they never offend anyone (I:3, 141–42). Juan Maldonado's paternalistic benevolence would emphasize both the primitive Indians' innate "goodness," and the civilized Spaniards' obligation to educate them. Maldonado explained to the arts faculty at the University of Burgos in 1545 that the Indians who lived without laws or letters (read: European laws or letters) may have lacked culture or humanity not because of their defective nature but because they lacked tutors to guide them (Pagden, *The Fall* 92). In his earlier *Somnium* of 1532, Maldonado had explained the Indians' "edenic existence" ["existencia paradisíaca"] as the result of their freedom from hypocrisy and fraud, and as the basis for their supposed willingness to absorb Christian teachings (Bataillon 645–46). Similarly, Vasco de Quiroga would contrast the golden age in which the peoples of the New World lived with the decadent "age of iron" of the Europeans (Bataillon 820).[6]

The tenacity of the myth is witnessed to by the fact that the sites of the New World continued to be regarded as "edenic regions" ["comarcas paradisíacas" (Anghiera Decade IV: bk. 10, 434)] despite recurrent eye-witness accounts of "a hostile continent peopled with armed warriors rushing out of the tropical forests or strange cities . . ." (Hanke 6); Cortés's written reports of the ferocious enmity that existed between the Tlaxcalans and Aztecs in Mexico; Peter Martyr himself describing—almost apologetically—the existence of *some* cannibalism (III:1, 290), institutionalized sodomy (III:1, 290), and child sacrifice (IV:8, 426); and what Anthony Pagden describes as the forcible "conquests which rapidly became, and have remained to this day, marked down as one of the most appalling chapters in the history of human brutality" (Pagden, *Lords* 65). Dr. Chanca, who would soon change his mind about the edenic quality of the New World, nevertheless describes it initially in his letter to the *cabildo* in Seville as "these lands . . . in which I am assured in my heart that the earthly paradise is" (quoted in Campbell 47). Even Bartolomé de las Casas, in his excoriation of the Spaniards' cruelty in *The Spanish Colonie Or Brief Chronicle of the Actes and gestes of the Spaniards in the West Indies, called the newe world*, uses tropes reminiscent of the Indies as a second and fallen Eden where "there might have been builded great Cities, by the Spanishe, in which they might have lived as in an earthly Paradise" (quoted in Campbell 207). And John Locke could still say: "[t]hus, in the beginning all the world was America, and more so than it is now" (*Treatise* 2: ch. 5, para. 49).[7]

The discovery of the New World certainly gave new vigor to the abstract myth, clothing the former in the visionary accoutrements of the latter. This can be discerned not only in the *Decades*, but in the letters of both Columbus to Santángel in 1493 and Pero Vaz de Caminhya to King Manuel in 1500 announcing the discovery of Brazil, and in

---

6. The trope of the "noble savage," living in the "natural" state of humankind, pervaded the European imaginary. For an interesting overview, see Roger Bartra's *El salvaje en el espejo* and *El salvaje artificial*.

7. There were those, of course, who argued instead that the Spaniards had destroyed this idyllic world (Brandon 43). For an interesting perspective on how ancient geographic myths and fictions attained new life against the voyages of exploration, see Romm, especially "Epilogue: After Columbus," 215–22.

Amerigo Vespucci's accounts of the Mundus novus (1503?) and in his *Quatuor navigationes* of 1504 (Milhou 149). In a Europe where Pierre d'Ailly's and Mandeville's accounts of exotic lands had long been part and parcel of its intellectual currency, the existence of such marvels was simply taken for granted. After all, Mandeville claimed to have *seen* lands populated by men with dog heads, people with one leg who could stand on their heads and use the one huge foot as an umbrella, pygmies and Amazons, and men with eyes in the backs of their heads and women with bearded faces.[8] And Walter Raleigh had approvingly affirmed in his *Discoverie of the large, rich and Bewtiful Empire of Guiana* that Mandeville's "reports were held for fables many yeares, and yet since the East *Indies* were discovered, wee find his relations true of such things as heertofore were held incredible" (quoted in Campbell 86). Such superimposition of familiar myths onto new discoveries was part of the cultural climate. Marco Polo had interpreted China. "Medieval Europe's expanding geographical scope and knowledge of the physical world was curtailed," Gregory Guzman tells us, "by its superimposition of sacred and profane myths and legends on newly acquired information about the Orient" (53). Columbus's descriptions of "Española," Mary Campbell rightly points out, "resonate with established legends: the vegetable fertility and abundance are found in the Land of Cockaigne, the gold is from the Garden of the Hesperides and Solomon's Ophir, [and] the spices (nonexistent in Haiti) had always given the 'fabulous East' a voluptuous as well as commercial appeal" (175).

This is Don Quixote's cultural legacy. Tzvetan Todorov and Anthony Grafton actually describe Columbus in terms that could easily be applied to Don Quixote. For Todorov, there is nothing of "the modern empiricist about Columbus: the decisive argument is an argument about authority, not of experience. He knows in advance what he will find; the concrete experience is there to illustrate a truth already pos-

---

8. Mandeville's reports were validated by more authoritative writings, most notably Pliny's *Natural History*; Caius Julius Solinus, *Collectanea Rerum Memorabilium*; Bartholomaeus Anglicus, *De Proprietatibus Rerum*; and the many redactions of the medieval *Physiologus*. Belief in such strange creatures persisted into the seventeenth century with Conrad Gesner's *Historia Animalium*, Ulisse Aldrovandi's multiple volumes on the natural world, and Edward Topsell's *The History of Four-Footed Beasts* (1607). See also T. H. White, *The Book of Beasts* (London: Cape, 1954).

sessed . . ." (Todorov 17). For Grafton, Columbus's pleasure lies "in the
fact that experience in the field confirmed the texts that he had preferred
to believe" (82). And so it is with Don Quixote, for whom the concrete
experience of everyday life merely serves to illustrate the chivalric truths
that he already possesses.[9]

---

9. Todorov reminds us that Columbus performed "a 'finalist' strategy of interpretation, in the same manner in which the Church Fathers interpreted the
Bible: the ultimate meaning is given from the start (this is Christian doctrine)"
[17]. Readers of *Don Quixote* may well wonder if under cover of his mad knight,
Cervantes's ironic humor is not exposing ideological inertia and presenting a sardonic portrayal of the intellectual bankruptcy of "finalist" interpretation in all its
official manifestations. Whether or not this is the case, it is nevertheless interesting
to see that, in contrast to Avellaneda's novel, which keeps Don Quixote immured
in dogmatic certitude lest his resilience threaten Authority (see Mariscal on this
topic), Cervantes's Don Quixote gradually assimilates experience, thereby becoming less aprioristic.

4
The Pan European
Land of Cockaigne

L ike Don Quixote, Sancho Panza is also the cultural product of his age. The legend of Prester John's inexhaustible wealth, probably enhanced by descriptions of the Earthly Paradise which Saint Jerome had translated as an *hortus voluptatis* and an *hortus deliciarum*, was ripe, then, for yet another appropriation. It would provide an imaginary means of decentering the cultural gaze onto other idealized sites of abundance and leisure. But before going on to demonstrate the effects of such decentering, we would like to provide an interesting example of how cultural crossovers can be arbitrarily legitimized. The transcription below sheds some light on how a concept like Cockaigne, accessible in folklore, could become a popular counterpart to Don Quixote's classical Golden Age.

In a document cited by Alain Milhou, a Spanish peasant from Toledo in May 1534 recounts the tale of the huge quantities of gold amassed by the Spaniards in the "ransom" of the Peruvian Inca Atahualpa. This is how the peasant transcribes the event:

> While I was at the village blacksmith's with some friends discussing the news of Peru and of all these amounts of gold and silver that were brought back from there, one of them said that this was the country where Our Lord Jesus Christ had lived, since the grass where he walked had changed into gold and silver and this was why there was so much of it to be found. (quoted in Milhou 151)

In such a way, one of the blackest instances of Spanish betrayal in the New World becomes elided, even "Christianized," in the popular mind.[1] Similarly, the concept of Cockaigne will be subject to cultural crossovers and adapted "for a variety of purposes . . . ridiculing existing institutions, alleviating fears . . . providing moral instruction" (Pleij 326). The trajectory of Cockaigne's discursive formations provides interesting illustrations of how specific practices become new cultural productions.

The Cockaigne myth had fed the cultural imagination everywhere. As a theme of popular folklore, it was known under different names in different milieux: Cockaigne, Pomona, Jauja (Xauxa). Gorman Beauchamp reminds us of how pervasive and constant the myth remains to our own day:

> The French, English, Italians, Spanish, Portugese [*sic*] and Dutch all have some variant of the word . . . denominating this mythic land where the pleasure-principle operates unobstructed by reality: the Germans have their Schlaraffia and Pfannkuckenberg (Pancake Hill) and Bauernhimmel (Peasants' Heaven); the Swedes their Lattingersland (Land of Loafers) and the Irish their Mag-Mell (Plain of Pleasure). In our own day Hobo's Heaven and the Big Rock Candy Mountain recapitulate all the motifs . . . For while the names and locales . . . may vary, the content does not: it remains remarkably constant from culture to culture and throughout the centuries. (358)

In early centuries, so magical a site could take imaginative shape in Sir John Mandeville's marvellous adventures in exotic lands; in the biblically promised Judeo-Christian New Jerusalem where all restlessness would one day be assuaged; in a Muslim paradise of gustatory and sensual pleasures; or, as in Spain, in the eponymous Peruvian "tierra de Xauxa." Traces of it can be found among such varied ideological and literary forms as Charles Kingsley's *Water Babies*, W. B. Yeats's *The Happy Townland*, or in the popular versions of contemporary American folk-song traditions. For Herbert Marcuse, in *Eros and Civilization*, such magical sites function as a challenge to the reality principle with which we are faced in everyday living (Whitebook 4); for A. L.

---

1. The Spanish destroyed the great temples of the Aztecs and Incas, and forbade the practice of their religious rituals "and, above all, the Aztecs' massive human sacrifices. And they carried out a massive human sacrifice of their own, deliberately killing and subjugating native peoples and inadvertently using the microbes they carried to depopulate the new lands" (Grafton 132).

Morton, their function is compensatory and their impact associated with the actual economic reality from which they emerge. Morton calls Cockaigne the "people's utopia." Without disputing these psychological and/or economic arguments, one of our foci lies in exploring how myths like Cockaigne and Don Quixote's Golden Age, apparently different because of the positionality of the two protagonists, nevertheless betray the "circularity" of their reciprocal influence.[2]

Regardless of the varied ideological uses to which we will see it put, the myth of Cockaigne evokes a world where scarcity is abolished. François Génin in his *Recréations Philologiques* describes one of Cockaigne's most popular contemporary representations:

> During the 16th and 17th centuries, on the occasion of public festivities, a mountain was set up in a square of Naples, supposedly representing Etna or Vesuvius. From the crater of this mock volcano there spewed forth an eruption of sausages, cooked meats, and especially macaroni; as these tumbled down they were dusted with grated cheese which lay like ashes on the slopes of the mountain. The crowd fought among themselves to catch them: that was called a Cockaigne.

> [Pendant le [XVIe et le XVIIe] siècle, dans les occasions de réjouissances publiques, on élevait sur une place de Naples une montagne qui était censée représenter l'Etna ou le Vésuve. Du cratère de ce volcan parodié jaillissait une éruption de saucisses, de viandes cuites, et surtout de macaronis qui, en dégringolant, s'enfarinaient de fromage râpé, dont les flancs de la montagne étaient revêtus en guise de cendres. Le peuple se battait pour en attraper: cela s'appelait une *cocagne*. (89)]

The first known reference to the myth is believed to occur in the thirteenth-century *Carmina Burana*, whose collection included older material (see Beauchamp 356–57), but the earliest complete text extant in Western European literature is the *Fabliau de Cocagne* (or *Coquaigne*)

---

2. We use the term "circularity" here in Carlo Ginzburg's sense (*The Cheese and the Worms*), already suggested by Mikhail Bakhtin, as counter to the notion of autonomy and to describe the reciprocity between dominant cultures and subordinate classes. In his book, Ginzburg describes the profound influence in the sixteenth century that the high culture had on the subordinated classes, and the latter, in turn, on the former.

of around 1250.[3] In this work we encounter the phrase that will charac-
terize all of its subsequent representations in the various languages: "The
country's name is Cocaigne; / Whoever sleeps most here earns most"
["*Li païs a a non Cocaingne; / Qui plus i dort, plus i gaaigne* (vv. 27–28,
ed. Väänänen 21)]. The narrative setting for this particular fantasy is
medieval and its pretext a pilgrimage. The narrator goes to Rome to do
penance, and the Pope sends him to Cockaigne, a country that has been
blessed by God and all his saints:

> I believe that God and all his saints
> have blessed it more than
> any other country

> [Je cuit que Diex et tuit si saint
> L'ont miex beneïe et sacrée
> Que il n'ont une autre contrée. (vv. 24–26)]

The commonplace medieval frame story of pilgrimage, travail, penance, and self-denial, or its secular equivalent of the solitary knight
venturing into perilous lands, is here reversed and turned into a praise
of sloth, indulgence and excess. In this carnivalesque overturning of
everyday life, the calendar is conveniently re-shaped and so is the ecclesiastical year in order to favor its inhabitants. Every day is a holiday,
the months have five weeks, the year has four Easters, four Saint John's
Days, four wine harvests, four Candlemasses, four Carnivaltides. Lent
comes only once every twenty years (vv. 80–88), fasting is made easy
(vv. 89–90), and its denizens can earn five and a half *sols* if they sleep
until noon. Following the French *fabliau,* we find the Cockaigne motto
repeated from text to text and from engraving to engraving in the Italian: "He who sleeps most here earns most" ["quello chi più ci dorme più
guadagna" (Zenatti 55; Cocchiara 166)].

In a sixteenth-century poem titled "Capitolo di Cuccagna" ([Si-
ena] 1581), Cockaigne is pictured as a land where all kinds of food

---

3. There are three manuscripts in existence: the Bibliothèque Nationale no. 837
(A); the Bibliothèque Nationale no. 1593 (B); and the Bibliothèque de la ville de
Berne no. 354 (C). The version published by Méon in 1808 is an eclectic text based
on A with substitutions from B. Veikko Väänänen gives preference to manuscript A
and also prints the variants from manuscripts B and C.

are available (Cocchiara 160). Cocchiara also reproduces an early seventeenth-century illustration of a country abounding in fields of marzipan, mounds of cooked foods, and rivers of wine, as well as another print which is dated 1703. Two Spanish *romances* of the seventeenth-century, *La Isla de Jauja* (ed. Durán no.1347) and *La Isla de la Chacona* (no.1733), "por otro nombre Cucaña" ["also known as Cockaigne"], exemplify recurrent characteristics of the land of Cockaigne in the Catholic south. Here it features a land of sumptuous palaces bedecked with gold and precious jewels (or in the Italian, with walls made of cheese and good food). Whatever version we encounter, Cockaige always defies age and mortality. It is a land in which everyone remains young or can be rejuvenated in the waters of a well or in a fountain of youth. The fantasy abolishes all kinds of material lack: food and wine abound; sheep, goats, and calves, are born in great numbers; caves or trees are hung with gorgeous clothes that are free for the taking. Like manna from heaven, the industrialized equivalent, cooked poultry and wild game, fall from trees. Gold nuggets lie abandoned under trees.

This is the age-old core of the Cockaigne material: non-aristocratic, non-heroic, the cultural construct that flourished in both urban and rural settings (Pleij 418) and in versions that exemplified the aspirations and desires of a people too simple to codify a utopian ideology (Demerson 545). Many of the "cultured" versions of Cockaigne are more transparent in their ideological formations and have less to do with the commonplace realities of hunger and backbreaking labor than with the communal sharing of property and women. They often betray the ancient traditions that have been conflated in order to clothe the "new" with familiar descriptions of the "old." Mandeville's account of his supposed travels in Sumatra, a "combination of Utopian ideal and savagery" (Grafton 72), provides a good example of this conflation. His description echoes the biblical Eden, Plato's Ideal City, and even the Tibullan Golden Age in *Elegy II* (Grafton 69–72) which, as Stagg puts it, becomes "filled with the open enjoyment of the delights of Venus" (87).[4] Here is Mandeville's account:

---

4. In satirical versions of the Golden Age, sex had already been featured as one of its blessings. As early as Lucian's *True History*, the narrator tells us: "They [the inhabitants of his *fortunatae insulae*] see nothing indecent in sexual intercourse, whether heterosexual or homosexual, and indulge in it quite openly, in full view of everyone . . . As for women, they are shared indiscriminately with all men, and

> In that land is full great heat. And the custom there is such that men and
> women go all naked, and they scorn when they see any strange folk going
> clothed. And they say that God made Adam and Eve all naked, and that no
> man should shame him to show him such as God made him, for nothing
> is foul that is of kindly nature . . . And they wed there no wives, for all the
> women there be common and they forsake no man. And they say they sin
> if they refuse any man. And so God commanded Adam and Eve and to all
> that come of him when He said, *Crescite et multiplicamini et replete terram*
> . . . And also all the land is common . . . And every man there taketh what
> he will without any contradiction, and as rich is one man there as is another
> . . . . (quoted in Grafton 72–73)

Goods are not the only thing these inhabitants share in common, "for
they eat more gladly man's flesh than any other flesh" (quoted in Grafton 73).

The Tibullan erotic fantasy that Mandeville echoes, elaborated upon
and perpetuated in Jean de Meung's parodic (and misogynistic) continuation (ca. 1275–1280) of the *Roman de la rose*, becomes integral to
the bliss of subsequent "popular" and "cultured" versions of Cockaigne.
In the Spanish *Romancero*, we find that in the land of Xauxa, ten beautiful damsels are at each man's disposal "to serve and delight him" ["para
asistir a su servicio y regalo" (ed. Durán nos. 1347, 394)]. These damsels are replaced weekly or monthly. In *La Isla de la Chacona* Cucaña
(ed. Durán no. 1, 733), each man "has at his command" ["tiene a su
mando"] six beautiful maidens who are replaced weekly (573). In the
"cultured" version, Brussels Rhyming Text B, *Narratio de terra suaviter
viventium* (ca. 1500–1510), the usual background frame of plenty is
reiterated. And the narrator adds,

> There's another bonus to be had,
> Which cannot fail to make you glad.
> Neither men nor women offer excuses,
> There is no one who refuses
> To sleep with another tenderly . . .

---

there are no such things as jealous husbands" (280). He adds an addendum, ex-
cised in subsequent formulations of the myth: "Similarly, the boys cooperate freely
with anyone who makes advances to them, and never raise the slightest objection"
(280).

Lovely women and girls may be taken to bed,   .
Without the encumbrance of having to wed

[Daer en roept wijff noch man,
dye den anderen geweygeren kan
om eyn fruntelick slaepen gaen
. . . .
Schoene wrouven ende jonfrouwen,
Die mach ellick hebben all sonder truwen
(lines 105–7; 111–12, quoted in Pleij 437; trans. 39)

The Prose Text G from Ghent dating from the second half of the fifteenth century expresses it more crudely:

> Loose women are highly thought of in the country, and the more wanton
> and frolicsome they are, the more they're loved. Even though it's said that
> lecherous whores are expensive to keep, this is certainly not the case in that
> land, where all sensual pleasures are readily available and at no cost what-
> soever. (Pleij 43)

> [De vroukens die van lichter munte zijn, die worden in dit lant seer hoogh
> geachtet. Ende hoe dat se luyer ende leckerder zijn, hoe men se daer liever
> heeft. Want al is't dat men seyt dat leckere hoeren veel costen te houden,
> 't selfve en is nochtans in dit landt soo niedt, omdatter alle gheneughlijcke
> leckerheyt soo overvloedich wasset, die men lichtelijck sonder eenighe koste
> krijgen mach. (Pleij 441)]

The French variant [A] is almost identical with the Dutch rhyming
text: the men "take without resistance, whomever their heart desires"
["sanz contredit et sanz desfensse / Prent chascuns quanques son cuer
pensse" (ed. Väänänen MS A, p. 22, lines 49–50)]. The Italian text simply declares:

> There are many maidens who are
> always ready to give pleasure.
> You never saw more beautiful ones!

> [Et evvi ancora di molte zitelle
> Che seco stanno sempre a sollazzare
> Che non vedesti mai forse più belle! (quoted in Cocchiara 166)]

In Hans Sachs's disapproving German version, *Schlaraffenland*, Cockaigne's folkloric fountain of youth is not the source of magical healing and regeneration but instead a means of prolonging men's lust. In a modern illustrated version for children (!), we read: "A Fount of Youth flows down past benches / filled with oldsters mad for wenches" (Hinrichs 8). A late seventeenth-century anonymous poem, "An Invitation to Lubberland," repeats the now familiar characteristics of Cockaigne: "There you may lead a lazy life / free from all kinds of labor / and he that is without a wife / may borrow from his neighbor" (quoted in Beauchamp 359). It is clear, then, that woman, once eroticized in the *locus amoenus*, becomes an integral part of the myth. The fabliau, variant C, shows women providing men sexual pleasure, "without any commitment" on the men's part ["[sans] sairemanz ne foiz" (ed. Väänänen MS C, p. 25, line 8)]. Seigoffo's Italian map of 1703 shows them rocking the men to sleep. Taken at face value, these ideological formations seem to embody what Mumford claims to be Everyman's erotic fantasy: "What man has not had this utopia from the dawn of adolescence onwards—the desire to possess and be possessed by a beautiful woman?" (18).[5]

Once again the so-called autonomy of "cultured" or "popular" cultural constructs is put in question. Carlo Ginzburg's story of the sixteenth-century miller, Domenico Scandella (Menocchio), demonstrates the hybridity of such cultural images as the Golden Age, Prester John's Earthly Paradise, Cockaigne, and even the Mohammedan paradise of Mandeville's travel books. Since Menocchio would be burned as a heretic in 1599, he could not have been responding lightly to the Inquisitors' interrogation as to the meaning of paradise: "[P]aradise," Menocchio explained, conflating these separate traditions, "is a gentle

---

5. Even Marco Polo's description of the marvels of the East is interesting in this regard. Marco includes tribes where adultery and polygamy are integral to their way of being and where promiscuous women are valued as brides (Campbell 110), and his advice is that "into that country the young gentle-men from sixteen years to twenty four will do well to go" (quoted in Campbell 115). In a modern instance of *plus ça change plus c'est la même chose*, a Detroit newspaper puts it thus: "Ask most guys to describe Utopia . . . and they'll say something about being stretched out in a hammock on a tropical island . . . while Raquel Welch peels you a grape . . . That's Utopia all right!" (quoted in Beauchamp 345). Frank E. and Fritzie P. Manuel, on the other hand, see freedom from toil and the abundance of food as fundamental to utopian fantasies.

place where one finds every kind of fruit in every season and rivers forever flowing with milk, honey, wine, and sweet water; and . . . there are beautiful and lordly houses befitting the merit of each, decorated with precious stones, gold, and silver. Each person will have maidens and make use of them and will find them always more beautiful . . ." (quoted in Ginzburg 77).

At times the gendered message of utopia is complicated by traces of the misogyny of Jean de Meung's erotic fantasy. In the opening lines of *Trionfo della Cuccagna* of the sixteenth century, for example, amid a scene of wholesale merriment, the proverbial topos is echoed:

There's never any problem with ladies and young girls;
    they are all beautiful there, and you'll fall in love with them

[Et mai ci si fa briga per donne e per donzelle
Là ci son tutte belle, te ne innamoreresti (quoted in Cocchiara, 170)]

The phrase "*mai ci si fa briga*" makes the topos more ambiguous and polyvalent. It can be interpreted in two ways, either way reflecting what the male narrator interprets as a utopian dream. *Cuccagna* is where beautiful women and girls can be found "without trouble" whenever men want them, or *Cuccagna* is an ideal world because in it men are "free from the troubles" that women cause them in the real world.

The only compensation provided for woman in Cockaigne's erotic fantasy appears in the Italian 1703 engraving where, apparently free of pain, she sings and dances after childbirth. As Ruth Levitas points out, in Cockaigne "while Adam's labour is abolished, Eve's is unmentioned" (162).

We pause here to modify somewhat the gendered perspective we have been presenting. Three elements must be factored into Cockaigne's figuration of desire and of woman. In the light of what Frank E. and Fritzie P. Manuel believe to be the basic ingredients of utopian desire—freedom from the compulsion to work and from the fear of starvation—we must keep in mind that Cockaigne, unlike the Golden Age, is a fantasy of the *present*, though projected onto the future. In the idealized world of Cockaigne, responsibilities of all kinds are abolished, thereby radically simplifying the significance and representation of woman.

The first element is psychological. Competition constitutes the greatest source of strife for man in the real world and so a male-authored and male-directed utopian fantasy seeks to eliminate all forms of possession (Pleij 295). Both the past eutopia Don Quixote conjures up and the hedonistic Cockaigne of popular folklore simply render rivalry non-existent. As Plato had done with regard to the Guardians in his ideal commonwealth, in subsequent ones, both private property and the private possession of woman are abolished in ideal commonwealths. Woman is consequently limited to three figurations: as sexually available to all; or, as the virgin of Don Quixote's evocation, who in her chaste inaccessibility poses no problem of male rivalry; or, *mirabile dictu*, as an impossible combination of both virgin and wife as in Sir John Mandeville's Muslim paradise where "[e]very man shall have four score wives, who will be beautiful damsels, and he shall lie with them whenever he wishes, and he will always find them virgins" (*Travels* 104).[6]

Even women-authored utopias, addressing the question of possession, but in terms of the "conflicting needs for both community and individual autonomy," struggle with the issue (Williams, Lynn 132). In an interesting survey of feminist utopias, in which she calls the elimination of all forms of possession in utopia a "preference . . . for extended families rather than the sexual exclusiveness of marriage," Lynn F. Williams nevertheless arrives at a similar conclusion for these utopias as we have for the male-authored ones. Williams concedes that the "sexual mores" in women-authored utopias may also "vary from the comparatively puritanical to the overtly lusty, [but] there is a general agreement that loves, like possessions, are to be shared, not enjoyed privately" (128).

The second factor we proffer for the representation of woman in the utopian fantasy could be called socio-economic. As Gardiner insists, "utopias [cannot] be viewed as fantasies of ideal cities, forms of social organization, or mythical lands which are the product of an individual's creative imagination; rather they are construed as *manifestations of per-*

---

6. This playful vision receives severe condemnation in the seventeenth-century work of the theologian Pedro Aznar Cardona justifying the expulsion of the Spanish Moors. Aznar Cardona contrasts the Christian paradise, a "shining vision of God and contemplation of his essence" ["clara visiō y contemplacion de Dios essential"] with the perversity of the Muslim paradise: "not food or fleshly delights, as the lecherous Muhammad claims" ["y no por comidas, ni deleytes carnales, como pret[en]de el libidinoso Mahoma" (32 recto)].

vasive social and ideological conflicts with respect to the desired trajectory of social change" (22: emphasis added). And as Louis Marin demonstrates in his discussion of Rabelais, no matter how much utopian fantasies try to alter the real by fabricating a "replica" of the absent real, two realities are always present in the literary product, traces of the everyday real and the altered "real" of the utopian fantasy ("un autre récit se substitue au récit manquant: à celui de l'histoire, celui d'une autre histoire." [Marin, "Les corps utopiques" 49–50]). Could this then account for the restricted representation of woman in these fantasies?

Utopian fantasies are first and foremost shelters from the instabilities of the real world. The economic travails of a man's everyday life in that world, after all, are primarily allied to his condition as *homo faber*. Unable to enjoy what he produces, a working man either sells his labor or skill or he must give it to his landlord or master. In such an economy, man's desire for woman assumes less importance than does his freedom from back-breaking labor, from unpredictable weather conditions that can destroy his means of livelihood, and from the insecurity of not having enough food. The connection between food and eros is poignantly put in Italo Calvino's *The Path to the Nest of spiders* (*Il sentiero dei nidi di ragno*): "The dreams of the partisans [read: Cockaigne dreamers] are short and rare, dreams born of nights of hunger, linked to food which is always scarce and to be divided among so many; dreams about chewing bits of bread and putting them away in drawers . . . Only when the men's stomachs are full . . . can they dream of naked women" (74; quoted in Biasin 102).

The third factor that may explain the figuration of woman in Cockaigne is also historical and may be seen as a corollary of the second. In the real world of the laboring man of the early modern period, marriage seldom occurred before the age of thirty. Man needed woman as helper on the farm, in his workshop, and as producer of additional helpers and heirs. Woman might be co-producer in such an economy, but she and the children were pieces of necessary equipment without which the familial machine could not function. Cockaigne inverts the needs of the everyday world. It abolishes all kinds of work and, as a result, the requirement of women's or sons' labor. Man's need of woman for continuity in posterity is simply rendered irrelevant since Cockaigne's restorative magic wells and fountains of youth defy age and mortality. And so the pleasures of sex, when depicted, function as acts quite separate from the social institution of marriage or from woman as biological reproducer.

Here we permit ourselves an excursus: the issue of gender, though treated more obliquely in *Don Quixote* than was the text's trivializing of pastoral love, also serves to expose the "real" in the text vis-à-vis its eutopic present. Sancho is seen bonding happily in his utopian quest—male to male and servant to master—with Don Quixote in their chivalric adventure and their respective dreams of wealth and fame. Like the milkmaid La Perette in La Fontaine's fable, Sancho has already secured, in fantasy, his social ascent. In fact, in the repertory of proverbs that anticipate Sancho Panza in Cervantes's novel, we saw a mocking reference to the illusions of the Sancho figure in folklore: "Sancho has hidalgo delusions" ["Rebienta Sancho de hidalgo"] (Márquez Villanueva, 51). But the text's utopian discourse exposes Sancho's fantasy by figuring Teresa Panza in her own setting: she is left to mind the home and guarantee the continuity of the family according to the hierarchical status quo, and she lacks, as we have pointed out, the means even to offer a simple supper to the page who brings the letters from the Duchess (II:1, 628). Again, while Sancho fantasizes his peasant daughter as the wife of a Count, the text confirms the always already dispensation of Sanchica's social positioning. Her only choice, in the Panza family's "real" situation, is to marry her equal, the neighbor Juan Tocho (II:5).

The myth of Cockaigne, then, could be adapted *ad infinitum*. It could be transformed into what Pleij calls "elitist Cockaignes," an example being the fantastic theme park at Heslin Castle in northern France (destroyed in 1553 by Charles V's imperial armies) with its golden trees, metallic singing birds, and healing waters engineered to regale the eyes (Pleij 23–25). It could serve as a means of subverting the social order, that is, as imaginary compensation for what was perceived by the humbler classes as "normal," albeit unjust, in their everyday lives. Two fourteenth-century documents make this position clearer. One is a peasant declaration cited by Raymond Williams to the effect that "[w]e are men formed in Christ's likeness, and . . . kept like beasts" (*The Country* 42); the second, by Sir John Froissart, relates the oft-cited sermon supposedly delivered by John Ball every Sunday after mass. We quote John Ball:

> My good friends, matters cannot go on well in England until all things shall be in common; when there shall be neither vassals nor lords . . . Are we not

all descended from the same parents, Adam and Eve? And what can they
show, or what reason can they give, that they should be more masters than
ourselves? . . . They have handsome seats and manors, while we must brave
the wind and rain in our labours in the field; and it is by our labour that
they have wherewith to support their pomp. We are called slaves, and if we
do not perform our service we are beaten . . . . (Froissart 207–8)

This aspect of the myth becomes even more poignant in its "popularized" variants. We have an example six hundred years after John Ball's
sermon. It is the Cockaigne-like fantasy of the American folk song "Big
Rock Candy Mountain," in which the myth serves to exorcise the reality of hunger and poverty, if only temporarily, through the medium of
humor and fantasy.

> In the Big Rock Candy Mountain,
> There's a land that's fair and bright,
> Where the hand-outs grow on bushes,
> And you sleep out every night,
> Where the box-cars all are empty,
> And the sun shines ev'ry day
> Oh, the birds and the bees and the cigarette trees,
> The rock-and-rye springs where the whangdoodle sings,
> In the Big Rock Candy Mountain.
> In the Big Rock Candy Mountain
> All the cops have wooden legs,
> And the bulldogs all have rubber teeth,
> And the hen lays softboiled eggs.
> The farmer's trees are full of fruit,
> And the barns are full of hay.
> Oh, I'm bound to go where there ain't no snow,
> Where the sleet don't fall and the wind don't blow,
> In the Big Rock Candy Mountain (quoted in Bullough 35)

As Renato Poggioli pointed out a generation ago, abundance of food
and drink must be seen as integral to "the utopia of the pícaro." Such
abundance is "a projection of hunger's dreams, the wish-fulfillment of
the starving man's obsession with food" (Poggioli 248). Gian-Paolo Biasin, in *The Flavors of Modernity*, and in the same vein, shows that food
always signifies more than itself. Food links, Biasin tells us, "the literary
expression with the pretextual, historical or sociological level" (11), for

"[t]he discourse on food inevitably becomes a discourse on pleasure and on power" (27), and the abundance of food is usually a product of its semantic opposite—hunger (Biasin 31). Food as signifier, then, makes accessible to the reader signs of both the cultural experiences of the dreamer and of the ideologies that have shaped the dream.[7]

Cockaigne could become the basis of parody as well. If we go back to the Middle English poem "Land of Cockaigne", we find one of the best-known examples of a rarer version of Cockaigne, as a clerical, or anti-clerical, parody (in Bennett 136–44). It retains the evocation of a land blessed with the characteristic amenities. Unlike the French and Italian versions, however, it is now a place exclusive to young monks who escape from their "wel fair abbei," (140, line 51) which is also a luxurious abode, and disport themselves with the young nuns from "a gret fair nunnerie" (143, line 148) nearby. Sex and sloth figure prominently here. The monk who is most active in the former and who, echoing the recurrent phrase that characterizes the latter in the various languages, "slepith best"—["Qui plus i dort / plus i gaaigne" (*Fabliau*, vv. 27–28); "quello chi più ci dorme più guadagna" (in Cocchiara 166)]—may hope to become an abbot (Bennett 144).

In a fine discussion of this poem, Juliette de Caluwé-Dor sees it as a diatribe against religious orders in the form of a mock Paradise, typified by the licentious living of contemporary monks and nuns, an "anti-Paradis caractérisé surtout par les moeurs relâchées des moines et des nonnes" (116). Whatever interpretation is put upon it, the anonymous author clearly enjoyed creating this representation of Cockaigne. The curious condition imposed in the poem upon those who enter this blessed land—seven years spent in swine's dirt ("seve yere in swineis dritte")—may (or may not) be a comic metaphor for the wretched period spent as a novice. What is made clear is that the secular lordlings

---

7. Such a eu-topic and u-topic blissful *nowhere* as Cockaigne, upon which a powerless *peuple* (François Génin's designation, above) could sometimes stage its illusions, could become practical and disorderly realities, as in the 1525 peasants' revolts where they "ransacked monasteries, swilled wine . . . as they raided the cellars of abbeys along the Rhine, Neckar, and Mosel" (Mullett 98). But, as A. L. Morton explains, during such periods "in which revolution was not objectively possible though popular riots were, of course, frequent," Cockaigne-like fantasies "were the means of keeping alive hopes and aspirations that might otherwise have died away, and which at a later date would prove of immense value" (31).

in the poet's audience will never enter unless they first undertake a pre-scribed penance: "Lordinges gode and hend / Mot ye never of world wend / Fort ye stond to yure cheance / And fulfille that penance" (Bennett 144, lines 183–86). This clerical admonition may well display a trace of how Cockaigne is framed in its more moralistic variations. Despite its abundance, the land is no longer in the tradition of the kind upon which we have so far been focusing—what Sargent called "a body utopia or a utopia of sensual gratification." It is now conditional. For this reason Raymond Williams qualifies such versions of Cockaigne as "latently utopian," because a compensatory "sweet little world" may await the dreamer, but *only if and when* "the battle has been won" (Williams, *Problems* 204).

From the fourteenth through the sixteenth century, Cockaigne's mythical land becomes primarily a source of mirth. Boccaccio renames the place Bengodi and associates it with trickery.[8] In the *Decamerone* (Eighth day, Third story), Calandrino, the nickname of a famously simple-minded painter, is duped into believing in this bogus land supposedly full of priceless stones that have magical properties. Gian Francesco Straparola's rogues use Cockaigne's mythical abundance to trick the simpleton Campriana. In Spain, Mateo Alemán's Guzmán is proud to proclaim that his trickery with the cook has provided him with such pickings that the kitchen in which he worked, "seemed to me to be the land of Xauxa" ["parecióme la tierra de Jauja" (pt. I: bk. 2, ch. 6, 318]; and Lope de Rueda has similar fun with the myth in his *Paso Quinto*.

But an interesting feature of Rueda's variation on this fabulous place is that it is developed within the dramatic situation of the interlude. Unlike the French and Italian Cockaignes, Rueda's Xauxa is not an independent, free-floating fantasy, elaborated with rich detailing in order to engage the wishful desires of the listener. Instead, Rueda has the audience watch the deception as he distances the spectator from the trickery taking place. Consequently, it is not we—the spectators/readers—who are to be seduced by this wondrous land. It is the simpleton Mendrugo

---

8. Boccaccio's Castilian contemporary Juan Ruiz also uses *cucaña* to convey deceit and trickery in his *Libro de Buen Amor*: "I wrote that song about the greedy student, my companion in the easy life . . ." ["Del escolar goloso conpañero de cucaña fize esta otra troba . . ." (st. 122a)]; "Sir Monkey went home, and many went with him; the litigants went with him, a slippery crew" . . . ["Don Ximio fue a su casa, con él mucha conpaña, / con él fueron las partes, conçejo de cucaña" (st. 341b)].

whom we see as complicit in his deception. The thieves succeed because Mendrugo is only too willing to be duped by his own desires. It is not surprising that Cervantes admiringly recalled the comic artistry of Rueda —"famous for his performance and his intelligence" ["varón insigne en la representación y en el entendimiento" (*Teatro completo* 8)—since it anticipates his own skill in presenting willing dupes not only in *El retablo de las maravillas* but in *Don Quixote* as well.

As in Boccaccio's and Straparola's work, in the *Paso Quinto*, titled *La Tierra de Xauxa,* Rueda dramatizes how the two thieves, Honzigera and Panarizo, trick the simpleton with the promise of easy living in the fabulous mythic place. The thieves' depiction of Xauxa for the credulous Mendrugo is one familiar to us, and consists of the alluring characteristics of the "popularized" Cockaigne. In Rueda's mythical land "men are paid for sleeping" ["pagan soldada a los hombres por dormir"] and they "are whipped for working" ["azotan los hombres porque trabajan"]. The proverbial rivers of honey and of milk give forth their abundance, and between the two rivers there is a platter of butter and curds which tumble into the river of honey, seemingly saying "eat me, eat me" ["hay un río de miel y junto a él, otro de leche, y entre río y río hay una fuente [9] de mantequillas encadenada de requesones y caen en aquel río de la miel, que no paresce sino que están diciendo: 'cómeme, cómeme'"]. The trees in Rueda's Xauxa have trunks made of salt pork ["hay unos árboles que los troncos son de tocino"], the leaves are pancakes, and the fruit are fritters that fall into the river of honey, also saying "chew me, chew me" ["Y las hojas son hojuelas, y el fruto destos árboles son buñuelos, y caen en aquel río de miel, quellos mismos están diciendo 'máscame, máscame'"]. Xauxa's streets are paved with egg yolks, and between each egg yolk is a pork pie ["las calles están empedradas con yemas de huevos, y entre yema y yema un pastel con lonjas de tocino"]. There are barbecue pits three hundred paces long, loaded with hens, capons, partridges, rabbits, and woodcocks ["hay unos asadores de trescientos pasos de largo, con muchas gallinas y capones, perdices, conejos, francolines"]. Beside each bird is a sucking pig, ready for carving, saying "gobble me down" ["Y junto a cada ave un cochinillo, que no es menester más que cortar,

---

9. Marín Martínez in his edition of Rueda has amended *fuente* "platter" to *puente* "bridge" which is more difficult to visualize.

quello mismo dice 'engollíme, engollíme'" (ed. García Pavón 85–88)]. There follow boxes of preserved fruits, marzipan, and glasses of wine. Absent from Rueda's Xauja, however, are characteristics found in other Cockaigne variations: there is no river of wine flowing through it, no community of women for men's pleasure, no mounds of gold, and no fountain of eternal youth.

The two sharpers, Honzigera and Panarizo, meet Mendrugo on the road as he carries a pot of stew to his wife, who is in jail for procuring. In order to deprive him of what he has, each of them, by turn, takes Mendrugo aside and mesmerizes him with *what he could have* as they describe the mouth-watering details of Xauja. Mendrugo's attention is distracted, the two sharpers accomplish their purpose, and Mendrugo loses his pot of stew. Unlike in the French and Italian models, Rueda's adaptation does not play to the audience. It exposes the vision of Xauja/Cockaigne as fraudulent, dramatizes it as a hoax, and has the audience witness it as a hoax.

If we may digress briefly: by investing the traditional free-floating Cockaigne material with motivation, Rueda exposes the lie on which Cockaigne-like fantasies are based. More importantly, he enables a static, future-less fantasy, with dialogic possibilities that Cervantes will exploit in *Don Quixote*. Cervantes shows the reader, as Rueda had done before him, the very process by which deception is perpetrated on the credulous. It is the product of their own desires. The laborer Sancho Panza, for example, is led from the start by Don Quixote's promises of social ascent coupled with the accompanying allurements of a life of ease. Don Quixote, the impoverished hidalgo, is motivated by the fantasy of resurrecting a past chivalric world in which the privileges once enjoyed by his class will form no small part. Neither knight nor squire, of course, thinks of these fantasies as fantasies, but the utopian discourse discloses them for what they are. Once Sancho is installed in Barataria the utopian fantasy is ironized. The reader watches Sancho being tantalized, and then bamboozled, by delicious dish after dish that is set before him only to be snatched away. That first meal can be said to be metonymic of Sancho's entire experience as governor as he laments the lack of ease, of gain, of sleep, ("pagan soldada a los hombres por dormir" [Rueda 85]/ "Qui plus i dort / plus i gaaigne" [ed. Väänänen, line 28]/ "quello chi più ci dorme più guadagna" [in Cocchiara 166]) in his wished-for utopia. In similar fashion, the text discloses the reverse situation that will cause Don Quixote's unhappiness. In his case, it is the interminable otium (the ease his squire covets) of the life that has been recreated for him in the Duke's and Duchess's palace.

The comic diversion of the Cockaigne tradition by Boccaccio, Straparola, and especially by Rueda, is continued in two other ways in *Don Quixote*, thereby interrogating the utopian idyll constructed in the text. First, the overwhelming abundance of Camacho's Cockaigne-like wedding feast is placed in a "realistic" setting, which could plausibly accommodate Rueda's hyperbolic 300-yard barbecue pits. But the same "realistic" landscape, with its arbors, garlands, and music, is simultaneously reminiscent of an idyllic pleasance. The utopian discourse's juxtaposition of idyll and gross abundance, as well as Sancho's gormandizing, introduces conflicting readerly keys which destabilize both verisimilitude and idyll. Second, the text ironizes the myth in its deliberate reversal of spectators'/readers' expectations. That is, the poor laborer Sancho is filled to satiety. The rich Camacho, on the other hand, who has harbored the delusion of spiritual and emotional plenitude by deploying his Cockaigne-like resources, is the one who ends up empty-handed.

After this brief excursion, we return to Cockaigne and its trajectory, now in the Northern countries. Here the land of plenty is condemned as a land of sluggards. Hans Sachs's *Schlaraffenland* of the sixteenth century depicts the mythic land as "The Glutton's Paradise," and a land of licentiousness.

> Whoever is shiftless and refuses to learn,
> he comes to great honors in this land;
> whoever is acclaimed as the laziest,
> in this land he is king.
> Whoever is savage, wild, and senseless,
> who stupidly eats everything,
> in this land he becomes a prince.
> He who gladly fights with Liverwurst,
> he is made a knight.
> Whoever is a slob and cares for nothing
> but eating, drinking, and lots of sleeping
> in this land is made a count.

[Wer unnuetz ist, wil nichts nit lehrn,
Der kombt im Land zu grossen ehrn;
Wann wer der faulest wirdt erkant,
Derselb ist koenig inn dem Landt.
Wer wuest, wild und vnsinnig ist
Grob, unuerstanden alle frist,
Auss dem macht man im Land ein Fuerstn.
Wer geren ficht mit Leberwuerstn,
Auss dem ein Ritter wird gemacht.
Wer schluechtisch ist und nichtzen acht,
Dann essen, trincken und vil schlaffn
Auss dem macht man im land ein Graffn. (Sachs 10)]

Even before Sachs's text of 1530, a German print of 1520 had represented Cockaigne as a den of promiscuity in which a good-for-nothing citizen of this mythical land simply fritters his time away cavorting with promiscuous women (Pleij 339–40). This text was the model for the Dutch prose text G (ca. 1546), to which we have alluded. It warns its readers that "[e]ating and drinking and lazing around / These are three things that ought to have bounds" ["Luy en lecker en veel te meughen, / Dat zijn drie dinghen die niet en deughen" (Pleij 40; 438)].

According to Geoffrey Bullough, the German satire of Cockaigne is the one that prevails in England, where "Cockaigne" becomes known as "Lubberland" (Dutch *Luilekkerland*). Bullough cites John Florio's definition of 1598: "*Cucagna*, the epicures or glutton home, the land of all delights: so taken in mockerie"; "*Cocagna*, as we say, Lubberland" (quoted in Bullough 24–25). Cockaigne has come a long way in these variations from the blessed and "playful image" presented in the thirteenth-century *Le fabliau de Cocagne*—a country blessed ["beneïe et sacrée"] by "God and all his saints" ["Diex et tuit se saint" (vv. 24–26)], from the poignant idyll of the "people's utopia," and especially from the land of easy living mirthfully evoked by Boccaccio, Straparola, Mateo Alemán, and Rueda.

The mythic land now becomes the object of serious moralistic disapprobation in countries affected by the Protestant reformation. In 1605, the English Bishop Joseph Hall's *Mundus Alter et Idem* was published under the pseudonym Mercurius Britannicus and translated into English by John Healy in 1609. It went through two editions in the English translation, two Latin editions, and one German edition (Leslie 126). The condemnation of Cockaigne in this popular book is severe. The *Mundus* depicts a voyage to Terra Australis in which Crapulia or the Land of Excess is discovered. Hall's Crapulia is divided into two provinces: Pamphagoia, also called Glutton's Land or Tenter-Belly, and Yvronia or Drunkards' Land. In one of Pamphagoia's towns, we encounter the familiar picture of our hedonistic Cockaigne now described as a disgusting place. An attendant daily opens the lazy master's eyes when he awakens for "the master onley exerciseth but eating, digesting, and laying out" (Morton 34).

The reception given Hall's *Mundus*, however, is particularly interesting in three ways. It continues to demonstrate how Cockaigne becomes reformulated as a means of meaning production under specific conditions of cultural circulation. It shows how a dominant order renders alternative or oppositional forms non-threatening through incorporation or co-optation (Williams, *Marxism and Literature* 123–25), as well as the way in which the processual nature of hegemony always entails the Gramscian notion of struggle for meaning.

In France, Gabriel Naudé, Cardinal Mazarin's librarian, simply dismisses the *Mundus* as a mere "satire on the corrupt morals of this age" (Brown, introduction to Hall p. xxxi). This "inadequate description," as Huntington Brown calls it, of the *Mundus*, "repeated with slight variations at intervals ever since" (p. xxxii), is staunchly condemned in England by John Milton. Milton, only too aware perhaps as Englishman and Puritan, of the attractiveness of a land of ideal climatic conditions, where work is non-existent, food and drink excellent, and women sexually willing, attacks the *Mundus* as "the idlest and the paltriest Mime that ever mounted upon banke" (quoted in Hall p. xxxiii). Of course both Cockaigne and Arcadian fantasies are equally distasteful to the dour Puritan. In his *Eikonoklastes* (1649), he attacks King Charles for making Pamela's prayer from Sidney's *Arcadia* his own before dying: "For he [King Charles] certainly whose mind could serve him to seek a Christian prayer out of a Pagan Legend [Arcadia], and assume it for his own, might gather up the rest God knows from whence; one perhaps out of the French *Astraea*, another out of the Spanish *Diana; Amadis* and *Palmerín* could hardly escape him . . ." (quoted in Doody 264).

Ben Jonson's well-known treatment of Cockaigne-like fantasies in

Bartholomew Fair, as well as Pieter Bruegel the Elder's notable painting *Luilekkerland* (from 1567) in the Alte Pinakothek in Munich, also dismiss Cockaigne as a land of good-for-nothings. In Bruegel's portrayal every level of society is represented as having already fallen prey to the pervasive influence of Cockaigne. In the painting, the peasant, the warrior, and the scholar, representing the three estates, have all succumbed to gluttony and sloth.

In his essay on "Symbolic Power" in *Language and Symbolic Power,* Pierre Bourdieu makes a distinction between myth and ideology: "Unlike myth," he says, "which is a collective and collectively appropriated product, ideologies serve particular interests which they tend to present as universal whole" (167). But, *pace* Bourdieu, myth too can be transformed, as we see, in order to serve the particular interests of particular groups. The written versions of Cockaigne bear witness to ideological transformation and circulation, and imply an intellectualized mode of appropriation that dissimulates the very contradictions that produced the myth in the first place. Poggioli may have called Cockaigne "the utopia of the *pícaro*" (248), and with some reason, but specific practices have consistently transformed it into interesting and unexpected cultural productions.

It is important to keep in mind that Cockaigne as a folkloric land of leisure was never circumscribed to a laboring audience. The projected desires of the *peuple* were appropriated for a different audience and structured by different social conditions. Consequently, although it is often said, by Peter Burke and others, that "the culture of the lower classes (*Unterschicht*) is an out-of-date imitation of the culture of the upper classes" (*Oberschicht*) [Burke 58], the converse can also be true. Since neither "culture" constitutes an autonomous construct, it is the purpose for which the construct is used that becomes significant—that is, its function, not its content nor the impulse from which it springs.

Written, and later printed, texts of Cockaigne, for example, actually exist alongside whatever traditions of oral performance were familiar to the illiterate classes. The fabliaux, as Paul Zumthor notes, may have been bourgeois in production. These fabliaux appear to mark the emergence of a literature especially suited to the urban bourgeoisie ["semblent marquer l'émergence d'une littérature plus spécialement appropriée à la bourgeoisie citadine"]. The literate authors would have been clerics, perhaps, but mostly minstrels and even bourgeois ["par-fois des clercs, mais plus souvent des jongleurs, sinon des bourgeois" (Zumthor 138)]. Cockaigne, in our surviving fabliau (whose very clas-sification as a fabliau Veikko Väänänen finds open to question), has obvious marks of refinement, even of luxury. The tables are not rustic. They have white cloths on them "*blanches napes mises*" (v. 46)]. The author in his presentation of the rivers of wine stakes his claim to con-noisseurship: the red wine is the best that can be found "in Beaune or from beyond the sea" ["Du meillor que l'en puist trover / En Biausne ne de là la mer" (vv. 67–68)], and the white wine is "the best and fin-est that was ever produced in Auxerre, La Rochelle, or Tonnerre" ["le meillor et tout le plus fin / Qui onques creüst a Auçerre, / a Rocelle, ne a Tonnevrre" (vv. 70–72)]. The entire representation of food in this Cockaigne exemplifies the hierarchization that Bourdieu has pointed out in language use. In "The Economics of Linguistic Exchanges," he distinguishes between the manners symbolized by *la bouche* and *la gueule* when referring to "mouth" in French. The idioms that employ the former, *la bouche,* imply fastidiousness; the idioms for the latter, *la gueule,* vigor, even violence. It is by such means that the "higher" culture "aristocratizes" food—by emphasizing form and style in its representation. Popular or "low" culture, on the other hand, priori-tizes plenty and food as a "nourishing substance" (Bourdieu, *Distinc-tion* 197) that provides for the body's "brutal needs" (*Distinction* ch. 1; 192–94).

The pleasures depicted in such Cockaignes, therefore, are sensual, but not sexually coarse. Quality becomes more important than quantity (*Distinction* 196). The women are gentle ladies ["dames" and "damoi-seles" (v. 110)] and not wenches. The clothes that can be had are in-tended as much for fashionable display as they are for covering the body and for providing basic warmth. The fabrics described come in rich colors, are made of fine wool, camel hair, silk from Alexandria (vv. 128–34), and the traders are courteous gentlemen ["mout sont cortois" (v. 125)]. Conversely, when we discuss the hybridity of Cockaigne as a cultural construct, it should be noted that the fact that a fabliau was performed by *jongleurs,* and in public places, indicates that Cockaigne could never have been exclusively bourgeois or exclusively plebeian, ei-ther in circulation or in reception.

The written Italian versions, though they occur much later than the

French, make clear the hybridity which may have characterized these French fabliaux. They bear witness to a tradition of oral performances by *cantastorie* (singers of tales), indicating that Cockaigne must have circulated among "popular" and bourgeois audiences. Tomasso Garzini, in his *Piazza universale di tutte le professsioni del mondo* (Venice 1587), refers to such stories as the proverbial "stuff" of travellers' and pilgrims' tales (Rossi in Calmo 399; Cocchiara 162). By the same token, when the erudite polymath and cultured letter writer Andrea Calmo allows himself a flight of fancy in one of his epistles, a vision of abundance that clearly evokes the familiar characteristics of Cockaigne (*Libro* II, *lettera* 34), his editor Vittorio Rossi comments: "We have here a fine example of a description of the land of Cockaigne, a dream dear to the people of all times" ["Abbiamo qui un bell'essempio di descrizione del paese di Cuccagna, sogno tanto caro al popolo di ogni tempo" (Rossi in Calmo 143 n. 9)]. Rossi also cites the opening lines of the early seventeenth-century text, *Trionfo della Cuccagna* by Martin da Lucca, as an example of the universal theme of a land of abundance and carefree existence where work has been abolished:

> Laughing and singing we'll go to Cockaigne,
> where you get a living without hard work

> [Ridendo e cantando andremo in cuccagna,
> Là ci si guadagna senza dura fatica (quoted in Calmo 400)]

We note, however, that even in these imaginary constructs the utopian discourse often casts doubt on the utopian fantasy it has set up. For example, in Cockaigne, we are told, nothing is bought and nothing is sold "[n]us n'i achate ne ne vent" (ed. Väänänen MS A, 1. 108; 25). Nothing here is beyond anyone's capacity to possess, whether it be a measure of wheat or a cask of wine:

> A measure of wheat is got for a farthing,
> and a cask of Trebbiano for almost nothing

> [Il moggio di formento si dà per un quattrino
> E per un bagattino la botte del trebbiano (quoted in Calmo 400)]

Everything is available in this land of plenty where

> a hundred slices of marzipan go for a farthing,
> and for a pittance you can buy
> a roasted calf and good biscuit to go with it
>
> [e cento marzapani se dan per un quatrino
> e con un sol terlino si compra un vitel cotto
> con certo bon biscotto . . . .
> (Faustino da Terdocio, *Testamento*; quoted in Calmo 404)]

Then what is the purpose/value of the mountains of gold and heaps of coins that are figured there? The supposedly neutralized real is very much present in the utopian fantasy, for the "representation constantly displays a tendency to transgress its borders" (Marin, *Food for Thought* 89*)*. Gold thereby becomes a sign that reveals what it symbolizes (*Food* 25), namely, the inability of the dispossessed to pay off incurred debts. The lack of money in the real world is thus displaced by a superfluity in the utopian fantasy in which it is neither needed nor valued.

The same can be said of the treatment of work as a punishable crime in Cockaigne. In the illustrated version of this land of pervasive leisure—"pagan soldada a los hombres por dormir"/ "Qui plus i dort, plus i gaaigne" / "quello chi più ci dorme più guadagna"—the prison to which those who work go is given prominence by being placed in the foreground. But the apparent tautology of forbidding work where none is needed, however, has an analogous effect to that of the superfluity of money. This is particularly discernible in the seventeenth-century engraving and in Seigoffo's of 1703. Both show the imprudent wretches who have been caught working being dragged off to jail. In Seigoffo's version the overdetermined moat of "vino dolce" and the cannons that fire bottles of wine (with which the fortified prison is defended) are signifying practices. The utopian discourse exposes the contradiction that the utopian fantasy elides. It reminds the reader of an everyday reality that exposes the contradictions from which the fantasy initially emerges.[10]

---

10. Campbell's already cited description of the impulse behind Columbus's "imposition" of gold and spices (which were wholly lacking there) onto the islands of the West Indies is germane here. Such "factual inconsistencies," she suggests, are

Although the myth's function is somewhat clear, its origin and development are not. We cannot expect to answer the question of how the literary versions of Cockaigne came into existence. But we can allude briefly to some of the crossover problems between "higher" and "popularized" versions of Cockaigne in this regard. For Antonio Cornejo Polar, such cultural crossovers (*entrecruzamientos*), however limited in scope, become important because they expose conflicts and alterities usually concealed in "transculturation" (55). For Susan Willis, such instances of alien inscriptions do not inhibit the production of viable cultural statements (Joannou 181) for, as Paul Ricoeur reminds us, it is the function of imaginary constructs, and not their origins, that is culturally significant. "Does not the fantasy of an alternative society and its exteriorization 'nowhere,'" he asks rhetorically, "work as one of the most formidable contestations of what is?" (16).

We cannot say that Cockaigne originates in folk tradition, nor that the myth has been subsequently appropriated by the literary culture. The reason is that there is no evidence in the myth itself of essential characteristics that scientific folklorists attribute to folk culture. Among them are orality and practical functionality. Oral culture is collective, communitarian, and is also subject to the variability with which collectors of ballads, stories, and anecdotes are familiar. A ballad, a traditional *romance*, collected, printed in a sixteenth-century *romancero* or *cancionero*, divorced from its music and perhaps its dance, is no longer participating in the traditional culture from which it was taken, and where it functioned within a shared communal consciousness. It is, in fact, marked with a radically different sign. We have no evidence for the transformation of such an oral tradition in the literary examples of Cockaigne. The myth also lacks the known functionality of folk culture in its connection of popular songs, stories, etc. with the peoples' rhythms of work, the boredom of repetitive tasks, and moments of shared relaxation (Soriano 484–89).

The Cockaigne narratives may be compared, instead, to the seventeenth-century Spanish *literatura de cordel*. The stories and ballads, cheaply printed as broadsheets and sold on the streets of Spanish cities, catered to the newly literate or barely literate populace (see Caro

_____

"part of a literary landscape generated over several centuries by the specific needs and scarcities of the actual landscape of Home" (183).

Baroja, *Literatura de cordel*, 56–57). That is, this type of literature, in Molho's words, is subliterary and *aimed at* the *pueblo*, not *drawn from* the *pueblo* ["literatura infraculta escrita de cara al pueblo"]. It is "popularized" ["popularizada"], rather than popular in the sense understood by folklorists and historians of culture because it lacks organic function in the life of the *pueblo* (Molho 30). Like the *littérature de colportage* in France, it is a literature designed to amuse and to bring imaginary comfort, even tranquillity, to the poor and the dispossessed.

The Cockaigne myth exists primarily in its literary, written manifestations, and these may have served the function of the *littérature de colportage*, namely, to assuage the desires and defuse the frustrations of the alienated poor through fantasy. Visions of Cockaigne, like the French *Bibliothèque Bleu* of a later century, "in reality served to put a brake or an obstacle in the way of a true awareness of the social and political conditions to which the common people were subjected" ["ont pu constituer, dans la realité, un frein, un obstacle à la prise de conscience des conditions sociales et politiques auxquelles etaient soumis les milieux populaires" (Robert Mandrou, *De la culture populaire*; quoted in Molho 32)].

So, although we cannot satisfactorily answer the question of how the literary versions of Cockaigne came into existence, and can only describe some of its "higher" and its more "popularized" cultural variants, two things can be said of it with a modicum of certainty: that the Cockaigne myth is a visual or textual form of desire—the impulse Levitas ascribes to all utopian fantasies (*The Concept of Utopia*); and that whatever its transformations, Cockaigne differs from Arcadia or the Golden Age in that it is an anarchic eden, a collective dream evoked to gratify unlimited *personal* wants (Demerson 535, 545). A myth like Don Quixote's Golden Age, on the other hand, focuses on the *common*-weal and so aims at the restriction, not the gratification, of human desires. As Alexandre Cioranescu explains, "[t]he Age of Gold promises its citizens subsistence and contentment, but on the same strict conditions as in the earthly Paradise: one must not eat the forbidden fruit, one must not create new needs . . . because happiness has always been the art of being satisfied with what one has." ["L'âge d'or assure la subsistance, le bonheur de ses citoyens, mais c'est avec la même condition drastique du Paradis terrestre. Il ne faut pas mordre au fruit défendu, il ne faut pas se créer de nouveaux besoins . . . car le bonheur a été toujours l'art de se contenter de ce que l'on possède" ("Utopie" 88)].[11] Cockaigne's pleasures, on the other hand, (with the exception of those we find in the ones Raymond Williams calls "latent utopias") are unconditional.

But in other respects the myths of the Golden Age and of Cockaigne are similar. Despite the apparently different forms they take, both are fantasies of containment, temporary disavowals of the here and now, and therefore imaginary shelters from the instability of the everyday world.[12] And both are myths of satiety. In Sancho's case, the image of Cockaigne offers a compensatory shelter and a symbolic overturning of his everyday life. The wealth and rank he will acquire as governor simply ensure his fundamental desire, to have "hot food and cold drinks" (II:51, 795) ["comer caliente y beber frío"] and to "please my body with linen sheets and featherbeds" (795) ["y a recrear el cuerpo entre sábanas de holanda, sobre colchones de pluma" (1051)]. In Don Quixote's case,

---

11. Roland Greene speaks of similar utopias as "literary inventions" of the period that serve in part "as measures to manage desire" (233).

12. Guy Demerson points out the protean nature of both "popularized" and "cultural" Cockaignes:

> The legend of Cockaigne can just as easily evoke the exasperation of the conscientious before the laziness of the drunken worker as the suspicion of orthodox moral theology before heretical mores that ignore the redemptive value of work. Cockaigne can stand for the compensatory collective dream of groups seized by hunger, the fantasy elicited by envy of the riches of others . . . an Earthly Paradise impugning the prohibitions and virtues of 'official' social morality, a repugnant ghetto for banished dissolutes and cowards, Cockaigne can discredit the institution of Lent or serve to remind us of Lent's sanctity.

> [La légende de Cockaigne peut traduire aussi bien . . . l'exaspération du travailleur sérieux devant la paresse des saoûls d'ouvrer ou même ma [sic] méfiance d'une théologie morale orthodoxe envers les comportements hérétiques qui ignorent la valeur rédemptrice du travail. Cocagne, c'est aussi bien le rêve collectif compensatoire de foules saisies par le vertige de la faim que les fantasmes secrétés par la jalousie a l'égard des riches . . . aussi bien Paradis terrestre récusant en esprits les interdits et les vertus de la morale sociale 'officielle' que ghetto répugnant où l'on relègue débauchés et poltrons, Cocagne peut discréditer l'institution de Carême ou en rappeler la sainteté. (551)]

the golden world he evokes of simple abundance is not fundamentally different from Sancho's myth of sumptuous abundance. Both myths are "circular" in their influence and hybrids of pervasive cultural constructs of the time. Given the tales Sancho has heard of the magical Indies and the experience of abundance in which he has participated among the country folk at Camacho's Wedding Feast (II:20), he has good reason to believe in the reality of his master's promised *ínsula*.

5

Sancho Panza and the
Material World

The source of Don Quixote's utopian vision has been seen to lie in the cultural imaginary of a privileged minority. In contrast to Don Quixote's myth of a past golden age of austerity, the myth we associate with Sancho Panza, that of Cockaigne/Jauja (or Xauxa), has been seen instead to be projective, open to everyone, at least imaginarily, to have constituted part of the collective memory for centuries, and to compensate for what Sancho lacks, namely, food, money, and a life of leisure.

We remember that the squire's justification for following Don Quixote is the thought of possessing an island of abundant food and leisure. The memory of the coins he obtained from Cardenio's suitcase (I:23) has encouraged him, he tells Tomé Cecial, and so "tempted and lured by a purse with a hundred *ducados* that I found one day in the heart of the Sierra Morena; . . . at every step I take I seem to touch it with my hand, and put my arms around it, and take it to my house, and hold mortgages, and collect rents, and live like a prince . . ." (II:8, 535) ["cebado y engañado de una bolsa con cien ducados que me hallé un día en el corazón de Sierra Morena . . . me parece que a cada paso le toco con la mano y me abrazo con él, y lo llevo a mi casa, y echo censos y fundo rentas, y vivo como un príncipe . . ." (729–30)].

Hermeneutically, the myth of Cockaigne becomes relevant to the typology of Sancho as it implicates the world of his desires and serves as counterpart to the world of Don Quixote. The myth's compensatory allure, namely, the pleasure principle, is what also constitutes Sancho's modus operandi throughout the novel. Sancho is described as indolent, a glutton whose name is synonymous with the love of food and drink. Don Quixote sums up his squire's priorities with such statements as:

"I, Sancho, was born to live by dying, and you to die by eating" (II:59, 842) ["Yo, Sancho, nací para vivir muriendo, y tú para morir comiendo" (1107)]. Gullible, at least when his gluttony is engaged, Sancho is happiest when surrounded by culinary excesses like the "paradise" of Camacho's Wedding Feast, or when duped into believing in a "paradisal" *insula* of which he is to take possession.

In discussing Sancho, we are not concerned with the squire's possible literary antecedents, though much valuable and interesting work has been devoted to placing him in the tradition of literary buffoons. Nor are we going to trace his possible ancestry in folklore among, for example, such wise fools as the legendary Marcolf. Instead, we turn our attention to the "reversibility" (Molho's adjective) of the two protagonists—one a *loco-sabio* (wise madman) and the other a *tonto-listo* (smart fool) which makes them such complicated characters. This reversibility rescues them from being literary buffoons, safeguards the book's humor from becoming farcical, and prevents the readers from feeling superior even as they laugh at the antics of the two characters.

The essential orality of *Don Quixote*, the elements of folklore that Cervantes uses, especially in his characterization of Sancho Panza, and the carnivalesque features of the novel have all been pointed out. Molho, however, is prescient in showing that the novel does not imitate any specific model of the comic rustic of literature or of folk tale, but incorporates, especially in the figure of Sancho Panza, a set of basic folkloric structural elements (231). These are the elements of the simpleton (*bobo, tonto, simple*), combined with the smart or clever man (*listo*). As a result, the character is given the added complexity of "reversibility."

The narrator first introduces Sancho to us as a simpleton, "a good man—if that title can be given to someone who is poor—but without much in the way of brains" (I:7) ["hombre de bien—si es que este título se puede dar al que es pobre—pero de muy poca sal en la mollera" (91)]. His own wife Teresa Panza describes the villagers' view of Sancho to the Duchess: " . . . in this village everybody takes my husband for a fool, and except for governing a herd of goats, they can't imagine what governorship he'd be good for" (II:52, 801) [" . . . en este pueblo todos tienen a mi marido por un porro, y que sacado de gobernar un hato de cabras, no pueden imaginar para qué gobierno pueda ser bueno" (1057–58)]. Yet this simpleton is also a *listo* who knows how to *hacerse el tonto* ["act the fool"] in order to derive profit or to keep out of harm's way (Molho 255–336). The canny Sancho is willing to give up the hypothetical ínsula Don Quixote has promised him for more immediate rewards in securing the recipe for the balm of Fierabrás. As he explains to the knight: "I renounce here and now the governorship of the ínsula you have promised and want nothing else in payment of my many good services but that your grace give me the recipe for this marvelous potion, for I think an ounce of it will bring more than two *reales* anywhere, and I don't need more than that to live an easy and honorable life" (I:10, 72) ["yo renuncio desde aquí el gobierno de la prometida ínsula, y no quiero otra cosa en pago de mis muchos y buenos servicios sino que vuestra merced me dé la receta de ese estremado licor, que para mí tengo que valdrá la onza adondequiera más de a dos reales, y no he menester yo más para pasar esta vida honrada y descansadamente" (115)]. We have already seen how adroitly he uses proverbs in specific circumstances, so much so that Don Quixote is frustrated by his mastery of them (II:43).[1] The intuitive Sancho sees through people in ways that consistently surprise the other characters. We hear the narrator and characters say that "his words and actions indicated an extraordinary mixture of intelligence and foolishness" (II:51, 790) [" andaban mezcladas sus palabras y sus acciones, con asomos tontos y discretos" (1045)]; in Barataria, the steward who comes to scoff remains instead to praise Sancho, "astonished by his deeds and speech" (II:51, 790) ["tan admirados de sus hechos como de sus dichos" (1045)]; the citizens are "amazed at the judgments and verdicts of their new governor" (II:45, 752) ["quedaron admirados de nuevo de los juicios y sentencias de su nuevo gobernador" (998)]; and Sancho himself realizes how perceptive and even wise he can be at times: "This master of mine, when I talk about things of pith and substance, usually says that I could take a pulpit in hand and go through the world preaching fine sermons" (II:22, 598) ["Este mi amo, cuando yo hablo cosas de meollo y de sustancia suele decir que podría yo tomar un púlpito en las manos y irme por ese mundo adelante predicando lindezas" (810)].

It is the complex combination with which Cervantes has fashioned

---

1. These *refranes*, as we said earlier, become stratagems that empower Sancho, and with them he makes up for the lack of cultural capital so unevenly distributed among his class. "It is his oral heritage's answer to Don Quixote's written Cultural dicta" (Rivers 79).

him that makes Sancho interesting to us.[2] Whereas W. S. Hendrix, Maxime Chevalier, and Francisco Márquez Villanueva have related him to comic literary types of the sixteenth century, Maurice Molho places Sancho firmly in the tradition of folklore. For him, the conventional literary *bobo* is often univalent, depicted as either a *bobo* or a *listo*, and, as *bobo,* functions as comic relief or spokesman for the dramatist/author. The folkloric figure of Sancho, on the other hand, he sees as polyvalent precisely because of his reversibility. In the tradition of the Czech Good Soldier Švejk (or Schweik), the German Til Eulenspiegel or Simplex Simplicissimus, and the French Jean Sot or the hispanic Juan Bobo, Sancho, makes us laugh because he can be simple and child-like one moment and then disarm us, and even get the better of us, the next. Sancho turns situations to his own advantage, subverts our expectations, defies generic logic, confuses readerly keys, and, because of his reversibility, seems to slip adroitly from our control. The allegedly proverbial cunning of such folkloric figures as Sancho, Til, or Švejk is, in fact, the basis of the dominant culture's stereotypes of the humbler classes. Michael Mullett describes the view that city-dwellers have of peasants: "When it came to folly, the peasant—our word 'clown' originally meant a countryman—entered his own domain, but it was one in which ambiguity ruled: for if the peasant was regarded as the butt of jokes involving foolish credulity, and general slow-wittedness, we should bear in mind a tradition . . . in which stupidity affords the means of survival" (98). The very survival of peasants—as the adversarial pairing of *tonto/listo* illustrates—is always, so the argument goes, at someone else's expense. Thus Leon Battista Alberti finds "incredible how malicious are these ploughmen who have grown up amongst clods. Their whole study is devoted to diddling you . . ." (quoted in Mullett 73). Don Quixote tells the Duchess that one must be wary of Sancho for "Sancho Panza is one of the most amusing squires who ever served a knight errant; at times his simpleness is so clever that deciding if he is simple or clever is a cause of no small pleasure; his slyness condemns him for a rogue, and his thoughtlessness confirms him as a simpleton; . . . when I think that he is about to plunge headlong into foolishness, he comes out with perceptions

---

2. And of course this is also true of Don Quixote, as the reversibility of *loco* and *sabio* makes him so interesting a figure in the novel.

that raise him to the skies" (II:32, 674) ["Sancho Panza es uno de los más graciosos escuderos que jamás sirvió a caballero andante: tiene a veces unas simplicidades tan agudas, que el pensar si es simple o agudo causa no pequeño contento; tiene malicias que le condenan por bellaco y descuidos que le confirman por bobo; . . . cuando pienso que se va a despeñar de tonto, sale con unas discreciones, que le levantan al cielo" (900)]. Sancho says of himself: "I have some guile in me, and a touch of cunning" (II:8, 505) ["bien es verdad que soy algo malicioso" (688)].

It is an upside-down world that can be seen as a *temporary* shelter for just such a survivor as Sancho. As Mikhail Bakhtin explains, the festivities of "popular" culture represent a subversion of order and a temporary reversal of hierarchy. Such a reversal is ambiguous, however, since it occurs only in a symbolic mode—a distinction that Bakhtin blurs. As Grigorii Pomerants asks us to keep in mind in his critique of Bakhtin, "[i]f the carnival was celebrated in the Cathedral square, the very existence of the square depend[ed] upon the existence of the Cathedral" (quoted in Averintsev 18).[3] Piero Camporesi also emphasizes the fact that even the most enduring myths of popular culture do not effect a genuine transformation. "Even the great myth of the Land of Cockaigne," Camporesi explains in *Bread of Dreams,* "whether in its general desire for fair community ownership of material goods and property, or in the dream of eternal youth and love, not socially controlled, of non-institutionalized *eros*—never remotely entails authentic political and social renewal" (36). Carnivalesque performance, then, even if regarded as a product of popular culture, has often been appropriated by the dominant order for its own use (Stallybrass 13; Maravall, *Teatro* ch. 2). And the many learned glosses on popular verses and songs, the cultured imitations of the *romances germanescos,* and the gentrification of popular dances such as the saraband are our constant reminders of this, namely, the continual dynamic reciprocity and hybridity of seemingly autonomous traditions (see Burke, *Popular Culture* ch. 2).

To return to Sancho Panza: let us briefly review the socio-economic culture from which the figure in the novel would have emerged in order

---

3. More serious perhaps is Bakhtin's failure to acknowledge the fact that carnival has different meanings for different participants, and that it can have victims (see Burke, *Varieties* 117, 129, 151).

to understand the powerful attraction the abundance of his promised *ínsula* would have exerted on him. The novel refers to Sancho as a *labrador* (I:7, 91). The term is as imprecise as its English equivalent "peasant." According to Sebastián de Covarrubias,

> it applies not only to him who tills the soil, but also to him who lives in the village, because villages were created so that those who worked the land nearby could have refuge with their oxen, their mules, and their herds. So, when many came together in one place, they created villages and hamlets.
>
> [Se dice no sólo el que actualmente labra la tierra, pero el que vive en la aldea; porque las aldeas se hizieron para que en ellas se recogiessen con sus bueyes, mulas y hato los que labravan las tierras vezinas, y concurriendo muchos en un puesto hizieron sus lugares y aldeas. (746b)]

The imprecision lies in the fact that, although *labrador* denotes a person who worked the land and, since he was not a member of the nobility, paid taxes (a *pechero*, as contrasted with the tax-exempt hidalgo), it was an umbrella term that included rich farmers, poor tenants, and landless peasants.[4] A *labrador* might typically occupy a hovel with a dirt floor (Salomon, *Vida rural* 271), work a small plot of land for which he would pay with a proportion of his crops, and own a work animal such as a donkey, a mule, or perhaps a pair of oxen. His position in the rural economy was a lowly and unenviable one: "[t]he overall impression is that the majority of *labradores* were renters" ["[l]a impresión de conjunto es que la mayor parte de labradores eran renteros" (*Vida rural* 278)]. Noël Salomon goes on to observe that "on the whole, the *labradores,* whether they were renters or owners of a small plot, were poor . . . The majority of the reports give the impression of uniform poverty among the peasants" ["En su conjunto, los *labradores*—tanto si eran renteros como proprietarios de una parcela—eran pobres . . . De la mayoría de las relaciones se saca la impresión de una uniforme pobreza campesina" (278)]. A recent reader of the *Relaciones topográficas* sums up the reports gathered from the inhabitants of the Campo de Montiel

---

4. Philip II's survey of towns and villages of Castile, the *Relaciones histórico-geográficas de los pueblos de España,* has been analyzed by Noël Salomon in *La vida rural castellana.* This work is invaluable for local details as well as for the general conditions of rural life in the late sixteenth century.

(where Quixote sets out, [I:2, 47]): "there is a universal outcry expressed in dramatic terms against the poverty in which they exist: bad harvests, tiny plots, poor soil, harsh climate . . ." ["existe un clamor generalizado, con acentos dramáticos, por la pobreza en que viven: malas cosechas, pequeñez de los términos, baja calidad de la tierra, dureza del clima . . ." (Campos y Fernández 66)]. In short, "the condition of Spanish peasants in these times is the poorest, most extreme, wretched and downtrodden of any class and it is as if all the rest had joined together and conspired to destroy and ruin them . . ." ["el estado de los labradores de España en estos tiempos está el más pobre y acabado, miserable y abatido de todos los demás estados, que parece que todos ellos juntos se han armado y conjurado a destruirlo y arruinarlo . . ." (Fray Benito de Peñalosa, quoted in C. Blanco Aguinaga et al. vol. I:286)]. Even so, the poor *labrador* was better off than the man who had nothing to offer but his physical labor, that is, the *trabajador*, *jornalero*, or *bracero* (day-laborer).

Although Cervantes describes Sancho as poor (I:7), and illiterate (I:26), he does not make him one of the impoverished villagers who roam the country and go into towns to beg. Sancho owns a donkey, but apart from that, as he says, "I don't own enough for anybody to envy me" (II:8, 504–5) ["ni tengo tantos bienes que pueda ser envidiado" (689)], and keeps a family who add to the domestic economy through spinning and needlepoint. He is not starving, although otherwise his situation is vague. He has worked as a day laborer (II:41–42). Carroll Johnson calculates his monetary income as consisting of forty-eight or fifty-one maravedís per day, in comparison with the two hundred maravedís earned by a carpenter (*Cervantes and the Material World* 22). What little Sancho may have produced or earned in kind would not have added significantly to his family's level of comfort.

The tables of wheat production compiled by Salomon from the *Relaciones* show that the part of New Castile familiar to Sancho, and in which he would have worked, was *relatively* productive—Tembleque, Campocritana, Argamasilla de Alba. But the local peasants would not necessarily benefit from such productivity. Middlemen, speculators, and large landowners could hoard crops in order to force up the price of grain. The wealthy landowners could keep fields out of production. The price of bread, the staple food of country people, could thus be illegally raised and, as a result, the grim situation of the rural proletariat could continue without relief. In 1571, Philip II would have to enforce his *Pragmatica* of 1558 because it was being systematically ignored. He berates the middle men who exploit the poor: "employing various swindles, tricks and subterfuges . . . they publicly defraud and contravene the aforementioned Proclamation and sell bread at a price above that which is set by law . . . to the great detriment of the customer. . . ." ["usando para ello de diversos fraudes, vías y modos . . . publicamente defraudan y contravienen a la dicha Pragmatica y venden el pan a mas precio de la dicha tassa . . . en perjuycio y daño de las personas a quien se vende" (*Pragmatica y Provision,* A2 verso)]. And the poor were deprived not only of bread by such covetousness, but also of the flour to make it themselves: "in many districts and towns of this kingdom, it has been and continues to be sold at excessive and exorbitant prices . . . with the authorities turning a blind eye, permitting and authorizing it" ["en muchas partes y lugares destos reynos, se ha vendido y vende a excesivos e immoderados precios . . . con dissimulacion, permission y autoridad de las justicias" (*Pragmatica* A3 recto-verso)]. During the reign of his successor, Philip III, the records show that the situation becomes worse. During the years that Cervantes was engaged in writing *Don Quixote*, Pedro de Valencia (1550–1620) would protest repeatedly to King Philip and to the royal chaplain Diego de Mardones against the rapacity of powerful men (*los poderosos*).

If we look beyond the fictional Sancho Panza, then, to the circumstances in which his real-life counterparts would have existed, we find that this was a time of strong, often bitter, and sometimes violent tensions in village communities. At this critical juncture in the rural economy of Castile, pressure was being exerted by big landowners to privatize the common lands on which villagers had the right to graze their animals. Time after time, the *relaciones* confirm what was known through other sources, that village communities were losing common lands to private (noble, or simply wealthy) landowners eager to extend their properties (Salomon, *Vida rural* 140–47), and to the Church, which was always interested in acquiring land (168–70). The resulting inequity aroused indignation among social analysts and moralists over more than two centuries. Pedro de Valencia complained of the situation in Spain in his *Discurso sobre el acrecentamiento de la labor de la tierra* (1607): " . . . this inequality in the possession of land, whereby a few have huge tracts and almost everyone else has not even a hand's breadth or a clod of dirt, is the most pernicious state of affairs for the community . . . God condemned it, and forbade it among his people, and every lawgiver in his republic has warned against it . . ." [" . . . esta desigualdad de la posesión de la tierra, con que unos pocos tienen dehesas larguísimas y otros, o casi todos no alcanzan ni un palmo ni un terrón, es la cosa más perniciosa a la comunidad . . . Dios la condenó y prohibió en su pueblo, y cada legislador la previno en sus repúblicas . . ." (*Escritos sociales I: Escritos económicos* 150)].[5]

The nobility not only purchased or forcibly acquired common lands, but they frequently destroyed the peasants' crops as they hunted deer and wild boar. In 1569 Tomás de Mercado exploded with indignation at the depredations inflicted by the nobility in their hunting forays:

Much could be said about the wrongs committed by these gentlemen who own these copses and woods, given the damage that the ordinary people suffer, the great amount of land they occupy, and the havoc wrought by the stags and other wild animals that eat and destroy the crops and the fruits of the neighborhood. Moreover, the poor peasant is so discouraged that he is unwilling to sow or plow his land, seeing that all his eight months' labor will inevitably be devoured by pigs, boars, fawns, and deer. The worst of it is that no peasant dare open his mouth to complain, so they abandon agriculture and become mule-drivers or cry out to God demanding justice for these wrongs . . .

[Mucho más cierto habría que decir en la culpa que cometen estos señores en tener semejantes sotos y bosques, que según el daño que la gente común recibe, así de la mucha tierra que ocupan, como del estrago que los ciervos y otras alimañas hacen en los trigos y frutos comarcanos, comiéndolos y destrozándolos. Y principalmente desganando y desanimando al pobre labrador que no siembre ni cultive la tierra, porque viendo que lo que trabaja en ocho meses se lo han de pacer al mejor tiempo puercos, jabalíes, corcetas, venados, sobre todo, aún no han de chistar, desamparan el agricultura y dan en ser arrieros o en dar voces a Dios y pedirle justicia destos agravios . . . . (quoted in Viñas y Mey, 67–68)]

---

5. For discussions of Pedro de Valencia's interesting and forceful arguments for agrarian reform, see José Antonio Maravall's 1970 article and the introduction to the 1994 edition of Pedro de Valencia's *Escritos Sociales*.

And yet manifest peasant discontent and the destruction wrought by the nobility is consistently elided in *Don Quixote*. When we read of the Duke's extravagant hunting party (II:34), for example, the anger of a Tomás de Mercado is nowhere discernible. The only reaction of the *pobre labrador* Sancho Panza is to lament the tear in the hunting coat provided for him by the Duke. However, there are some traces of disconformity. When the Duke offers a complacent and platitudinous defense of the hunt as "an image of war" and a builder of character (war being the traditional raison d'être of the aristocracy), and a sport "that harms no one and gives pleasure to many" (686) ["se puede hacer sin perjuicio de nadie y con gusto de muchos" (915)], it is of course Sancho who is quick to respond. A governor, he retorts sharply, should not neglect the business of government for such frivolities: "How nice if weary merchants came to see him and he was in the woods enjoying himself! What a misfortune for the governorship! By my faith, Señor, hunting and those pastimes are more for idlers than for governors" (686). ["¡Así enhoramala andaría el gobierno! Bueno sería que viniesen los negociantes a buscarle fatigados, y el estuviese en el monte holgándose!" (915–16)]. Sancho's comments are airily dismissed. The Duke's claim that the hunt is carried on "sin perjuicio de nadie" is passed over in silence. But a sense of cultural unease has momentarily surfaced in the text.[6]

The absence of resentment in either Sancho or Don Quixote towards what Pedro de Valencia saw as the unequal possession of land also invites comment. The ostentatious wealth of the *labrador rico* Camacho, and the political muscle that such wealth allows him to wield, seems to elicit awe, not criticism. Yet, in the real time from which Cervantes's novel emerges, there were acute tensions in village life, and animosity between rich farmers (*labradores ricos* such as the figures represented in *Don Quixote* by the families of Marcela, Dorotea, Leandra, and Camacho, characterized by Salomon as "burguesía rural" [171] or "burguesía agraria" [280]) and the down-at-heel but tax-exempt local gentry who controlled the village councils. The wealthy farmers would try to remove the hidalgos from the councils by economic leverage, alliances, or force of numbers (Salomon, *Vida rural* 261), and they were at odds

---

6. David Quint discusses this episode as a critique of the aristocrats' inherited right to exercise violence against both animals and the lower orders (*Cervantes's Novel* 136–38).

with both the small village gentry (the class to which Don Quixote belongs) and the landless peasants.[7]

This state of affairs is manifestly absent from *Don Quixote*. Traces nevertheless remain as the utopian discourse calls the utopian fantasy into question. Classist categories are alluded to in passing: the knight's own niece and housekeeper complain of Don Quixote's self-imposed label (II:6), for example, and Don Quixote is simply too poor, they insist, to think of calling himself a *caballero* (II:2). Others follow suit. We are made aware of the resentment of the local *caballeros* at Don Quixote's adoption of the title "Don" given his meagre holdings. Sancho's wife Teresa also reinforces Quixote's transgression in this regard (II:5). Again, despite the apparent contentment of peasants like Teresa with their lot (II:5), traces of the real friction that existed between *labradoras* and *hidalgas* are disclosed in the ways in which the latter supposedly put the former down (II:1).

The utopian discourse exposes economic realities of material life elided in Don Quixote's communitarian fantasy in the same way. Innkeepers demand money (I:44) as indeed they must in the everyday world; Zoraida, despite her characterization within the romantic genre of the Moorish tale, must buy her release by stealing money and jewels from her father (I:41); Don Quixote is warned that in contemporary reality even medieval knights must sally forth equipped with money for their travels (I:3); Leandra's money and jewels are obviously more important to her lover than the "jewel" of her virginity (I:51); and squires like Sancho demand a salary for their services (I:20; II:7, 28). Sancho even goes so far as to demand payment if he is to free Dulcinea from her enchantment (II:71), and the Princess Dulcinea herself will ask Don Quixote for money when he encounters her in the Cave of Montesinos (II:23). In this way topical allusions to the real economic problems of the contemporary moment from which the novel emerges destabilize both Don Quixote's textual fantasy of resurrecting the values of a

---

7. Hostility between landless *jornaleros* and the farmers who employed them as migrant labor was of course not new to the century we are discussing (see Salomon, *Vida rural* 313–18), and Don Quixote is not the only instance of the literary media's elision of the everyday sufferings of the peasants in the century. The elegiac vision of the worldly bishop Antonio de Guevara in *Menosprecio de corte y alabanza de aldea*, as well as the world of happy peasants singing and dancing and making witty repartee in the plays of Lope de Vega, are two obvious examples.

golden world free from lucre and a chivalric order where salaries and money supposedly have no relevance. "What can be left of heroism, as well as love," David Quint asks, "in a world in which money dominates and transforms all human activity?" (60; see also 57–76). Besides the allusions to the historical moment's fixation on economic issues, the age's obsession with *pureza de sangre* is also reflected, though more obliquely, in the text. The knight may eulogize a past age of equality when no one judged and no one was judged, but Sancho can confidently proclaim: "I am an Old Christian, and that alone is enough for me to be a count" (I:21, 161) ["yo cristiano viejo soy, y para ser conde esto me basta" (234)], to which Don Quixote replies, "More than enough" (161) ["Y aún te sobra" (234)].[8] And the goatherd Eugenio tells his listeners that he is a worthy suitor for the wealthy Leandra because he is "pure of blood" ["limpio en sangre"] (I:51, 434; 577).

On the manifest level, nevertheless, the world of *Don Quixote* is a transparent one in which the different groups are sealed off from one another and the conflicted social reality we are describing does not exist. Sancho, Don Quixote, Dorotea, Don Fernando, and the rest simply become part of a storytelling community in which social differences scarcely matter. We are not looking in *Don Quixote* for explicit evidence of everyday experiences, but simply pointing out how the utopian discourse fractures the apparently seamless surface of the novel's utopian fantasy. These conflicts and contradictions are indices, we shall point out, of the issues debated in the documents of the period.

It is from within the socio-economic background we have been describing that the fictional Sancho Panza's desire for the *insula* is to be understood. If the pre-lapsarian fantasy of modest insufficiency has been naturalized as an earthly Paradise or Arcadia for Don Quixote, such a fantasy has no counterpart in Sancho Panza's desire. Sancho covets, instead, "the delicious offerings" of a myth of abundance, where work is abolished, where peasants like him can enjoy "the ease with which all can continually satisfy their desires" ["la facilité avec laquelle chacun satisfait ses désirs sans cesse sollicités par des offres succulentes" (Demerson 531)].

---

8. Old Christians were those who fell within the statutes of *pureza de sangre/* purity of blood because they were not tainted with Semitic blood. New Christians constituted a category that included converted Jews (*conversos*) and converted Moors (*moriscos*).

6

Discursive Formations in Sixteenth-Century Spain

We have been discussing the hybridity and relative arbitrariness of supposedly separate cultural constructs such as the Age of Gold or Cockaigne/Jauja, and how they expose "the limits of any claim to a singular or autonomous sign of difference" (Bhabha). In this chapter we commence the second level of our inquiry, which is to interrogate the historical record in order to uncover the discursive formations of the nation that produced *Don Quixote* and to suggest a match between them and the novel.

Conceptual shifts and socio-historical changes begin to take place in Spain during the sixteenth century: a semantic shift in the humanists' meaning of "nobility"; a change in attitude toward work and the work ethic; and discussions on the "natural" condition of humankind. The last, as we shall see, were especially intense since they impinged on Spain's ever-worsening economic problems as well as on the legitimacy of her colonization of the New World.

In pre-modern societies riches had accompanied noble status. Titles of nobility were always allied to grants of land, the most tangible and durable source of wealth in feudal Europe. In medieval Castilian texts the high nobility were routinely referred to as *ricos omnes,* that is to say, as "great" or "powerful" men.[1] The humanist debate on the defini-

---

1. The *Oxford English Dictionary* still gives as its first definition of *rich*: "Of persons: powerful, mighty, exalted, noble, great. (Obsolete)." The word *rico,* cognate with French *riche* and English *rich,* has its origin in the Frankish *riki* and is also the root of the modern German *Reich.* In Old French, *riche* = "powerful," and *richesse* = "power"; in Old English *rice* = "powerful." This sense of the word *rico* is attested throughout the medieval period, from 900 to 1535 C.E.

tion of *nobilitas,* which we discussed briefly in chapter 1, on whether private property and wealth were necessary attributes of nobility, had been summed up in John Tiptoft's 1460s translation of Buonaccorso de Montemagna's *Controversi de nobilitate*: "noblesse resteth in blood and riches." By this Tiptoft of course meant inherited riches. The wealth of the self-made man was cause only for contempt (quoted in Skinner 135–37).

By the time of Covarrubias the debate had lost its urgency. Even so, as late as 1611, Covarrubias would still give the first definition of *rico* as ["noble and of high degree" ["noble y de alto linage"]; his second would link *rico* with intrinsic worth. Thus, the rich person is "someone who because of excellent personal qualities deserves honor and respect" ["ser bueno, que por su persona merece ser honrado y estimado"]. Covarrubias cites the *Siete Partidas* of Alfonso X (law 6, title 9, part 2) to reinforce his point: "Nobles are of two kinds: some are noble because of their lineage and others because of their goodness. Although lineage is a noble quality, goodness surpasses it, but he who has both can truly be called a *rico hombre,* since he is rich by lineage and worthy by virtue of his goodness" ["Nobles son llamados en dos maneras, o por linage o por bondad, y como quier que el linage es noble cosa, la bondad passa y vence; mas quien las [h]a de ambas, éste puede ser dicho en verdad rico hombre, pues que es rico por linage e hombre cumplido por la bondad"]. In the same article, Covarrubias cites law 10, title 25, part 4 to the effect that *"Ricos homes,* according to Spanish custom, are those who in other countries are called counts or barons" ["En la ley dézima, tít. 25, p. 4, dize assí: Ricos homes, según costumbre de España son llamados los que en las otras tierras dizen condes o barones"].

Covarrubias now records with evident distaste the change that is taking place in Spain even as he writes. *Rico* has declined in meaning from "noble" (hence wealthy), to merely "wealthy," or worse, noble *because* wealthy: "Nowadays men with a lot of money and property have taken over the title 'ricos'; these are the nobles, the knights, the counts and dukes, because money secures everything" ["Oy día se han alçado con este nombre de ricos los que tienen mucho dinero y hazienda, y estos son los nobles y los cavalleros, y los condes y duques, porque todo lo sujeta el dinero" (910a)]. Traces of this societal change can be detected in Sancho Panza's cynical comment on the reality of his time: "You're worth what you have, and what you have is what you're worth" (II:20, 589) ["tanto vales cuanto tienes y tanto tienes cuanto vales" (799)].

The semantic shift from "noble and wealthy" to "noble because wealthy" records an analogous shift in social categories. The traditional division between nobles and non-nobles is multiplied, with divisions and subdivisions, as finer distinctions are claimed by status-hungry men. But as pragmatic *arbitristas* impatient with such theoretical distinctions affirm, in reality there was but one great divide: between those who own property and those who do not (Salomon, *Recherches* 772–74). This shift effects a social dichotomy that supersedes the theoretical three estates: *oratores* (clergy and scholars), *bellatores* (the warrior nobles), and *aratores* (laborers). Given the concentration of land in the hands of powerful nobles and the Church, and the expropriation of small owners, the division is reduced to two, the rich and the poor, the haves and the have-nots (Maravall, *Estado Moderno* vol. II, 37–38). Against this background, the egalitarian dream of Don Quixote evoked in his oration on the golden age, the land of plenty that Sancho Panza craves for his promised "island," and the novel itself, gain in significance.

Theorists from the late sixteenth century forward now become involved in deliberations on how to equalize the country's disparities and how to bring about a more just society. In reformist discussions on the need for an intermediate class to bridge the widening gap between wealthy landowners and the rest of the population, the value of work is emphasized. In particular, we find stress upon the need to return to the land and to stimulate manufacturing and commerce, activities that were traditionally considered incompatible with nobility. The valorizing of these productive activities is especially relevant at a time when the influx of American bullion and the Spaniards' dependence on money begin to take precedence as the primary source of wealth.

Maravall provides a fine demonstration of how at least one aspect of the issue— how to bring about a more just society—is treated in the century (*Estado moderno*). To do so he uses the sixteenth-century dialogue of *El crotalón* (mid-1550s). This work, whose authorship is still in dispute, consists of a Lucianesque dialogue between a poor shoemaker, Milicio, who is eager to work for a nobleman in order to be paid a salary, and the talking Cock (Gallo), a reincarnation of the philosopher Pythagoras, who elaborates instead on the virtues of self-employment. Given the contrast the author sets up, the ensuing interchange takes the form of *apologias*, but it is Gallo's argument that becomes more interesting for us. Life is not sweeter for one employed in noble houses, Gallo cautions Milicio, for masters are arrogant, demanding, and stingy. They are contemptuous of those who must grovel for a pittance from them. It is better to be self-employed and thereby retain one's freedom in honest poverty than to suffer the ceaseless humiliations of servitude to another (*El crotalón*, canto 19, quoted in Maravall, *Estado* 422, 432–33).[2]

Work is commended here for the dignity, freedom, and contentment it provides the self-employed. As Maravall points out, for Gallo work "enables him to live independently, [and so] must be reckoned as the greatest happiness" ["le permite vivir libremente . . . y por eso hay que reconocerlo como el estado de felicidad suprema" (vol. II, 370)]. *El crotalón* notwithstanding, Maravall concedes the ambiguity that pervades the notion of work in a period in which work and dignity are seen as fundamentally incompatible. Thomas More, whose *Utopia* limits work to six hours per day, and Juan Luis Vives (1492–1540), both recognize work as necessary though unpleasant in an ideal community (Maravall 370–71).

The century's thinkers were conflicted in their attitude to work. If labor provides the means for an individual to gain freedom from dependency, as some social thinkers argued, it is also a fact that work is a form of servitude. Who, then, is more free, he who obtains his freedom by accepting the *obligation* to work, or the self-employed man who, by having others work for him, supposedly lives a life of leisure? Traces of this double bind (work as freedom or as obligation) are discernible in Don Quixote's utopian fantasy (I:11) where the issue of work is merely rendered irrelevant. It is the backdrop for Sancho Panza's dream of buying a *censo* and living off the interest it accrues (II:13), and of his acquiring black slaves and bringing them to Spain, "where I can sell them, and

---

2. Somewhat earlier, Guevara cites the classical example of a search for the world's happiest man. This turns out to be the humble Aglaon who works his little plot of land in Arcadia, and has never left it. Guevara comments: "Only the man who never has to serve another can be called happy" ["Áquel solo se puede llamar bienauenturado que no se pone en necessidad de seruir a otro" (*Aviso de privados y doctrina de cortesanos*. In *Obras*, 1515)].

I'll be paid for them in cash, and with that money I'll be able to buy some title or office and live on that for the rest of my life" (I:29, 245) ["de cuyo dinero podré comprar algún título o algun oficio con que vivir descansado todos los días de mi vida" (340)].

The issue was not merely theoretical. This emphasis on work had practical consequences for the problem of widespread poverty. Every region had its hungry unemployed, but the situation was most visible to legislators in the principal cities. The influx of poor people from the countryside had various causes: natural causes such as disastrous harvests; the actions of great absentee landlords who left their lands in order to seek lucrative positions at court; and the fact that when the land that comprised the few enormous *latifundios* was actually cultivated, the productivity was very low (Fernández Álvarez 79). By the year 1595, according to Philip II's *Relaciones topográficas*, as much as one third of Castile's arable land had ceased to be cultivated. The price of wheat, a standard economic measure, had risen nearly threefold between 1595 and 1598 (Elliott, *Imperial Spain* 292) and the price of foodstuffs rose proportionately. Legislation enacted in the first half of the century had achieved little. As the situation became acute, new measures which would supposedly produce economic benefits for society were proposed, and with them came a shift in the century's changing attitude towards the poor.

From the Christian perspective, beggars had been traditionally entitled to receive alms, and almsgiving was a Christian duty.[3] There was a shift in the century from the Christian respect for beggars as agents of salvation to an alternative and secular view with its outcome in programs of social engineering. Beggars were becoming a menace, a cause of social unrest; therefore they had to be contained and, if possible, made productive. It was against this background that the deliberations concerning the need for a productive work force arose. The reformists sought measures that would relieve the nation of idlers, change

---

3. So normalized is this Christian perspective, that in 1612 the theologian Pedro Aznar Cardona can metaphorize it in requesting "charity" of reception for his "poor" book, because "the poverty and worthlessness [of his book] is the means [for the reader] to display and exercise his generosity and mercy" ["la pobreza y miseria es el sujeto do se emplea y descubre la liberalidad y misericordia." Aznar Cardona preface, n.p.].

the societal perception of beggars, and grant them the dignity of self-sustaining laborers.[4] The text reflects these concerns, briefly addressed, in "Las constituciones del gran gobernador Sancho Panza" (II:61, 1053), when, as governor of Barataria, Sancho legislates against speculators and monopolistic price fixers, and creates protection for the poor while persecuting idlers.

On this subject, the attention of the Cortes of Castile was continually being solicited by memoranda and personal testimony. [The Cortes urged landowners living on their rents in Madrid to go back to their estates in order to make them productive, and businessmen were exhorted to revive lost industries and establish new ones. While these voices grew more insistent, the situation deteriorated. When Pedro Fernández Navarrete wrote his *Conservación de Monarquías* (published some years later, in 1626), he described a dismal situation: abandoned fields, crumbling towns, and deserted villages, to which he ascribed a number of reasons and prescribed several remedies. In these desperate conditions, radical measures were proposed. Navarrete would encourage the immigration of skilled labor and give incentive to enterprising *labradores* by granting them privileges of nobility (Fernández Navarrete 5, 51, 67–68, 104, 273). In 1600, González de Cellorigo had gone further: if the Spaniards could not be made to cultivate the land, then slaves should be brought in to do the work (65, 98).

But these incentives were never as strong as the country's deep ideological resistance. A cultural imaginary in which work was considered beneath the dignity of a noble man retained its onus for agricultural and commercial activities. So, by the latter half of the sixteenth century, the manufacturing industries of northern Castile (which had flourished in the first half of that century), and the great international fairs and banking ventures of Medina del Campo and Medina de Rioseco, had declined to the point of extinction (Elliott, *Imperial Spain*

---

4. See Fr. Juan de Robles (or Medina), *De la orden que en algunos pueblos de España se ha puesto en la limosna para remedio de los verdaderos pobres* (1545); Miguel Giginta, *Tratado de remedio de pobres*, 1579; and Cristóbal Pérez de Herrera, *Discursos del amparo de los legítimos pobres y reducción de los fingidos*, 1598. For a detailed study of the issues of poverty, vagrancy, and the control of beggars see Martz; Cavillac, introduction to Pérez de Herrera; Cruz.

281). The reformists' need to valorize the notion of work was becoming crucial.[5]

It is perhaps not surprising that a Catalan, Jerónimo Merola, rather than a Castilian, would insist in 1597 upon the nobility of the activities in which merchants and traders were involved. Success in business and its accompanying productivity, he asserted, actually *produced* honor and respect for "honor is measured by profit" ["[l]a honra se mide por el provecho" (Cavillac 376)]. Indeed, there existed in Catalan cities a class of *ciutadans honrats*, distinguished bourgeois, who had been admitted into the urban aristocracy (Elliott, *Revolt* 68). In Castile, by contrast, men who had become rich from trade, speculation, or usury (*los poderosos*) lacked social legitimacy.

Despite deliberate and insistent direction among less traditional thinkers, and regardless of the fact that noble families in Seville dominated the transatlantic trade (Pike 110), and that the lower nobility continued to make alliances with non-noble merchants (Pike 33), the notion that trade and nobility were fundamentally incompatible prevailed. As Ruth Pike explains, this attitude was not restricted to Castile. The same phenomenon prevailed in France (though not in Italian or Dutch cities), and this despite the fact that the aristocratization of the bourgeois had already become a European phenomenon in the late sixteenth century (Braudel vol. II:729). Nobles were already marrying into wealthy bourgeois families "with a yen for nobility and rank" ["con apetito de nobleza e hidalguía" (Tomás Mercado, quoted in Cavillac 55). Intermarriage, however, instead of altering the status quo, actually served to reinforce the rigidity of the social structure. Many bourgeois, in emulation of the nobles, privileged property over commerce and trade, turning "to land as a prime safe investment, thus reinforcing a social order based on aristocratic privilege" (Braudel vol. II:732).

Conditions in Castile, unlike those in Italian and Dutch cities, were

---

5. However, as late as 1554, Saravia de la Calle could state that manufacturing and commerce were socially acceptable occupations in Spain: "Not only townsmen, farmers, and merchants but gentry . . . live by business and trade" ["no sólo ciudadanos, labradores, y mercaderes, mas hidalgos . . . se mantienen en tratos y mercaderías" (*Instrucción de mercaderes*, quoted in Cavillac 54)]. And around the year 1568, Jean Bodin reportedly declared that the people of Spain have no other occupation but commerce (Cavillac 54).

never favorable to the formation of merchant dynasties. Government policies actually discouraged it. To cite but one example: in dealing with cases of debt, private capital in Castile could be confiscated and compulsory loans repaid with annuities rather than cash, thereby depriving merchants de facto of their capital (Pike 109). Land, on the other hand, was a much safer investment.

Spanish sons still followed their fathers in business in the early sixteenth century but, as Pike explains, though they might continue to invest in trading ventures, "the social prejudice against trade and toward nobility grew stonger, fewer merchants' sons went into business, and more began to enter the professions, church, and government" (Pike 110). Perhaps the frequently mentioned incident involving the Castilian merchant Simón Ruiz demonstrates more clearly what Braudel was to call the century's "trahison de la bourgeoisie" ["defection of the bourgeoisie" in the English version, vol. II:729]. Ruiz married twice, each time to a lady of noble family. He left no sons, and before dying sent for a nephew, Pero, to carry on his business. Ruiz's generous gesture was rejected because, as Pero's father informed Ruiz in a letter, the son "does not wish to be a merchant but a nobleman" ["no quiere ser mercader, sino caballero" (Lapeyre 95)]. Hence the insistence with which the reformist agendas of the period's *arbitristas* argued for the nobility of work and the necessity of agriculture and commerce. It is an insistence Maravall claimed, in his *Utopia and Counterutopia*, that Cervantes satirized.

But Don Quixote's eloquent speech on a primitive utopia that supposedly prevailed before the hoe existed and before Mother Earth had been plowed would have been wholly irrelevant to the issues with which contemporary thinkers were struggling. The mad knight's "communitarian" oration to the dumbfounded goatherds, which translates "equality" into an eutopia of abundantly available and shared material goods, is a vision of a very different order from the carefully reasoned proposals of practical economists and planners. And so, *pace* Maravall, Don Quixote's agenda, if such it can be called, is part of no one's reformist principles and cannot be read as a satirical distortion of any plan by an *arbitrista*. It elicits laughter precisely because of its incongruity and lack of practicality.

One of the most articulate of the reformists promoting the work ethic, González de Cellorigo, introduces a plan that he suggests would mitigate the problem by creating a middle group between the haves and the have-nots. He perceives the problem as two-fold: a declining population and a great gap between the titled wealthy and the poor. His solution entails the formation of a middle group which would be made up of urban traders and farmers. As an incentive, Cellorigo explains, the trade of merchants would be recognized as honorable and merchants would be ennobled (85–86). Farmers who work their own land (but not those who work for a landlord) would also be recognized as noble (82). Cellorigo cites as precedent examples from antiquity of kings and emperors who cultivated their estates or who sprang from families of merchants (81–82). Not only does he cite precedent, as befits a man of his time, but he leans upon Biblical analogies and exhortations to reinforce his proposal (112–13).

Cellorigo nevertheless takes for granted the traditional tripartite division of society, now no longer operative (if it ever was so), in advocating that each person must know and keep her/his place in the social order. Any deviation, he fears, could only cause disorder and unruliness. We have echoes here of the ideologies discussed in chapter 1 underlying the concept of true *nobilitas*, namely, the Aristotelian and Scholastic argument on "the indispensability of private property in any well ordered commonwealth" (Skinner 138). And so Cellorigo steps warily: "Though it would not be right to say that all people should be equal, it would be reasonable for the extremes to be brought within measure. But the desire to have everyone be equal is the cause of the greatest disorder; the State becomes a confusion of the lowest and the middle and the highest, with everyone out of step and out of the rank that they should observe in conformity with each one's property, occupation and estate" ["Y aunque no sería bien decir que todos hayan de ser iguales, no sería fuera de razón que estos dos extremos se acompasasen, pues el quererse todos igualar es lo que los tiene más desconcertados, y confundida la República de menores a medianos y de medianos a mayores, saliendo todos de su compás y orden que conforme a la calidad de sus haciendas, de sus oficios y estado de cada uno, debieran guardar" (52)].

It is clear that Cellorigo's aim, like that of his fellow reformists, is to mitigate the extremes of rich and poor and to restore a middle rank. But to achieve this end, he still holds to a neo-Platonist paradigm of a "perfect" social order in which everyone keeps her and his place under the strict supervision of a Guardian of sorts who ensures its stability.

The "Guardian" in Cellorigo's model is the Prince who, in a musical allegory or conceit, maintains the harmony of voices emanating from the diverse but fixed classes: "The prince must ensure that the social ranks not change, alter, become confused or made equal, but *that each one keep its place, order and relation, so that the diverse voices may make a perfect harmony.* The prince will adjust the high and low notes to the harmony of his governance, making it melodious and orderly, and will follow the example of the skilled musician who, if the strings play a false note, removes or destroys them . . ." ["las cuales [clases] el Príncipe ha de disponer de manera que no se muden, que no se alteren, confundan, ni igualen, sino *que cada uno conserve su lugar, su orden, su concierto, de suerte que con diversas voces hagan consonancia perfecta;* acomodando el Príncipe los sones agudos y graves a la concordia de su gobierno, para hacerle sonoro y bien concertado, tomando el aviso del diestro músico que, cuando las cuerdas son falsas, o las quita o hace pedazos . . ." (124: emphasis added)]. This "harmony," which we will hear insisted upon, is for Cellorigo and many of his fellow reformers what constitutes an ideal society.

The rapid growth of a monetary economy in the sixteenth century, then, had created new relations of power from the purchase of high positions and honors all the way down to the bribery of jailers and lawyers' clerks. Traces of the latter are reflected in many of Cervantes's works, and not less so in *Don Quixote* where money, as we have said, seems to be the consistent arbiter of the social order. Referring to Ana Félix's using the story of her father Ricote's buried riches to gain the Governor's favor for her lover Don Gregorio (II:63), Georges Güntert observes that it is "an obvious sign that in this new world the passport is money" ["señal evidente de que el pasaporte en el mundo nuevo es efectivamente el dinero" (99)]. In the incident involving Ricote himself (II:54), Sancho declines the Morisco's offer of two hundred escudos as payment for helping to recover Ricote's buried treasure, either through fear of governmental retribution or because of Old Christian scruples (814–15). The scene, however, is ironic both generically and historically. Generically, because this conversation about money and ethnic cleansing is allowed to take place in the *locus amoenus* of a poplar grove, under the proverbial beech tree ["al pie de una haya" (1071)], at the foot of which Sancho and Ricote are seated. Historically, because it is in the person of the exiled Ricote that the text gives us an exemplar of the very program the reformists claimed they were seeking—hard work, abstemious living, and the resultant accumulation of wealth which would be vital to the welfare of the nation. Once again, the utopian discourse discloses the contradictions that the text elides.

Here we must allude to the Morisco situation. A. W. Lovett notes that observers "were struck to the point of indignation by the frugality of the community. The Moriscos would build up savings even from their minuscule incomes" (272). What was perhaps even more offensive to Castilian Old Christians was the Moriscos' failure to spend their earnings, and to create, instead, economically self-sufficient communities. To the great annoyance of clerics like the bishop of Segorbe, it was this ideological disconformity that such Morisco behaviour represented that provoked hostility. The "honorable" way would have been to flaunt money in personal ostentation (carriages, a retinue of servants, dress, gifts) and in donations to religious institutions (Johnson, "Ortodoxia" 289).[6] And we know that Spain's religious centres added to the bleeding of Spanish wealth into the hands of foreigners. When Sancho encounters Ricote, for example, the latter is in the company of German pilgrims who travel the country explicitly "to visit the shrines which they think of as their Indies: as sure profit and certain gain" (II:54, 814) ["a visitar los santuarios della, que los tienen por sus Indias, y por certísima granjería y conocida ganancia" (1073)]. As Carroll Johnson points out in his analysis of the incident of the Morisco, it is in Ricote that "we see in miniature, on the individual, human level, the typical route taken by Spanish capital in the sixteenth century: America, through Spain, to end up in the hands of German bankers" ["En él se representa en miniatura, a nivel individual y humano, la clásica trayectoria del capital español en el siglo XVI: desde América a través de España, a parar en manos de los banqueros alemanes" (Johnson, "Ortodoxia" 293)]. The expulsion of the Moriscos, then, was to prove a human and an economic disaster for Spain. Not only was a great pool of skilled labor lost, but it signified "the stillbirth of a native petit-bourgeois capitalism based on values and life-style that triumphed in northern countries, and could have helped to prevent the decline of Spain" [la expulsión viene a significar . . . la

---

6. In Cervantes's *Dialogue of the Dogs* [*Coloquio de los perros*], the dog Berganza also complains of the stinginess of the "morisco rabble" ["la canalla morisca" (*Novelas* 349–50).]

muerte—antes que pudiera nacer—de un capitalismo nativo pequeño-burgués basado en valores y estilos de vida que triunfaron en los países del norte, que pudiera haber contribuido poderosamente a evitar la decadencia española" (Johnson, "Ortodoxia" 291)]. Cervantes's text figures the poignancy of the human disaster while seemingly eliding its economic consequences.[7]

In their continued efforts to equalize society, the reformists explored other issues besides that of the work ethic, namely, how and why social divisions and property rights had come about in the first place; what constituted a just society; and what legitimated authority. In what follows, we acknowledge that Don Quixote's Golden Age speech is nothing other than a poetic fantasy which the bucolic scene evokes in the knight's mind. We suggest, however, that the issues addressed in his oration, distorted as they may be, can most fruitfully be read against the novel's historical record. As such, they are consistent with an an-

---

7. Güntert remarks that "Philip III's Spain still pursues its abstract ideal based on the unity of faith, language, and the nation . . . Only in northern Europe does a gradual ripening of new attitudes become possible, which will permit the rise of completely new conditions of life. Faced with these two realities, one unifying and intolerant, the other diversifying, with respect for the individual conscience, Don Quixote remains silent. The dream of the golden age has departed forever." ["la España de Felipe III continúa persiguiendo su abstracto ideal, basado en la unidad de la fe, de la lengua y de la nación . . . Sólo en el Norte de Europa se hace posible la paulatina maduración de nuevas mentalidades, que van a permitir el auge de unas condiciones de vida en todo diferentes. Frente a estas dos realidades, unificadora e intolerante la una, dispersadora y respetuosa de la conciencia individual la otra, Don Quijote calla. El sueño de la edad de oro se ha alejado definitivamente" (Güntert 99)]. Before the irony of this most ironic of novels we pause. The jury may still be out on whether to take at face value Ricote's view of Germany as a country in which one enjoys freedom of conscience ("se vive con libertad de consciencia" (1073) at the same moment that he praises Philip III for expelling him and his fellow moriscos. But Güntert's suggestion of a parallel between the dream of the age of gold which Quixote has lost, with "respect for the individual conscience" (99), seems to us untenable. Don Quixote's harmonious Golden Age and the "harmony" Cellorigo and his contemporaries idealize for Spain conjure instead images of the price one always pays for ideal commonwealths, namely, the "tyrannical unanimity" (Jameson in *Diacritics*, 1977) of those "literary inventions" which function, in part, as "measures to manage [individual] desire" (Greene 233).

thropology of the law and political theory that remained pervasive and contestatorial throughout the sixteenth-century and which, in this and the following chapter, we will demonstrate to be current in the period.

We know that the trope of a pre-lapsarian humanity of social justice, where no one was subject to the will of another, consistently motivates the knight's most "chivalric" actions. Seven instances that come readily to mind are the case of Juan Haldudo and Andrés, in which Don Quixote demands justice for the boy whose owner refuses to pay what he owes him (I:4); that of the lady in Part I, chapter 8 whom Don Quiixote frees from her supposed abductors so that she can now "do with thy person as thou wishest" (63) ["puede facer de su persona lo que más le viniere en talante" (101)]; his defense of Marcela's desire for personal freedom in withdrawing into her pre-social natural world (I:14); his intervention in terms of the "natural" justice that gives poor Basilio his only sheep Quiteria (II:21, 596) ["no tiene más desta oveja" (807)] while the rich Camacho "can buy whenever, and wherever, and whatever he desires" (596) ["podrá comprar su gusto cuando, donde y como quisiere" (807)]; his assuring Eugenio that "despite the abbess and all those who might wish to prevent it, I wouldst [sic] rescue Leandra from the convent, where she is certainly held against her will" (I:52, 438) ["que yo sacara del monasterio (donde sin duda alguna debe de estar contra su voluntad) a Leandra, a pesar de la abadesa y de cuantos quisieran estorbarlo" (583)]; his rescuing the statue of the Virgin Mary whose sad demeanor showed that she was being taken "against her will" (I:52, 440) ["contra su voluntad" (586)]; and his challenging the laws of the King and liberating the chain gang—one of the most "insane" of his actions—for "it seems harsh to make slaves of those whom God and nature made free" (I:22, 170) ["porque me parece duro caso hacer esclavos a los que Dios y naturaleza hizo libres" (244)]. Whether this emphasis of Don Quixote's on the free will of the individual makes him a hero (Ortega y Gasset 148–49) or simply "a menace to the state and to the Catholic Faith" (Quint 101) is not our concern. What interests us is that the same trope of primordial social justice in which, originally, no one was subject to the will of another, provided the reformists a heuristic device for grounding the concept of "natural law." Even though such recourse to a pre-social stage in human history must certainly have been taken metaphorically, it did not prevent the reformists from using it in formulating their legal and political theories.

This concept of natural law, or *ius naturale*, underwent numerous transformations since its enunciation by Roman legists and has been understood in several contradictory senses. Since the late eighteenth century, for instance, "natural law" has been subsumed into the argument for "natural rights" or the "rights of man." But this is a development of more recent history. We are concerned here with the notion of *ius naturale* as it was understood in Cervantes's time, that is, as a strand of jurisprudence with roots in Roman law. This strand grew in importance in the late middle ages and nourished a political theory in sixteenth-century Spain of a lawless, propertyless humanity as the foundation for theoretical origins of society and for the constitution of authority.

The term "natural law," from Roman antiquity on, was used in two principal and rather different senses, though these were at times confused. The more familiar use of the term was the one associated with Stoic philosophy, which the Roman writers took from their Greek mentors. Thus Cicero writes: "True law is right reason [*recta ratio*] in agreement with nature; it is of universal application, unchanging and everlasting . . . . We cannot be freed from its obligations by senate or people, and we need not look outside ourselves for an expounder or interpreter of it . . . [O]ne eternal and unchangeable law will be valid for all nations and for all times, and *there will be one master and one ruler, that is, God, over us all, for he is the author of this law, its promulgator, and its enforcing judg*e" (*De re Publica*], [bk. III: sec. 22, para. 33: emphasis added). To the idea of the oneness and the universality of the law, immutable and eternal and over which there was only one "enforcing judge," Cicero added the Stoics' insistence on the fundamental equality of all humankind. This was seen as contrary to Aristotle's doctrine in the *Politics*, as interpreted by the Paris Scholastic, John Major, which affirmed that some humans were inferior and feebleminded and needed to be governed. Even the Bible seemed to concur with the Aristotelian position: "the fool will be servant to the wise" (Prov. 11:29 RSV). Cicero's position suggested that because all are subject to one universal law and are fellow-citizens, it could be inferred that they must in some sense be equal (Sabine 165). The implications are spelled out in a well-known passage from his *De Legibus (On Laws)*: "For those creatures that have received the gift of reason from Nature have also received right reason, and therefore they have also received the gift of Law, which is right reason [*recta ratio*] applied to command and prohibition. And if they received law, they have received Justice also. Now all men have received reason; therefore all men have received Justice" (I:12, 33).

This concept would, in the course of time, be assimilated into Christian philosophy. Natural law would come to be identified with the law given by God to Adam. The fact that pagan philosophers had propounded a universal law of nature as well was taken to confirm both its universality and its permanence. "Natural law," Thomas Aquinas affirmed, "is nothing else than the participation of the Eternal law in rational creatures" (*Summa Theologica*, 1a 2ae, quae. 91, art.2; quoted in D'Entrèves 43); for Domingo de Soto, "[t]he natural law is an imprint made at the creation of nature itself" (*De justitia et jure* (1553–1554), bk. I, q. 3, art. 9: quoted in Hamilton, 15). The light of natural reason enables us to discern good from evil (D'Entrèves 43), and hence, according to Saint Thomas, to "do good and avoid evil." From this a sequence of other precepts is logically derived. For humans, natural law encompasses "the inclination to know the truth about God" and to live in society (D'Entrèves 44). As such, it is an aspect of the divine order and unalterable even by God himself (Gierke, *Natural Law* 235 n. 32). Such, in excessively brief and schematic terms, is what we might call the dominant conception of natural law. It is this conception which found favor particularly among theologians who wrote on political theory. In the later seventeenth century secular political theorists would turn it towards other ends (Troeltsch 206–7; Tuck; D'Entrèves ch. 3).[8]

There is another and less-known tradition of *ius naturale*, however, that is pertinent in examining the match effected between *Don Quixote* and the century's discursive formations. Like the tradition that we have just outlined, it was codified in Late Antiquity and developed throughout the Middle Ages and into the sixteenth century. It is relevant to the knight's conflation of a mythic golden past with his desire for a good society. Its legal origins are to be found in the Emperor Justinian's codified *Corpus Iuris Civilis* (534 C.E.) in the section known as the *Digest* (533 C.E.), which had been rediscovered in the eleventh century. Among the jurists whose work was incorporated into it was Ulpian (Domitius Ul-

---

8. The identification of natural law with Christian moral philosophy was confirmed by Samuel Pufendorf (1634–1692; see Stein 108).

pianus, ca. 160–228), whose writings constitute about one third of the *Digest*.

Ulpian's *ius naturale* differs substantially from that which we have been discussing so far. It goes beyond Cicero's inference that because all are subject to one universal law we must therefore in some sense be equal. Ulpian is anticipated, to some extent, by Seneca's *Letter 90*, to Lucillus, in claiming the originary condition of all people to be free and equal, bound only by ties of family relationships, and having equal right to all the goods of nature. But Seneca wrote as a moralist; Ulpian the jurist was necessarily less diffuse. Ulpian described the law of nature, or natural law, as "that which nature has taught to all animals; for it is not a law specific to mankind but is common to all animals . . . Out of this comes the union of man and woman which we call marriage, and the procreation of children and their rearing . . ." ["Ius naturale est, quod natura omnia animalia docuit: nam istud non humani generis proprium, sed omnium animalium . . . hinc descendit maris atque feminae coniunctio, quam nos matrimonium appellamus, hinc liberorum procreatio, hinc educatio" (*Digest* bk. I: title i, 1)]. Ulpian cites by counter-example to the *ius naturale* the manumission of slaves which, he says, pertains to the stage following that of natural law, namely, the *ius gentium*, or law of peoples: "since, of course, everyone would be born free by the natural law, and manumission would not be known when slavery was unknown" (*Digest* I:1, 4) ["[Q]uae res a iure gentium originem sumpsit, utpote cum iure naturali omnes liberi nascerentur nec esset non manumissio, cum servitus esset incognita" (cf. Gierke 233 n. 25; Megías Quirós 23)]. He states this even more directly in *Digest* Book I, title 5, paragraph 4: "Slavery is an institution of the *ius gentium* whereby someone is made subject to the ownership of another" ["[S]eruitus est constitutio iuris gentium qua quis dominio alieno contra naturam subicitur"].

Ulpian's argument proceeds as follows. A hypothetical *in illo tempore* in which all peoples were born and lived free and equal is succeeded by human societies organized by, and subjected to, specific laws which embodied authority. It is this authority that then apportioned power and distributed land. This is the *ius gentium* which is said to have superseded the *ius naturale*. The former would have come into existence in one of two ways. According to the first theory, there was a kind of rational progress from simple to complex: as the number of people increased and filled the earth, they recognized the need for a social contract. Government and the subsequent distribution of resources then ensued. The consequences were far reaching and acquired their own momentum. In the view of Hermogenianus, a fourth-century jurist whose opinions contributed to the *Digest*, the "harmony" Don Quixote predicated of the originary condition gave way to the *ius gentium*, and "[a]s a consequence of this *ius gentium*, wars were introduced, nations differentiated, kingdoms founded, properties individuated, estate boundaries settled, buildings put up, and commerce established . . ." ["ex hoc iure gentium introducta bella, discretae gentes, regna condita, dominia distincta, agries termini positi, aedificia collocata, commercium, emptiones, venditiones, locationes conductiones, obligationes institutae . . ." (*Digest* I:1, 5)].[9] It is in such a world that civil law is said to have been developed and systematized, with its prohibitions and sanctions. In the *Institutes*, Justinian's textbook for law students, the transition from the *ius naturale* to the *ius gentium* is likewise ascribed to "the reality of the human condition" ["[N]am usu exigente et humanis necessitatibus gentes humanae quaedam sibi constituerunt: bella enim orta, captivitates secutae et seruitutes, quae sunt iuri naturali contrariae. Iuri enim na-

---

9. Ulpian's idea of an original state of nature (before the *ius gentium* and its consequences are imposed, namely, division of property, wars, slavery, political rule), is repeated in the formulae of Isidore of Seville (d. 636) as one in which there was "liberty for all" and "all things [were shared] in common" [*omnium una libertas* and *communis omnium possessio*]. That is, the "*ius naturale* is common to all nations; it is what is received everywhere by natural instinct, and not by any convention. It includes the union of men and women, the bringing up of children, common possession of everything and freedom for everyone." ["Ius naturale est comune omnium nationum, et quod ubique instinctu naturae, non constitutione aliqua habetur, ut: viri et feminae coniunctio, liberorum susceptio et educatio, communio omnium possessionum et omnium una libertas." (Migne 82, col. 199, quoted in Tuck 18).] The tradition is continued into the sixteenth century with Gregorio López Madera's authoritative gloss on the *Siete Partidas*. López Madera reminds his readers, as the peasant will remind the king in the *Disputa* of the 1400s which we examine below, "that dominion over men is not the law of nature, where freedom is shared by all." ["Et adverte etiam, quo dominium super homines non est de iure naturae, cum omnium sit libertas . . . " (Partida 3, tít. 18, ley 31). López Madera continues his gloss by citing the familiar words of Augustine, in *De civitate dei*, that God set men over all other creatures, but not over other men.

turale ab initio omnes homines liberi nascebantur" (bk. I: title i, para. 1)].

But another theory of how the *ius gentium* came into existence held that primordial freedom and communal possession were terminated not by consensus but by forcible imposition. This second theory, echoes of which can be heard in Quixote's argument, recalls John Ball's poignant reminder in the sermon we cited in chapter 4 to the effect that all humans are created in God's image, and yet some are treated as beasts. Ball's view, and the way the story is told according to this second theory, is beautifully manifested in an anonymous and untitled Spanish manuscript from the late 1400s published by José Amador de los Ríos as the *Libro de los pensamientos variables* in volume seven of his *Historia crítica de la literatura española* (1865). The anonymous text warrants citing at length in order to show how subversive this second theory on natural law could be. The fictional dialogue takes place between a peasant and a king. Maravall calls it *Disputa del rey y el labrador* (*Estado moderno* vol. II, 240). We shall refer to it as the *Disputa*.

The *Disputa*'s premise is threefold: (1) that the powerful have usurped what in God's economy was originally distributed to all equally; (2) that the rich strive to become richer, unceasingly exploiting the poor in the process; and(3) that what has been taken by force can be legitimately reclaimed by force. The manuscript makes the Narrator/Spectator, who dismounts from his horse to rest by a cool spring, an eavesdropper on the dialogue.

The anonymous author first creates the background for the *Disputa* by meditating on the diversity of societies and the fact that the ends of government are everywhere the same: " . . . as I was pondering on the great variety of provinces, lands, regions, kingdoms and lordships that there are in the world, and on how diverse are their forms of governance, I marveled greatly because it seemed to me that there was only one form or principle of governing. And the more a form of governance diverges from that principle, the more flawed it is" [" . . . é como considerasse tantas diferençias de prouinçias, tierras, rregiones, rreynos é señoríos, quantas en el mundo vuiese, é asimesmo quán diuersos sus rregimientos fuessen, muncho me marauillaua, porque a mí pareçia no ser más de vna la forma ó rregla de gouernar. É que tanto quanto más de aquella cada un regimiento se desuiase, tanto más era rregimiento errado" (Amador de los Ríos 581)]. His meditation is interrupted by the arrival of a man of obviously high rank, richly attired, who dismounts at a distance. Then there comes a poor and sweaty peasant who ignores the gentleman and is rebuked for his lack of respect, which immediately highlights the hierarchical social dispensation the manuscript depicts.

When the peasant realizes that the noble is in fact the king, he resists the rebuke, and thus the social and textual order, by informing the king of another order. This order is the one that is traced in what we have referred to as the second version of how the *ius gentium* is said to have superseded the *ius naturale*, namely, the forcible usurpation of an originary egalitarian state of humanity. The peasant describes humankind's earliest condition as one of equality and justice wherein all were masters of what is in the world. It is the rich and powerful nobles, he claims, who subsequently usurped this natural condition and forcibly seized goods that were once communal: "All men who were born into this wretched world were equally masters of what, before they were created, God made for them and so, if one may say so without offence, *people like me are bound to have great enmity towards great nobles because, having seized power by force they made slaves of us*" ["Los onbres en este mísero mundo venidos todos fueron ygualmente señores de lo que Dios, antes de su formacion, para ellos auia criado, é desta manera si onestamente dezir se puede, *gran enemiga deuemos auer é tener los tales como yo con los altos varones, pues forçosamente auiéndosse usurpado el señorío, nos han hecho sieruos*" (583: emphasis added)].

The tone becomes more aggressive as the peasant slips from the "history" of humankind's beginnings in equality and its subsequent "fall" into serfdom, to a veiled threat to the king that what has been taken by force can also be reclaimed by force: "know that by those same laws that set up the state of affairs we have mentioned, we wish to undo it, *because anything that is done by force, must be undone by force*" ["sepa que por aquellas leyes por donde lo dicho se prinçipió, querriamos el contrario rehacer, *porque toda cosa que con fuerça se haze, con fuerça deshacer se tiene*" (584: emphasis added)].[10] He describes the growing impatience

---

10. In the sixteenth-century work of Guevara, *El villano del Danubio*, in an episode in his *Vida de Marco Aurelio*, a barbarian informs the Roman senate that their greed and pride have deprived the Danubians of what was theirs and, consequently, warns them in words that echo the medieval peasant's threat, that "tenemos por infalible regla, que el hombre que toma por fuerza lo ajeno, pierda el derecho que tiene a lo suyo proprio" [we take it as an absolute rule that the man who takes

of the poor towards the excesses of the wealthy; granting that human-kind needs leadership, it has to be based on virtue: "only he who is vir-tuous deserves to rule" ["por solo virtuoso, mereçer es bien que señoree" (584)].

In words reminiscent of Don Quixote's communitarian golden age, the King replies that common ownership was a consequence of human-kind's primitive state, of the natural abundance of food at its disposal and of its fewer needs. But he then resorts to the age-old distinction be-tween two versions of humankind's beginnings. The peasant has evoked the image of a harmonious originary state, as Quixote does in his ora-tion. The king prefers the Lucretian version of humankind's originary state which we have seen capitalized upon in the sixteenth- and seven-teenth-centuries by Ioannes Boemus and Jean Bodin and, in Thomas Hobbes's well known words, as "nasty, brutish, and short."[11] It is this *ius naturale,* this primitive state, according to the king, that the *ius gentium* with all its built-in discontents has mercifully remedied: "although in the first ages of the world all things were held in common, this was more the result of the brutishness of the inhabitants than because it was to anyone's benefit" [" . . . que bien que en las primeras edades del mundo todas las cosas fuessen comunes, que más era por la bestialidad de los habitantes, que por ser provechoso a ninguno" (584)].[12]

A communitarian society would still exist, the king continues, if all men were of good will ("de sana intención"), but he maintains that it is human resentment which accounts for present power relations. In

---

another's property by force loses the right to his own" (3)]. In his introduction to the episode, Américo Castro also points out the resonance in Guevara's work of the medieval dialogue (p. xxiv). The Bolognese legist Azo had written, in reference to the hypothetical voluntary transfer of power at the beginning of human society, that even then, "the people did not completely abdicate their power, for what is transferred may be taken back" (Pennington 432).

11. On the "state of nature," Hobbes writes: "No arts; no letters; no society; and which is worst of all, continual fear and danger of violent death; and the life of man, solitary, poor, nasty, brutish, and short" (*Leviathan* pt. I: ch. 13).

12. Two centuries later, Montesquieu still distinguishes between the "primitiv-ism" of common ownership and the "civilizing" influence of land distribution: "It is the distribution of land which is responsible for the increase in the civil code. Among nations where there is no such distribution there are few civil laws." See Montesquieu, *Oeuvres complètes* vol. II:538.

a rhetorical tour de force he blames the poor—those who work—for resenting the rich who enjoy the fruit of their labor, asserting that those who believe themselves to be better must necessarily rule over those who are less worthy: "It is true that if everyone had been well intentioned, things would still exist in communal possession, but since that cannot be, *he who labors takes it hard that someone else enjoys the fruits, and this is why those who have high ambition master lesser men and force them into servitude*" ["verdad es que si todos fuessen de sana intençion, aun durarían las cosas en ley de comunidad; mas como aquesto ser non pueda, *aquel que más trabaja á por graue que otro lo goze, lo qual es causa que aquellos que para más se piensan ser, forzosamente se enseñoreen de los menores e de aquellos se sirvan.*" (584: emphasis added)]. In conclusion, the king affirms, presumably restricting his statement to the noble class: "there is nothing wrong in each getting whatever he can" ["que cada uno procure el proprio provecho no es ylícito" (584)].

The peasant becomes more aggressive and asks the king if he realizes the pain the poor feel "on seeing those who have made themselves great enjoy our hard labors? . . . Oppressed with burdens and cares, we spend our days without any pleasure; oppressed by a thousand woes, we are rejected in every way; we are oppressed by the heavy labor *from which you kings and nobles carry off all the profit.* Given the way things are, there can be no love lost between us . . ." ["veyendo a los que mayores se han hecho de nuestros afanes goçar? . . . Nosotros, llenos del afán e del cuydado, passamos los dias sin ningun plazer: nosotros, llenos de mil miserias, somos por muchas maneras despechados; nosotros, llenos del *creçido trabajo de que los reyes é grandes os lleuais todo el prouecho.* Pues, sigun estas obras, pequeña enemiga os tenemos . . ." (585: emphasis added)]. Nature herself, he adds, requires that those who toil should enjoy the fruits of their labor.

In his defense and that of the peasant's "betters," the king first alludes to the intellectual and corporal superiority of the noble class. He enumerates the cares, anxieties, responsibilities, and sleepless nights that they suffer. Who has the greater labor, he asks rhetorically, "he who only has to maintain his body, or he who strives with his mind?" ["¿aquel que solo el cuerpo sostiene, ó aquel que con el espíritu se aflige?" (586)], and who would defend the realm against its enemies if the warrior nobles did not exist? He then compares the "idyllic" rural life of the peasant with the burdens of his own: "I tell you truly that many are the nights when you sleep more soundly on delightful lawns than I do on linen sheets. Because you rest after your physical labor, all food is pleasant, and the murmur of the rushing streams lulls you to delightful sleep on the cool grass" ["Que en verdad te digo ser muchas las noches que duermes tú muy más holgadamente sobre viçiossos çespedes, que yo sobre las sáuanas de Olanda. Porque a tí después del corpóreo trabajo descansas: todo comer te es tenplado, é el murmurable son de los huyentes arroyos sobre la fresca yerua acostado, te administra sabroso dormir" (586)].[13] The king insists that the delightful dishes he is served, and the luxurious beds to which he has access, cannot assuage his cares. Which of you [peasants], he again asks rhetorically, would choose this life? ["¿Pues cuál de vos querria tal vida . . . ?" (586)]. Such aggravations, supposedly suffered by men of power according to the king, will be actually visited upon the governor Sancho in *Barataria*. They are part of the Duke's cruel practical joke on an ignorant peasant who should never have aspired to the position of leadership of his "betters." Don Quixote adopts a similar stance in his soliloquy to the sleeping Sancho:

> O thou, more fortunate than all those who live on the face of the earth . . . Ambition doth not disturb thee, nor doth the vain pomp of the world trouble thee, for the limits of thy desires extendeth not beyond caring for thy donkey; thou hast placed care for thine own person on my shoulders, a weight and a burden that nature and custom hath given to masters. The servant sleepeth, and the master standeth watch, thinking of how he may sustain him, and improve him, and grant him favors" (II:20, 583).

> ["Ni la ambición te inquieta, ni la pompa vana del mundo te fatiga, pues los límites de tus deseos no se estienden a más que a pensar tu jumento, que el de tu persona sobre mis hombros lo tienes puesto, contrapeso y carga que puso la naturaleza y la costumbre a los señores. Duerme el criado, y

---

13. The sixteenth-century theologian Domigo de Soto will simply take for granted this divinely-ordained chain of being in his analogy of the relation between the body and the soul: "This was the wisdom and the providence of God," Soto claimed in his *Deliberacion en la causa de los pobres* of 1545, "that there should be rich men who, like the soul, should be able to sustain and rule the poor, and poor men who, like the body, would serve the rich by working the land and performing the other tasks that are necessary for the republic" (quoted in Pagden, *Fall* 98).

está velando el señor, pensando cómo le ha de sustentar, mejorar y hacer mercedes" (791)].

A similar paternalistic justification for subordination resonates in Erasmus's *Encomium moriae*, in Shakespeare's *Henry IV* as the king describes the burdens of the great, and even his Henry V as he sees his low-born subjects sleeping before the battle of Agincourt (Kaiser 283).

So insistent is this justification in the sixteenth century that we may imagine the resistance it must have met. Traces of resistance can be detected in *Don Quixote* when Sancho quarrels with his master who insists that Sancho flog himself in order to disenchant Dulcinea. When the squire knocks the knight to the ground Don Quixote cries: "What, you traitor? You dare to raise your hand against your *natural lord* and master? You presume to defy the person who gives you your bread?" (II:60, 851: emphasis added) ["¿Cómo traidor? ¿Contra tu amo y *señor natural* te desmandas? ¿Con quien te da su pan te atreves?" (1117)]. And Sancho replies: "I depose no king, I impose no king, . . . but I'll help myself, for I'm my own lord" (851) ["Ni quito rey ni pongo rey . . . sino ayúdome a mí que soy mi señor" (1118)].

With the invention of the printing press, and after the Reformation, feudal submission to natural lords and blind obedience to the Church were bound to lose some of their power. Carlo Ginzberg gives us a sixteenth-century example of this, again in the case of the miller Domenico Scandella (Menocchio) whom we have encountered in this study. Railing, as Ginzburg tells it, against the "enormous edifice built on the exploitation of the poor, Menocchio set forth a very different religion, where all members were equal because the spirit of God was in all of them" (Ginzburg 17). Menocchio told the Inquisitors that even a "miller may claim to be able to expound the truths of the faith to the pope, to a king, to a prince, because he has within himself that spirit which God has imparted to all men" (Ginzburg 17). Menocchio was to pay with his life for such unwary audacity.

In view of the price the plain-speaking miller paid for his daring, it is not possible to read the incongruous ending of the *Disputa* as anything other than sardonic. In verses addressed to Queen Isabella, and despite the dialogue's consistently subversive message, the narrator celebrates a society in which, as Cellorigo would affirm, each class remains in its "natural" place:

So, noble Queen, I beg Your Highness
not to command the poor
to serve as the rich do,
and not to demand of the small
what only the great have.

[Pues, alta Reyna, suplico
Que Vuestra Alteza non mande
Sirua el pobre como el rico,
Nin pida nel lugar chico
Las cosas que son del grande. (589–90)][14]

Such divergent and conflicting views of *ius naturale* and *ius gentium* would result in heated controversies among theorists for the next two hundred years.

---

14. In Spain, especially in moments of popular unrest, the *Disputa*'s subversive conception of the *ius naturale*, in Don Quixote's words, that "[a]ll things were shared in that holy age" (59), comes explosively to the surface in communities of have-nots. Maravall sees in this text, plausibly perhaps, the "social program of the demands of the Comuneros" ["programa social de reivindicaciones de los comuneros" (*Estado moderno* vol. II:241)]. Whether or not this text crystallizes sentiments that were to take a more direct form of revolutionary expression forty years on, as Maravall believes, its representation of social resentment is clear. We note here that during periods of social unrest (i.e. the peasants' revolts of the late middle ages and early modern Europe), millenarian movements frequently emerge proclaiming the dissolution of existing social structures and the establishment of classless paradises on earth (see Cohn ch. 10–12).

7

The *ius naturale* and "The Indian Question"

We turn from the professional legists and theologians of the century to continue our interrogation of the historical record and the discursive formations of the period that produced *Don Quixote*. What we might now refer to as the Quixotic view of human institutional history was widely disseminated and discussed in Cervantes's time. A significant example of this is the Trinitarian friar Alonso de Castrillo, whose *Tractado de República* was published in 1521 in Burgos. What makes Castrillo especially valuable in our effort to demonstrate the match between *Don Quixote* and the ideas current in his time is the fact that Castrillo was not a professional in the area of jurisprudence. Unlike the theorists we have cited, Castrillo was neither a lawyer nor a theologian in the Thomist tradition. Consequently, his *Tractado* is not a legal treatise nor is it a work of political philosophy, although it can be said to partake of both genres.

The *Tractado* was not reprinted nor was it widely disseminated. In fact, precisely because of its non-specialist accessibility, it can be seen as even more representative of ideas that were "in the air" in the century. To cite José Megías Quirós: "Castrillo seems to represent the 'common' feeling of his period concerning political and juridical matters; that is to say, the 'feeling' communally shared in the environment, that is in the air, and that rarely appears in primarily academic texts until those views have gained the necessary prestige" ["Castrillo parece ser un representante del sentir 'común' de su época acerca de materias políticas y jurídicas; es decir, de ese 'sentir' comúnmente compartido, que está en el ambiente, en el aire, y que rara vez aparece en textos propiamente universitarios hasta que esa mentalidad no ha alcanzado el prestigio suficiente" (Megías Quirós 27)].

The *Tractado* proceeds in Scholastic fashion from the lesser to the greater. So we have: Capítulo I: *Que trata de qué cosa sea casa* [*Concerning what is a house*]; Capítulo II: . . . *qué cosa sea cibdad* [*what is a city*]; Capítulo III . . . *qué cosa sea cibdadano y qué cosa sea república* [*what is a citizen and what is a republic*]. Castrillo thus appears to be preparing the way for a communitarian theory of the state, an impression that seems to be confirmed in the title of his chapter: *Que trata de cierta comparación de las abejas a los cibdadanos y gobernadores de la República* [*Which treats of a comparison of a beehive and the citizens and governors of the Republic*].

In the two chapters that follow, Castrillo adopts the political commonplace of the perfect organization of the hive, and the respect and obedience that all bees have for their "king."[1] In chapter 6 the argument is reversed. Castrillo states the case *against* the very status quo he has thus far been describing. The view he now elaborates actually resonates with the peasant's perspective in the *Disputa* on the originary equality of humankind and the subsequent and forcible imposition of hierarchy brought about by the *ius gentium*. In Castrillo's words: " . . . whereas nature created us all equal and free, there is nothing that so offends against nature as obeisance, which was introduced rather by force than by natural justice" [" . . . que como quiera que la natura a todos juntamente nos hubo criado iguales y libres, no hay cosa de que tanto se agravia la natura como de la obediencia, la cual fué introducida más por la fuerza que no por natural justicia" (*Tractado* 43)].

It is a view we have seen circulating in sixteenth-century Spain by recourse to the authority of both Aristotle and Cicero. A fuller reading of these ancient writers, however, would authorize a less "libertarian" theory of the origins of human society and of the meaning of natural law than Castrillo ascribes to them. In fact, Aristotle and Cicero argued that humans are by nature political animals and have established themselves in power relations from the very beginning. Castrillo's partial citations of these authoritative sources nevertheless serve to validate his

---

1. The universality of this topos is attested to by López Madera: "bees have always been taken as a sign and a symbol of the Kingdom" ["que fueron siempre tenidas [las abexas] por symbolo y señal de Reyno" (fol. 4v)].

argument that original freedom and the common possession of all material goods was sanctioned, even by the ancients. This is how he glosses their statements: "Aliis autem praeter naturam videtur esse dominatio quoniam natura nihil diferant sed lege dum taxat inductum sit ut alii liberi sint alii servi qua propter nec iustum, violentum enim," which he transcribes thus:

> . . . which is to say: other learned men find overlordship to be contrary to nature because by nature all are equal: it is only by law that it was established that some should be slaves and others free. Consequently it is not just, but truly duress. Just as nature created us all free, so nature created us all equal in possession of the world, *as Cicero teaches* . . . . (emphasis added)

> [. . . Que quiere decir: a otros sabios les parece ser cosa sobre natura el señorío, porque por natura todos son iguales, mas solamente por ley fue introducido, que unos fuesen siervos y otros fuesen libres, por lo cual no es cosa justa mas en verdad forzosa: y así como la natura a todos nos crió libres, así la natura a todos nos crió iguales en la posesión del mundo, *lo cual Marco Tulio nos enseña* . . . . (Tractado 44: emphasis added)]

In *De oficiis*, Book II, paragraph 73, however, which Castrillo does not mention, Cicero had actually declared that there could be no worse plague than the equal distribution of property.

What Cicero is made to teach in the following extract that Castrillo chooses to cite is that private property (always a consequence of the *ius gentium*) began by the occupation of empty spaces. This occupation, either by consensus or by force, then became law: " . . . from that time forth, as what had by nature belonged to all came to be the property of one, and as greed increased, so fellowship among people decayed and the passage of the ages has given birth to so many diverse and abominable species of greed that it seems that our world is being destroyed by greed rather than by the fire of the Last Judgment" [" . . . y dende allí adelante como comenzó a ser de uno lo que antes por natura fuera de muchos, como creció la cubdicia, corrompióse el concierto de las gentes, y las largas edades han engendrado tan diversos y abominables linajes de codicias, que ya parece nuestro mundo perderse por codicia que por fuego del postrero juicio" (44–45)].

It is in his postulating a past time when all things were held in common, and in contrasting that time with the "abominable" greed of the present time, that the sixteenth-century theorist Castrillo echoes Don Quixote in his speech to the goatherds. In saying "echoes" we suggest resonances, not replication. Like Castrillo and others who share his ideas, Don Quixote wishes to remedy the greed and inequalities of his "iron age." Unlike these theorists, however, he means to do so by resurrecting a chivalric order that is essentially aristocratic, and whose values are inconsistent with the egalitarian age he eulogizes in his oration. What they hold in common, and what for Castrillo is justified by ancient authority, is that the rule by force of one man over another is "contra natura," and thus, for Don Quixote, immoral.

Castrillo supports his assertion of the unjust passage from humankind's original communitarian enjoyment of nature's goods to its subjection to institutions of power by recourse to both pagan and Biblical narratives. The notion of obedience "in ancient times was certainly established by force and not by justice" ["cierto es que antiguamente fue introducida por fuerza y no por justicia" (48)]. In chapter 11 he explains his position by referring to literary myth and elaborates on the declining sequence of the Four Ages in Virgil's *Aeneid* bk. VIII and *Georgics* bk. I, and in Ovid's *Metamorphoses* bk. I. His position is also reinforced by Biblical precedent. Castrillo cites the passage in Genesis in which God sets Adam above all other creatures and underlines the fact that "God did not say let us make man to rule over other men" ["mas no dijo Dios hagamos al hombre para que sea señor de otro hombre" (48)]. Humankind's harmonious "communitarianism," where no man was subservient to another, continued, according to Castrillo, until Noah laid the curse on his son Canaan. It was sin that brought about hierarchical dispensation and the transition from universal equality to the enslavement of some men by others.[2]

---

2. When Castrillo experiences difficulty conciliating his pagan sources with Biblical history, he reiterates the Biblical precedent in order to demonstrate its superiority over the classical version (cap. lx): the pagans claimed that the world was immortal, he explains, and unlike the Biblical authorities, they are understandably vague about what preceded their own historical records. The Bible, on the other hand, is precise, for it enumerates the generations since the creation of the world. At times Castrillo conflates his sources in order to save his argument, proceeding without self-consciousness from Cicero's statement that all things were once held in common to Nimrod as the disrupter of the primordial peaceable condition (44–45).

Castrillo finds support for his position in Christian tradition as well as in the pagan and Biblical writings. Saint Augustine had said that "God did not will that man, possessing reason, should rule over other men, but over the beasts" ["No quiso Dios que el hombre razonable señorease al hombre, sino el hombre a las bestias" (Castrillo 48 citing Augustine *De civitate Dei,* bk. 19: ch.15)]. Castrillo's premise always remains the same—that the *ius gentium* is an aberration from the originary *ius naturale,*[3] and that inequality was not the original human condition: "the first cause of servitude was sin, making men subject to others, which could only come about as a judgment from God" ["la causa primera de servidumbre fue el pecado, porque el hombre por concierto de condición fuese subjeto a otro hombre, lo que no se hace sino por juicio de Dios" (49)].[4] The inconsistencies that sometimes intrude into Castrillo's treatise do not signify that he is negligent or negligible as a writer. He is, in fact, orderly, and engaging. They merely point to

---

3. As Megías Quirós explains, this was a subject that lacked clear and accepted definitions: "There was no uniformity. In the universities the texts of the most important jurists of the 12th–14th centuries, basically Bartolus and Baldus, continued to be studied. From these jurists and many others any law student would be familiar with Roman ideas of the primitive 'state of nature,' the artificial character of political power, laws, and the greater part of the legal institutes" ["Faltaba, pues, unidad de criterio: en las Universidades se seguían estudiando los textos de los juristas más importantes de los siglos XII—XIV, fundamentalmente Bártolo y Baldo, y de la mano de estos juristas entre otros muchos, cualquier estudiante de Derecho estaba familiarizado con las ideas romanas acerca del 'estado de naturaleza' primitivo, de la artificialidad del poder político, de las leyes, de la mayor parte de los institutos jurídicos" (Megías Quirós 37–38)]. López Madera, writing in the closing years of the reign of Philip II (1594), gives a benign, complacent, even disingenuous version of *ius gentium*: "it gave us Kings, the separation of kingdoms and of property, instituted *just* wars, taught us nearly all the kinds of contracts . . . " ["nos dio Reyes, las particiones de los Reynos, y de las cosas, introduxo las guerras *justas,* enseñonos casi todos los contratos . . ." (fol. 2r: emphasis added)].

4. So absorbed is Castrillo in his argument that at times he refers not to a hypothetical age of primal innocence and equality before the *ius gentium* prevailed over the *ius naturale,* but to a generalized present: ". . . apart from the obedience of children to parents and the respect of the young for their elders in all ages, *that other obedience is unjust by nature because we were all born free and equal*" [" . . . salvo la obediencia de los hijos a los padres y el acatamiento de los menores a los mayores en edad toda, *la otra obediencia es por natura injusta porque todos nacimos iguales y libres*" (167–69: emphasis added)].

the contradictions and confusions that surrounded these issues in the period.[5]

The Quixotic view that property was originally held in common and that no one lorded over any one else (in Don Quixote's words, that "entonces no había que juzgar, ni quien fuese juzgado" [I:11]) was reiterated throughout the period. There is Fernando Vázquez de Menchaca (1509–1566) who will be a witness to the 1550–1551 debate between Bartolomé de Las Casas and Juan Ginés de Sepúlveda on the *natural* status of the Indians of the New World. Vázquez de Menchaca, a law professor at the University of Valladolid, premisses his discussion of the perceived mutability of political authority on the *ius naturale*. That is to say, while the law of nature is universal and immutable, as experience has shown, all human forms of authority or of dispensation change, become obsolete, or are replaced (Carpintero Benítez 123). There is also the Aristotelian Martín de Azpilcueta of the University of Salamanca (ca. 1492–1586) whom we might have expected to naturalize royal authority. But he too joins the debate on the relation between power and authority—*potestas* and *imperium*—and declares in the presence of the Emperor Charles V that "[t]he kingdom does not belong to the king" because "power itself belongs *by natural right* to the community, not to the king, and therefore the community cannot abdicate its power" ["El reino no es del rey sino de la comunidad, y la misma potestad, *por derecho natural,* es de la comunidad y no del rey; por esta causa no puede aquélla abdicar de su poder" (quoted in Maravall, *Estado moderno* vol. I:264: emphasis added)].[6] Francisco Suárez declared that "power rests in the community as such, by the very nature of things" ["En la comunidad como tal, está la potestad, por la misma naturaleza de las cosas"

---

5. Indeed, just a decade after Castrillo's *Tractado,* Juan Luis Vives wrote in his *De subventione pauperum* (Paris 1630): "We in our wickedness have appropriated what a generous Nature gave to us in common. The things she openly laid forth we have enclosed and hidden away by means of doors, walls, locks, irons, arms, and finally laws. Thus our greed has brought want and hunger into the abundance of Nature, and poverty into the riches of God" (quoted in Grice-Hutchinson 132).

6. Azpilcueta, however, was not a model of consistency. He declared elsewhere that anyone who asserted that the kingdom and royal power contravened the law of nature must be mad: "Regnum et regiam potestatem qui dicunt esse contra ius naturae insaniunt" (*Relectio super cap. de iudiciis, Notabile III,* quoted in Megías Quirós 41 n. 45).

(Maravall, *Estado moderno* vol. I:264)]. The theory of the primeval state of the world consisting of individuals free from legislation and subject only to the "law of nature" was, then, not merely a madman's poetic fiction. The theory was to persist as an alternative view to the "natural" hierarchization of society right into the nineteenth century.[7]

It goes without saying that such theories arguing popular constraint upon royal authority would have little or no influence upon imperial policy where *Realpolitik* overrode moral argument. A letter of advice addressed to the Emperor Charles V by his ambassador Diego Hurtado de Mendoza illustrates how the concept of violent usurpation was naturalized and universalized in Cervantes's own century, giving the force of legitimacy to imperial policy. It concerns Charles's scrupulous hesitation over the legitimacy of keeping Milan in order to frustrate the French. The Pope had offered to buy the Duchy and restore it to the Farnese family. Hurtado, however, had a letter smuggled into the Emperor's room, urging him not only not to yield, but to make war against both the French and the Pope (Spivakovsky 124–26). The following lines contain the substance of Hurtado's argument.

> Your Majesty has reason and right to this kingdom by virtue of its being an Imperial feudatory . . . You have the same right to Italy as to Flanders and Spain, and consequently to the whole world . . . What right had the Romans to be lords over almost all the world? What right had the Goths to Spain, the Franks to France, the Vandals to Africa, the Huns to Hungary, and the Angles to England? Ambition sent these peoples out, pure valor made them lords over the properties of others, and by virtue and good government many of them kept it until now. Usurpation was violent, retention was violent . . . Holding on to the Empire is violent! . . . As the world was then, it is now. Force was the only right and reason of the kingdoms; hence the proverb *Jus est in armis* . . . One state is as legitimate as the next, only the usurpation of one is older than the other (translation in Spivakovsky 124–25).

---

7. Hugo Grotius (*De imperio*), Samuel Pufendorf (*De jure naturae et gentium*), Vico, Rousseau, and Kant, to name but five of its most illustrious exponents, would continue this tradition. As Otto von Gierke explains: "Vico and [Adam] Ferguson . . . never really break with the idea of a non-social primitive condition" (Gierke, *Natural Law* 105; Troeltsch 206–7); and "Kant accepts *communio fundi originaria* as a principle involving an original common ownership of the surface of the earth" (Gierke, 294 n. 36).

[La razón y derecho que vuestra majestad tiene a esos estados por virtud del feudo del imperio . . . el mismo derecho tenéis a Italia que a Flandes y España, y por consiguiente a todo el mundo. Pregunto a vuestra majestad: ¿qué razón hizo a los romanos señores de casi todo el mundo, después a los godos de España, a los franceses de Francia, y a los vándalos de Africa, a los hungos de Hungría, y a los anglos de Inglaterra? Por ambición salieron estas gentes de su casa, por pura valentía se hicieron señores de la ajena, y por virtud y buen gobierno la han conservado muchos dellos hasta agora. Violenta fue la usurpación de todos, violenta la retención, violenta la continuación . . . Desde que'l mundo es mundo hasta agora. No ha habido más razón ni derecho a los reinos que la fuerza; de donde nació el proverbio *Jus est in armis* . . . [N]o hay más diferencia de la propiedad de un señorío a otro, que ser la usurpación una más antigua que otra (Original in *Historiadores de sucesos particulares* I, ed. Cayetano Rosell in *BAE* XXI, p.xxiv. We have slightly altered the accentuation)].

The reformists' argument eventually came to this: *ius naturale* had in fact been superseded, regardless of how this came about, and humankind had consequently no other choice but *ius gentium* and its hierarchical dispensation. Given the reality of authority as irrevocably vested in a ruler and not in the people (as it supposedly was originally), the reformists' debates centered on the following issues: What is the relationship between those who rule and those who are ruled? What is the derivation and scope of present authority and legislative power? Is sovereignty absolute (*princeps legibus solutus*) ["the ruler is not bound by laws"] or is authority based on the consent of the governed?[8] The theorists' authoritative source, Justinian's texts, seemed to provide support for different views, as we shall see (Stein 60).

But these questions were far from new. Legists could, and did, turn for guidance to the authority of the twelfth-century Emperor Henry VI, who had asked two Bolognese legists, Lothair and Azo, a somewhat similar question. That is, whether supreme authority (*imperium*) belonged to the emperor alone or whether other magistrates enjoyed it.

---

8. In Bernice Hamilton's brief summary, the sixteenth-century discussions centered on: "How much power did the community hand over to the rulers? Could they reserve any of it? Was the grant of power, once made, irrevocable? . . . what part did God, and what the community play in the royal authority? And, finally, were all forms of government other than (direct) democracy in some sense usurpations?" (36).

Azo, in a decision that echoed down the Middle Ages, concluded that it was enjoyed by other office-holders. But he also denied the contention of earlier glossators that once the people had transferred legislative power to the emperor (the *lex Regia*) that they could not revoke it. Azo made a crucial distinction between the people as a group of individuals and the people as a community. As a group of individuals they were excluded from revoking legislative power, he said, but as an *universitas* the people retained legislative power. As Peter Stein explains: "Azo's conclusion was momentous for political theory: the emperor has greater power than any individual, but not than the people as a whole" (Stein 60). It meant that the ruler had to remain, however remotely, answerable to the people in the exercise of his power. *Digest*, Book I: title 4, paragraph 1, seemed to confirm the first view, namely, that the emperor had absolute power to *legislate*. On the other hand, *Digest* I:iii, 32 affirmed that legislation, like custom, derived its authority from popular consent. The *Code* known as *Digna vox*, a constitution dating from Theodosius II in 429 C.E., stated that "the emperor should declare himself bound by the laws since his authority depends on the laws and it is a mark of imperial authority to submit to the laws" (Stein 59–60).

Italy (where authority was fragmented among numerous autonomous cities) provided fertile soil for discussion concerning the authority of the people in legislation. Marsilius of Padua (ca. 1275–1342) had argued strongly for the sovereignty of the people in his *Defensor pacis* (1324) which was condemned as heretical by Pope John XXII in 1327 (Gewirth, ch. 5). Bartolus of Sassoferrato (1313–1357), building on the opinions of Azo, observed that although the emperor was, in law, ruler of the world, many people did not obey him. The Italian city states, as Bartolus knew at first hand, acknowledged no superior, and so they, too, possessed *imperium* (Stein 71). In sixteenth-century Spain, the question of the authority of the king and its dependence on the consent of the governed continued to occupy, in varying degrees, both theologians and political theorists. Some of the most notable among these were Francisco de Vitoria (ca. 1485–1546), Domingo de Soto (1494–1560), Juan de Mariana (1535–1624), Luis de Molina (1535–1600), and Francisco Suárez (1548–1617).[9]

---

9. The author of the fourteenth-century *Tractatus de legibus* (a work attributed to Durandus of St Pourçain) takes an unusual approach to the questions of the origin of human government and the origin of private property. He asks whether such

Throughout the sixteenth century, the resistance to the naturalizing of authority informed many legal and theological debates. An important transmitter of these ideas was the fourteenth-century jurist Baldo de Ubaldis (ca. 1327–1400) who declared that "from the beginning of rational nature, all men were born free, so that in nature God did not make one man the slave of another" ["ab initio rationalis naturae omnes homines liberi nascebantur, qua in natura pari Deus non fecit unum servum alterius" (150)].

Spanish students of law were familiar with Roman ideas on this question from the required textbooks of Bartolus and Baldus (Megías Quirós 37–38), and the authorities cited by Gregorio López Madera in his exhaustive Latin gloss on the *Siete Partidas* are a compendium of the entire history of ancient and medieval law. At the same time, the other and contrary view that man is "by nature" a political animal—*zoon politikon*—in Aristotle's well-known phrase, was also kept alive by many of the philosopher's followers. These were to be found predominantly among theologians who addressed questions of law.

These theoretical discussions on the origins of humankind and the derivation and legitimacy of legislative power were to be given urgency by the "Indian question." Francisco de Vitoria (*ca.* 1485–1546) was the first Catholic political theorist to incorporate Roman law into moral philosophy and within a discussion of the natural law (Pagden, introduction to Vitoria p. xiv). Vitoria and his pupils, down to the generation of the Jesuits Luis de Molina (1535–1600) and Francisco Suárez (1548–1617), sought to create a moral philosophy which would be based on the Aristotelian/Thomist perspective on the *ius naturale*: that is, that humankind's original freedom had been exchanged, consensually, for the security which government could provide. But, they insisted, the initial social contract retained the inalienable rights of what Vitoria and the scholastics termed humankind's *dominium rerum*, the

---

institutions were rooted in natural law or in expediency. He reaches his conclusion, that rulers are not constituted by natural law, by arguing in fact constituted by expediency. "It was conceivable that some one man might know more than any other individual about the direction of public affairs, but not that one man should know more than the whole collectivity of men, including himself and others. Therefore it was inherent in the nature of things that rights of government should reside in the whole community" (quoted in Tierney 175).

"natural dominion (*dominium*)" over one's possessions and liberty which was "a gift of God" (Vitoria 242). Christians, then, could not "dispossess the barbarians [the American Indians] of their goods and lands" (Vitoria 246) on the basis of what supposedly legitimized the power of the Spanish crown in the New World, namely, that the Indians were sinners (*peccatores*) because of their alleged cannibalism, sodomy, and human sacrifice (240–43), or that they were unbelievers (*infideles*). Vitoria argued that *dominium* "[could not] be annulled by lack of faith" (243–46).

Responding to the contention that the American Indians were irrational (*insensati)* or slow witted (*amentes*), Vitoria countered that they could not possibly be called either irrational (247–48) or slow-witted (249–51) given the organization of their cities. He added that if the American Indians "seem to us insensate and slow witted, I put it down mainly to their evil and barbarous education" (Vitoria 250), affirming unequivocally that "the foundation of dominium is the fact that we are [all] formed in the image of God" (Vitoria 249).

Pope Alexander VI, following Columbus's description of the American Indians, had spoken earlier of them not as depraved but *deprived*, "a people who live pacifically and, it is said, walk about naked and eat no meat . . . and believe in a God of creation who is in Heaven, and seem to be capable of receiving the Catholic faith and of being instructed in good customs" (quoted in Pagden, *The Fall* 30). Vitoria concludes, then, that "before arrival of the Spaniards" the American Indians indeed "possessed true dominion, both in public and private affairs" (251), so that no ruler was now "entitled on any . . . grounds to arrogate to himself the dominium . . . of these barbarians" (Vitoria 255).

When Vitoria turns to the related question of whether the conquest of the New World could be called "just," he cites Augustine's definition of just wars as those that "avenge injustices (*iniuriae*)," and determines that the conquest of the New World cannot then be called a just war: "If the barbarians have done no wrong, there is no just cause for war" (Vitoria 270). This was no mere intellectual exercise. Reports of colonists, missionaries, and administrators had continually called into question, from the earliest days of the colonization, both its legitimacy and the means by which it was carried out (Carpintero; Hamilton ch. 6; Hanke). In the meantime, in the Spanish American colonies themselves, utopian projects were going forward, propelled by the Joachite visions of Vasco de Quiroga, who became Bishop of Michoacán, and by the evangelizing program of Franciscan missionaries (Milhou 152).

The basis for the opposing argument used in the public debate in Valladolid in 1550–1551, as is well known, was the Thomist/Aristotelian version of the *ius naturale* espoused by Ginés de Sepúlveda (Hanke). Sepúlveda denied the originary equality of all humans and turned, instead, to the opinion of the Scottish Dominican John Mair (or Major), who had claimed in 1510 that the Castilian crown's rights in the Americas were legitimate because the Indians were "natural slaves." Before the Spaniards arrived, Sepúlveda argued, the American Indians had no laws (read: European laws), no rulers, were not "civil," and so had never enjoyed pre-contract rights. Their documented "perversions"—their alleged universal cannibalism, child sacrifice, and sodomy—violated the laws of human society. Even if such creatures had once been created in the image of God (which he denied) they had long ago destroyed that image. Waging war against them could therefore be called "just."

These ideas concerning the primordial nature and condition of humankind continued to be negotiated into the seventeenth century. Momentous conclusions followed from the answers that were given. Arguments set out by Vitoria and Soto could be said to have laid the foundations for the doctrine of the divine right of kings based on the *Digest*'s attribution of absolute authority to the Emperor (see *Digest* bk. I: title iii, para. 31, and the principle of *princeps legibus solutus*). But Justinian's *Digest* also provided grounds for the communitarian theory of power, as we have noted.

In his influential lecture *On the American Indian* (1539), which we have been citing, and *On the Law of War*, Vitoria examines another issue, namely, the right (*ius*) of the Spaniards to rule the inhabitants of the New World.[10] He does not dispute the idea of an originary state of humanity at the beginning of the world in which all things were held in common. What he rejects is the theory that humankind's passage from *ius naturale* to *ius gentium*—that is, from "freedom" to rule—was the result of usurpation. He predicates the transition instead on human

---

10. In the following section, we are especially indebted to Anthony Pagden for his edition of Francisco de Vitoria's *relections*, and for his various essays on American Indians and Spanish Imperialism in the New World.

fragility. In his "relection," *De potestate civile* (1528),[11] Vitoria addresses himself to the question of political authority and the legitimacy of royal power, and espouses the view that compared to animals, humans were from the very beginning of their existence unprotected and defenseless.[12] Consequently, "in order to make up for these natural deficiencies, mankind was obliged to give up the solitary nomadic life of animals and to live in partnerships (*societates*), each supporting the other" (Vitoria 7). Thus the "clear conclusion," for Vitoria, is that "the primitive origin of human cities and commonwealths was not a human invention . . . [as other thinkers had claimed] but a device implanted by Nature in man for his own safety and survival" (9).[13]

---

11. *Relectio*, literally a rereading, constituted a lecture upon a topic already dealt with in the preceding session's university lectures, or consisting of some pressing issue of law or doctrine (Pagden, introduction to Vitoria p. xvii).

12. [*Partida* II. tít. 1. ley 7: "Why there should be a King, and what is his function" ["Porque conuino que fuesse Rey, e que lugar tiene"] had already used this argument to justify the existence of kings by listing the protective coverings and offensive weapons that other creatures naturally have but humans lack. López Madera's Latin gloss greatly expands the list.

13. Having justified civil power, not as the result of a social contract, but by reference to natural law, Vitoria concludes that "if public power is founded on natural law, and if natural law acknowledges God as its only author, then it is obvious that public power is from God . . ." (10); consequently, "the greatest and best of all forms of rule and magistracy is monarchy or kingship" (12). Vitoria and other political theorists would have felt less compulsion to deal with this matter were it not for the persistence of the more radical ideas that we have outlined. Evidence for their continued circulation can be surmised in the repugnance with which Vitoria treats them (see 12–14). Eliding the fact that these ideas were not only part of a long tradition of Christian writing from Augustine, Isidore of Seville, and Giles of Rome, but that they enjoyed an equally strong legal heritage, Vitoria fulminates: "There have been some writers even among those who call themselves Christians, who have denied that kingly power or any kind of rule by a single person comes from God, affirming that all sovereigns, generals, and princes are tyrants and robbers of human liberty" (12). He even insinuates that only heretics, "men who have already apostatized from God and his church," and who desire to "stir up sedition against our rulers," could hold such opinions (14). Vitoria's views are passed on to his protégé Soto, who also claimed that "public civil power is an ordinance of God!" and that princes were set up "by divine instruction" (*De legibus* IV: 4, 1; quoted in Hamilton, 34). A generation later, the debates will still continue with Francisco Suárez (1548–1617) defending the contrary position—the Roman doctrine of the sovereignty of the people. In his *De legibus ac Deo legislatore*, Suárez

Vitoria's conclusion that cities and commonwealths originate for man's own safety and survival, will find a curious and unexpected corollary in Juan Maldonado's paternalistic benevolence toward the *barbari* of the New World in need of a civilizing education, and Bartolomé de las Casas' view of them as innocent and "primitive" Indians in need of protection from the Europeans. When the American Indians are "given a voice" in the first and only known instance in a dramatic representation (Ruiz Ramón 19) in 1557, they fare no better. A brief excursus is warranted here.[14]

The complete title of the 1557 work is: *Cortes de casto amor y Cortes de la Muerte con algunas obras en metro y prosa de las que compuso Luis Hurtado de Toledo, por él dirigidas al muy poderoso y muy alto señor Don Felipe, Rey de España y Inglaterra etc., su señor y Rey. Año 1557.* It is in the latter part of Luis Hurtado de Toledo's publication that we find the *Cortes de la Muerte* written by Michael (or Michel) de Carvajal which articulates the plight of the American Indians. The *Cortes de la Muerte* is interesting to us in that it encapsulates both the formal debates on the "Indian question," and the informal and contemporary views that surrounded such discussions right into the middle of the sixteenth century.

The Indians in the *Cortes de la Muerte* present themselves before Death to ask to be released from the sufferings they experience at the hands of the Spaniards:

Los indios ocidentales
Y estos caciques venimos
a tus Cortes triunfales
a quexarnos de los males
y agravios que recibimos
Que en el mundo no tenemos

---

asserts that "in the nature of things all men are born free; so that, consequently, no person has political jurisdiction over another person, even as no person has dominion over another" ([III:2, 3; quoted in Hamilton, 373). Given that "fact," for Suárez, "it is easy to deduce the second part of the assertion . . . that the power in question resides, by the sole force of natural law, in the whole body of mankind" (III:2, 3–4; quoted in Hamilton, 373–35).

14. We are indebted to Carlos Jáuregui for calling our attention to the *Cortes de la Muerte*. The remarks on Carvajal's text that follow have been enabled by Jáuregui's careful edition, and its fine introduction, of the work.

Rey ni roque que eche aparte
Las rabias que padecemos;
Y por lo tanto a ti queremos so,
Muerte, dar quexas del arte

[We Indians from the West
come with these chiefs
to your triumphal Cortes
to complain of the suffering
and the wrongs done to us.
We have no-one in the whole world
who will give satisfaction
for the insults that we suffer;
Death, we protest to you
at this betrayal (vv. 1–10).]

The Spaniards' perspective is dramatized by the figures of Satan, the Flesh, and the World. They justify the conquest in terms of the allure of the New World, the temptation it has held for poor Spaniards who need to eat and clothe themselves and their demanding wives. The Indians' genuine plight, their complaint at the social injustice which brings them to ask Death to release them from it, is simply "resolved," as social injustice was resolved in the medieval *Disputa,* and by a similar rhetorical tour de force, through resorption in the status quo. The *Cortes de la Muerte*, however, goes further than the *Disputa*. It not only passes over the harrowing conditions of the Indians at the hands of the colonizers, but "explains" the Indians' suffering by blaming the Indies for the natives' plight (See Ortega y Medina). It is *because of* the lushness of the New World, Saint Francis and Saint Dominic conclude, that the Old World has been corrupted. Its lucre has provoked the avarice and lust of the colonizing Spaniards:

¡Oh India, que diste puertas
A los míseros morales
Para males y reyertas!
¡Indias, que tienes abiertas
Las gargantas infernales!
¡India abismo de pecados!
¡India rica de maldades!
¡India de desventurados!

¡India que con tus ducados
Entraron las torpedades!

[O you Indies, who opened the
gates to moral depravity,
to evils and strife.
You Indies,
who opened the chasms of Hell!
Indies, a sink of iniquity!
Indies, abundant in evil!
Indies, land of wretches!
Indies, with your wealth
Came everything base! (vv. 401–10)]

It is disconcerting, given the views expressed in the *Cortes de la Muerte*, to be reminded that the issue of the legitimacy of the Spanish conquest of the Indies, and the treatment of the American Indians, had been going on for many years. The discussions had begun as early as 1513 under King Ferdinand. They were intensified with the colonization and apparent destruction of what appeared to be sovereign states— Mexico (1520–1522) and Peru (1531–1532) (Hanke, *Spanish Struggle*). Once the authority of the Bulls of Donation from Alexander VI was subjected to doubt because the Pope was said to have no temporal power to confer land (Vitoria 258–64, 273), the "Indian question" had been discussed in terms of humankind's natural rights (Pagden, *Spanish Imperialism* 97). And the discussions centered on whether the American Indians were living in their own age of the natural law, as some believed (Pagden, *Fall* 219 n. 110). If this were the case, should they be treated as free and equal, as theorists on one side of the *ius naturale* argument had described humankind's "natural" condition? Or should they be treated as natural slaves, in the language of the Aristotelians and proponents of the alternative view?

As we have seen, both interpretations of *ius naturale* had been legitimated in the century and simply developed with different emphases by medieval jurists and theologians. And it is in the context of the century's heated disputes that Don Quixote's insistence on free will and the rationale for liberating the galley slaves acquire historical depth. His rationale resonates with the ideas then common, and which can be encapsulated in Francisco Suárez's well-known assertion, that "in the nature of things all men are born free; so that, consequently, no person has political jurisdiction over another person, even as no person has dominion over another" (III. ii. 3, p. 373).

Equally notable is the form the argumentation takes in the period. When reformists and theologians deal with these questions of legal theory, ethics, and history, they too resort, as does Don Quixote, to poetic myth and to a hypothetical and primordial human condition as precedent. We have seen Castrillo explain his position on the *ius naturale* by reference to the declining sequence of the Four Ages in Virgil's *Aeneid* bk. VIII and *Georgics* bk. I, as well as in Ovid's *Metamorphoses* bk. I. In Cristoforo Landino's preface to *P. Vergilii Maronis operum interpretationes* of 1488, Virgil's Aeneas, like so many of Don Quixote's chivalric exemplars, becomes "the perfect man in every way—so that we might all take him as the sole exemplar of the living of our lives" (I:215; quoted in Hampton 20); and when Antonio de Guevara speaks of the historical Marcus Aurelius, he does so "in terms that recall Landino's depiction of Aeneas" (Hampton 21–22). Both Guevara and Juan del Encina declare that they saw the dawn of a new Age of Gold. In their case, it is postulated under the imperial administration of Charles the Fifth (Maravall, *Carlos V* 196, 225; Endress, 106–7, 122). In justifying the Spaniards' right to travel in foreign territories (and thus providing a legitimation of their presence in the Indies [the *ius perigrinandi*]), Vitoria's theological argument evokes the unwarranted and, for him, objectionable, refusal of the mythical king of Latium to grant the epic hero Aeneas access to their lands (Vitoria 278, citing *Aeneid* bk. I:539–40).[15] In 1546 Melchor Cano would refute this analogy with Aeneas, not because of the fictive reference, but on the grounds that the Spaniards came as conquerors, not as travelers (Pagden, *Spanish Imperialism* 23–24).

If we consider the pervasiveness of these ideas, the form the discussions take, and their adoption as heuristic tools by legists and theolo-

---

15. Such blurring of myth and the mundane is typical of the explorers of the time as well. In describing the real Mountain of Crystal in Guiana, Walter Raleigh resorts to poetic myth. In his *Discoverie* he speaks of the diamonds and precious stones he has been told the mountain possesses. As Campbell writes, "Although one might take this 'mountaine of Christall' as a member of the set whose instances run from folktale and medieval romance through the Big Rock Candy Mountain of the American hoboes, it is present in the *Discoverie* as a topographical encounter rather than merely as a sign of Paradise" (226).

gians in the period, then the recourse of Cervantes's knight to poetic myth—to a hypothetical originary condition for humankind, and to the conviction that "it seems harsh to make slaves of those whom God and nature made free" (I:22, 170)—diminishes somewhat his avowedly and "profoundly archaic silhouette" (Foucault 75). Of course, as we have been insisting, Don Quixote's words cannot be read as a serious plan for action. Of course the knight is a man who is uniquely mad (I:1), one who "inverts all values and all proportions" (Foucault 74). But his author is not. Contextualized within the still-viable history of judicial anthropology of the time, the Cervantine text resonates with the debates of the period from which it emerges.

Given the arguments we have cited from Castrillo, Vázquez de Menchaca, López Madera's commentary on the *Siete Partidas* of Alfonso X, and Francisco Suárez, as well as from their medieval antecedents in the history of Roman law—Azo, Scotus, Ockham, Bartolo—Cervantes shows us that as *Don Quixote* is product, so its knight is re-producer, of Early Modern Spain's most challenging discourses.

8

Sancho Panza's Utopia

Laurent Gervereau argues that books, "by virtue of [their] basal function of interpreting signs and transposing them into an imaginary construct," constitute "the ultimate utopian instrument" (357b). Even if this is applicable, with reservations, to the stylized and rural setting of Part I, it cannot be said of Part II. In the former setting Don Quixote can *perform* as a knight-errant, can refuse to test the "magical" transformations he brings about (I:1; I:21), and, when nothing else works, can lay the onus on his fictional enchanters. But as Quixote and Sancho travel away from the insular spaces of La Mancha in Part II, the novel as "imaginary construct" gives way to a mirroring of the dense and varied urban world of Barcelona, a setting far from utopian, and one in which the knight's functional mechanisms of disavowal become increasingly impotent. It is in this "real" world that Cervantes has both knight and squire play out their fantasies. It is in this world that each must become "the architect of his own fortune" (II:66, 893).

For Sancho, the ahistorical dream of Jauja/Cockaigne, which he anticipates in his promised *ínsula*, now becomes a tangible though fleeting reality on the occasion of the wedding of the wealthy peasant farmer Camacho (II:19–21). For Don Quixote, the welcome he receives in the ducal palace as a celebrated knight represents the fulfilment of his fantasies. We deal first with Sancho's experiences.

In the earthly Paradise of Camacho's wedding, pastoral and carnivalesque, literary and popular, courtly and rustic, the seriousness of death and comic resurrection interpenetrate and boundaries dissolve. Here Sancho is assured that "hunger has no jurisdiction today" (II:20, 585) ["este día no es de aquellos sobre quien tiene juridición la hambre"

(794)]. And so luscious is this abundance that even the knight's usual asceticism is disturbed at the sight of the myriad game and poultry hanging, Cockaigne-like, from trees: "the hares without their skins and the chickens without their feathers that were hanging from the trees, waiting to be buried in the cauldrons, were without number; . . . the various kinds of fowl and game hanging from the trees to cool in the breeze were infinite" (584) ["las liebres ya sin pellejo y las gallinas sin pluma que estaban colgadas por los árboles para sepultarlas en las ollas no tenían número . . . los pájaros y caza de diversos géneros eran infinitos, colgados de los árboles" (793)]. So much so that Sancho's "assault on his pot" even "awoke the appetite of Don Quijote" (II:20, 591) ["comenzó de nuevo a dar asalto a su caldero, con tan buenos alientos, que despertó los de don Quijote" (801)].

The announcement of the drama to come seems to recall that of an earlier pastoral company, just as the student's combination of "the marriage of rich Camacho" with "the funeral rites of Basilio" (II:19, 582) ["las bodas del rico Camacho" with "las exequias de Basilio" (790)] seems to parallel the imminent burial of this shepherd with that of the pseudo-shepherd Grisóstomo (I:11). The expectation of a similar tragic ending is reinforced by the narrator's prefiguring the Camacho/Basilio/Quiteria story with the somber tale of Pyramus and Thisbe (II:19, 458), and with that of Cardenio and Luscinda (I:24).

What is presented, however, is far from somber. Spectacular excess is displayed at Camacho's wedding, in the form of food, music, dance, and joyful festivities (II:20). The display of meats at the wedding feast is exorbitant and superabundant: "an entire steer on a roasting spit made of an entire elm" (584) ["espetado en un asador de un olmo entero, un entero novillo" (792)]. There are mountains of firewood, six enormous pots like no others, "each large enough to hold the contents of an entire slaughterhouse" (584) ["seis medias tinajas, que cada una cabía un rastro de carne" (792–93)], so huge that the whole rams being cooked in them seemed to be the size of pigeons. The hares and chickens are innumerable and game birds likewise "infinitos" (793). More than sixty wineskins, a wall built entirely of cheeses, and foodstuffs enough to provision an army ["tan abundante, que podía sustentar un ejército" (793)]. Sancho, who merely asks "to be allowed to dip a crust of bread into one of those cauldrons" (585), is given the "skimmings" (585) from a cooking pot, consisting of three chickens and two geese ["tres gallinas y dos gansos" (794)]. The sensuous display is not limited to food and drink. There is a variety of colorful dances and the sounds of a "thousand different kinds of musical instruments" (II:21, 591) ["mil géneros de instrumentos" (801)], flutes, drums, psalteries, pipes, tabors, rattles, and the din of separate bands fill the air—so unlike the plaintive flute of similar literary pastoral scenes or the single fiddle of the shepherd Antonio in Part II, chapter 11. Above all, without having to work or pay for it, Sancho experiences, for the first time in his life, a culinary feast whose abundance he could never have imagined, much less consumed. Camacho's sumptuous wedding feast has indeed rendered credible for Sancho that utopic no-where stored in the collective memory as the "people's utopia" and which Sancho envisions for his *ínsula*.

The salacious allusions that are part and parcel of Jauja/Cockaigne in many of its versions also hover over this Cockaigne-like analogue. The evocation of the innocent shepherdesses who roamed Don Quixote's pastoral utopia "wearing only the clothes needed to modestly cover that which modesty demands, and has always demanded" (I:11, 77) ["sin más vestidos de aquellos que eran menester para cubrir honestamente lo que la honestidad quiere y ha querido siempre que se cubra . . ." (122)] is replaced at Camacho's wedding with sexual innuendoes. The allegorical masque between Love and Money, composed by a maliciously risqué *beneficiado,* dramatizes the rivalry between Camacho and Basilio for the love of Quiteria. It involves a mock combat that alludes to classical double entendres.[1] The priest himself feels the need to warn the "dying" Basilio "to attend to the well-being of his soul rather than to the pleasures of his body" (II:21, 593) ["que atendiese a la salud del alma antes que a los gustos del cuerpo" (804)]; Camacho grudgingly allows Quiteria to give her hand to the "dying" Basilio because "it meant delaying only for a moment the fulfillment of his desires" (II:21, 594) ["pues todo era dilatar por un momento el cumplimiento de sus deseos"

---

1. Cupid's lines include: ". . . y en cuanto el abismo encierra / en su báratro espantoso . . ." (II:20, 796). *Báratro,* is derived from the Latin "barathrum," from the Greek "βαραθρον" (a pit near Athens into which criminals were thrown: hence, "infernal regions" in Virgil, *Aeneid* [bk.8, line 245). But when our "beneficiado socarrón," who would have read Latin, put this word into the mouth of Cupid, he could have had in mind the passage in Martial's *Epigrams,* Book 3, line 81, where *barathrum* is given the meaning of female genitalia (compare the English "down there").

(804)][2]; and even Sancho, usually sensitive to his master's decorous be-
havior, allows himself a few risqué moments as he proclaims the bride
Quiteria to be a lass "who can pass through the banks of Flanders"
(II:21, 592) ["una chapada moza, y que puede pasar por los bancos de
Flandes" (802)].[3]

Cockaigne's miraculous fountains of life, and its denial of death, are
also humorously metaphorized here into a new mode of magical healing
and resurrection.[4] Regaled with a crown of cypress and a red silk suit cut
to resemble flames, Basilio interrupts the ceremony, orating histrioni-
cally at the very moment that vows are about to be exchanged between
Camacho and Quiteria. His sartorial sumptuousness, his spectacular
mock suicide, and his marriage *in extremis,* add to the wedding feast's
excessive display, reinforcing the theatrical reversibility of the upside-
down world of "the people's utopia"—that carnivalesque world where
all things can become possible temporarily. At Camacho's wedding feast
it is the poor shepherd and underdog who becomes a latter-day King of
Misrule. Here death is transformed into life, Basilio takes possession of
his name ("king") to overturn the power of money and to reverse the
role of his wealthy competitor from privileged suitor to generous loser.
It is the poor suitor who wins the coveted "princess."

In this wondrous setting, the text discloses ideologies of which San-

---

2. See Parker for the double entendre implicit in the word "delay/*delatio.*" She
notes its erotic connotation from Andreas Capellanus as "deferral of coitus or con-
summation" (186–87; 207 n. 11).

3. See Murillo, *Don Quijote* II:21, 197 n. 9: Luis Murillo explains that Rodrí-
guez-Marín, *Apéndice* 26, sees this as a reference, albeit polyvalent, to an allusion
to the wedding night. "Bancos de Flandes"/"trestles of Flemish pine" were used in
Spain to make beds (196). For the erotic connotations of this complex wordplay,
see also Rico and Foradellas, *Don Quijote* I, 802. Edwin Williamson attributes
some of the salacious innuendoes in the novel to the unsuccessful attempts of the
chivalric novels to reconcile the "inherited profanity of love in their forbears in Arthurian romance" (50) with the subsequent emphasis on what he calls the "didactic
alibi," namely, ecclesiastically sanctioned moral values (37–50).

4. Magical healing is intrinsic to representations of the utopian mode. In *Don
Quixote* it is re-enacted in the folkloric healing of the knight's ear during the pastoral interlude (I:11) and in Basilio's "miraculous" resurrection. A. L. Morton finds
in the theme of the magic cure "the link between the Cockaygne of popular tradition and the mythological Fortunate Isles with their fountain or well of perpetual
youth" (37).

cho becomes aware. He witnesses for the first time cracks in an established order he had formerly taken for granted. Before a splendor he can hardly believe, Sancho sees that there is another way in which people, including his fellow peasants, live. His awe is analogous to the effect Michel de Certeau describes on those who are exposed to the wonder of miracle tales. The underlying subtext of such narratives discloses, for the recipients, both their "recognition of repression," and the unexpected comfort that "[i]n spite of everything, they provide the possible with a site that is impregnable, because it is a nowhere, a utopia . . . which coexists with that of an experience deprived of illusions" (Certeau 17). But the upside-down-world of Camacho's wedding feast is no myth. It is present in real time, and the pragmatist Sancho soon takes full advantage of its reality.

Because the young shepherd Basilio is of Sancho's world, not rich but excelling in the rustic sports of wrestling, running, tossing the bar, etc., Sancho initially favors him over the wealthy farmer Camacho whom Quiteria is to wed. Sancho can well understand Basilio's simple love for the country lass. But as soon as he sees the abundance that the wealthy farmer Camacho can provide, and sniffs the cooking, Sancho redefines his position, choosing him instead. Uttering aloud, "but when those talents fall to somebody who has good money, then that's the life I'd like to have" (II:20, 584) ["pero cuando las tales gracias caen sobre quien tiene buen dinero, tal sea mi vida como ellas parecen" (792)], he is reminded that social mobility is possible, even for him, so he privileges wealth and promptly changes his allegiance. He sees what Camacho has acquired here. If so sumptuous a display is possible for the peasant Camacho, then neither Camacho's particular wealth, nor wealth in general, need be the exclusive property of Sancho's "betters."

This blurring of distinctions on the basis of money is not peculiar to Sancho. Given the socio-historical changes we have described as taking place in the century, it seems to have been a well recognized cultural phenomenon, as it is reiterated by the students who are also heading for Camacho's wedding. They speak of "pedigrees," of the fact that "fair Quiteria's is superior to Camacho's" (II:19, 577) ["[el linaje] de la hermosa Quiteria se aventaja al de Camacho" (783) but that "nobody thinks about that nowadays: wealth has the power to mend a good many cracks" (II:19, 577) ["pero ya no se mira en esto, que las riquezas son poderosas de soldar muchas quiebras" (783)]. Traces of such realities, despite the absent real that the text alters, problematize the assumed autonomy of "high" and "low" cultural constructs, de-romanticize the underclasses, and render untenable the predication of monolithic cultural values.

The poor peasant Sancho is fully aware that the display at Camacho's wedding is not given by courtesy of an aristocrat's largesse but provided instead by a farmer, though a famously rich one. Sancho, the simple yet cunning *aprovechado*, is also aware that he has already enjoyed comfort, abundance, and monetary rewards during his travels with Don Quixote. The comfort of Don Diego de Miranda's house is one example, the windfall of gold coins and fine linen shirts from Cardenio's suitcase in the Sierra Morena is another. He can well assume that if he continues to follow Don Quixote, the knight's promises may become realities for him as well, and in the form of islands, even kingdoms, that grateful knights are known to bestow on loyal squires. The "learned" Don Quixote has repeatedly told him that people of low birth, like Sancho, have risen to positions of wealth and honor (II:6): "Innumerable men born of low family have risen to the highest pontifical and imperial dignity" (II:42, 730) ["[i]numerables son aquellos que de baja estirpe nacidos, han subido a la suma dignidad pontificia e imperatoria" (970)]. A respected village priest has confirmed it. As Sancho tells his wife Teresa: "And if a person whom fortune has lifted from his lowly state (these were the words of the preacher) to the height of prosperity were well bred, liberal, and courteous with everyone, and if he does not try to vie with those who were noble from ancient times, be assured, Teresa, that no one will remember what he was, but all will respect him for what he is" (our translation) ["Y si este a quien la fortuna sacó del borrador de su bajeza (que por estas mesmas razones lo dijo el padre) a la alteza de su prosperidad fuere bien criado, liberal y cortés con todos, y no se pusiere en cuentos con aquellos que por antigüedad son nobles, ten por cierto, Teresa, que no habrá quien se acuerde de lo que fue, sino que reverencien lo que es, . . ." (II:5, 670]. Sancho himself has witnessed, at first hand, the relative abundance enjoyed by other "squires." His fellow laborer, Tomé Cecial, unlike Sancho with his meager supply of food (II:13), has a saddle bag, as he tells Sancho, with "better provisions on my horse's rump than a general does when he goes marching" (II:13, 536) "[m]ejor repuesto traigo yo en las ancas de mi caballo que lleva consigo cuando va de camino un general"

(731)]. A poor soldier he later meets simply reinforces Sancho's belief that making money depends on the kind of master one happens to serve. The soldier explains to Sancho: "If I had served some grandee of Spain, or some distinguished nobleman . . . I'd certainly have one [an advantage] which is what you get when you serve good masters" (II:24, 618) ["Si yo hubiera servido a algún grande de España o algún principal personaje . . . a buen seguro que yo la llevara [la ventaja], que eso tiene el servir a los buenos" (833)]. But it is at Camacho's wedding feast that Sancho begins to give real credence to these possibilities, especially to his master's promises that his life could become a better one, that even he could become governor of an island. His burlesque reception later in the palace of the Duke and Duchess will seem to validate both the poor soldier's remark and Sancho's ambition, just as the same ducal experience will convince Don Quixote that he is no mere literary creation, but a genuine knight-errant.

The reversibility analyzed by Maurice Molho in *Don Quixote* as the structural dynamic of folktale types continues to come into play here. Far from displaying the submission attributed to the naive poor, who are supposedly conditioned by the dominant ideology, Sancho the pragmatist is enabled by his participation in Camacho's wedding feast. He demystifies power relations, subverts the divinely ordained social hierarchy, and affirms the superiority of money over lineage. His affirmation of wealth as the means of empowerment, of getting a higher place on the social ladder, challenges the permanence of class differences and posits them as contiguous and interlocked formations. Aware that he lacks his own means of social mobility, Sancho simply destabilizes the taken-for-grantedness of the power hierarchy by appropriating its monetary base. "With a good foundation you can build a good building," he affirms, "and the best foundation and groundwork in the world is money" (II:20, 584) ["[s]obre un buen cimiento se puede levantar un buen edificio, y el mejor cimiento y zanja del mundo es el dinero" (792)].

This may be the first time that Sancho realizes it is possible for him to succeed in his aspirations, but it is certainly not the first time that he has tried to "break rank." He initially left home in search of adventure precisely in order to appropriate some of the power and wealth which had been the monopoly of his "betters"—a wealth he too expected to acquire by being governor of an island where the sale of black subjects would enable him to live in wealth and comfort (I:29). At Camacho's wedding he affirms that the "natural" division of the world is between the haves and the have-nots, and he simply chooses the former. He makes clear that, given the opportunity, he and his dispossessed relatives would invariably choose to belong to the moneyed class (II:20, 467). It is a predilection he has already demonstrated in his humorous dispute with his wife Teresa in Part II, chapter five. Thus Sancho, with his enhanced self-confidence in Part II, can aspire to transgress social hierarchies based upon divinely ordained categories of class, and to replace them with pragmatic distinctions of social mobility based on wealth.

In highlighting Sancho's desire to fashion himself after the moneyed classes, the text discloses the quandary Sancho faces. What choices does he have? The consequences of his self-fashioning would ensure the reproduction of that very order that has subjugated laborers like him. Knowing that he has no possibility of radically changing the status quo, Sancho's ambition is merely to belong to the "haves"—not to change an order that produces "have-nots." But if he does not aspire to such self-fashioning, he would still reproduce the hegemonic order. A short time before he had resigned himself to just that reality: "a poor man should be content with whatever he finds and not go asking for the moon" (II:19, 583) ["el pobre debe de contentarse con lo que hallare y no pedir cotufas en el golfo" (791)]. He will eventually accept the latter stance, but only after he leaves Barataria in disillusion. As a result, the reader is made aware of what Lacan called "the play of history beyond its [a text's] edges encroaching on those edges" (Lacan 94) and of Raymond Williams's conviction that alternative forms of culture are always tied to the hegemonic order. "The dominant culture," Williams reminds us, "at once produces and limits its own forms of counter-culture" (*Marxism* 114).

Inevitably our attention is drawn towards Barataria. This "real" fulfillment of Sancho's utopic aspiration, which Camacho's wedding feast had merely anticipated, is introduced by a narrator who distances himself from the events and its consequences. He assures us of the mirth we are about to experience, "two bushels of laughter" (II:44, 739) ["espera dos fanegas de risa" (982)], as we follow Sancho's adventures on the "island."

Whatever we may think of the Duke's and Duchess's *burlas*, we must remember that their success is the consequence not merely of malice, but of cunning, intelligence, and art in shaping the utopian moments of the two protagonists. They have brilliantly diagnosed each man's desire. We recall how Rueda has the audience watch the deception of Mendrugo as he distances the spectator from the trickery taking place (*Paso quinto: La tierra de Jauja*). We saw how complicit the simpleton Mendrugo was in his own deception. The thieves succeed because Mendrugo is only too willing to be duped by his desires. So it is with Cervantes's two protagonists. The Duke and Duchess give to Don Quixote, in the palace, and to Sancho Panza, in Barataria, exactly what each has coveted. Don Quixote's dreams of being recognized and treated as a knight because of the renown of his chivalric adventures in Part I are now fulfilled. Sancho, who left home and family with the promise of an island he could govern, is now given the "island" of Barataria.

Turning to Sancho's utopian dream and its materialization in Barataria, we readily perceive the defining weaknesses upon which the ducal pair build their edifice of illusion. Throughout Part I, which the Duke and Duchess have read, Sancho is presented as a glutton, satiety as his primary goal, and cowardice as a salient attribute. These character traits do not change in Part II, and the ducal pair concentrate upon them in order to fulfill Sancho's desires. So they offer him an island of plenty where he can be at leisure while others work for him and do his bidding.

Sancho's surname, Panza, distinguishes him as a lover of food and drink. He is variously called a "greedy glutton" (II:2, 469) ["golosazo comilón" (640)] by Don Quixote's niece, and a "glutton" (II:20, 583) ["glotón" (791)] by Don Quixote. The false "Dulcinea" in the ducal palace orders him to "lash that hide, O savage beast, and liberate your energies from the sloth that inclines you only to eating and still more eating" (II:35, 693)] ["Date, date en esas carnazas, bestión indómito, y saca de harón ese brío, que a solo comer y más comer te inclina"(925)]. Don Quixote describes Sancho as "naturally a coward" (I:23, 173) ["[n]aturalmente eres cobarde, Sancho" (248)], a "coward" (II:29, 648) ["cobarde criatura" (869)], "spineless creature" (648) ["corazón de mantequillas" (869)], and "heart of a mouse" (649) ["ánimo de ratón casero" (869–70)]. The narrator calls him "naturally fearful and not very brave" (I:20, 141) ["naturalmente era medroso y de poco ánimo (208)]. The narrative itself validates these descriptions of him. Sancho declares to Sansón Carrasco that he is prepared to take care of his master's person, but that he will never become embroiled in his master's adventures: "but to think that I'll raise my sword, even against lowborn scoundrels with their caps and axes, is to think something that will never happen" (II:4, 483) ["pero pensar que tengo de poner mano a la espada, aunque sea contra villanos malandrines de hacha y capellina, es pensar en lo escusado" (660)]. The narrator reiterates how frightened Sancho becomes at each *burla* perpetrated on him in the Duke's palace (II:34, 545–46; II:35, 548; II:36, 555; II:41, 570). In the Clavileño episode, even Don Quixote remarks that "not since the memorable adventure" with the fulling hammers in Part I, chapter 20, "have I seen Sancho as fearful as he is now" (II:41, 720) ["nunca he visto a Sancho con tanto temor como ahora" (958)]. As governor of Barataria, Sancho refuses to fight for his "citizens" during the mock invasion, declaring that such encounters should be left to Don Quixote and not to him: "sinner that I am, I don't know anything about this kind of battle" (II:53, 805) ["yo, pecador . . . no se me entiende nada destas priesas" (1062)]. Indolent and shiftless, Sancho prefers to sleep rather than to work. Don Quixote has told him: "You sleep, for you were born to sleep" (I:20, 144) ["[d]uerme tú, que naciste para dormir" (211)], and Sancho, as we have said, sees his island as a hypothetical source of slave labor in which he need not work, and which will enable him to "buy some title or office and live on that for the rest of my life" (I:29, 245) ["comprar algún título o algún oficio con que vivir descansado todos los días de mi vida" (340)]. His motivation, he tells his wife Teresa, is to "make money, because I've been told that all new governors have this same desire" (II:36, 699) ["hacer dineros, porque me han dicho que todos los gobernadores nuevos van con este mesmo deseo" (931)].

Wily manipulator that he is, prevaricator, liar, exploiter of his master's credulity, the one thing Sancho has not yet coveted is power. His poverty and his lowly peasant existence have shielded him from that temptation. Now, the wielding of power is precisely what Barataria offers him, and the two authority figures he most admires spur his ambition. Don Quixote's promise of social mobility, that "many people rise from low birth" (II:42, 970), Sancho has observed in the extravagant display of wealth by the *labrador* Camacho. The Duke too encourages his ambition by telling him: "[i]f you try it once . . . you'll long to eat it again, because it is a very sweet thing to give orders and be obeyed" (II:42, 728) ["Si una vez lo probais . . . comeros heis las manos tras el gobierno, por ser dulcísima cosa el mandar y ser obedecido" (968)]. In this respect Sancho will, for the moment, even exceed Camacho. Camacho has the power conferred by wealth (e.g., to buy a bride); Sancho will enjoy *authority.*

When we isolate the means of discursive production in Part II, conflicting discourses rise to its surface. These contradictions occur especially in its liminal, lawless spaces. Both Camacho's wedding feast and the "island" of Barataria occur outside the social sphere and cut off from normative society. As Augustin Redondo has pointed out about the Basilio/Quiteria/Camacho episode, such spaces allow for the momentary suspension of serious social issues: a woman's (Quiteria's) reputation in an honor-code society; weighty theological issues such as the validity of marriage, of confession; and the seriousness of suicide, as well as the lightness with which the priest handles the ecclesiastical dogmas entailed in the episode. But once we leave the utopian space that has been cut off from normative society and we return to normality, traces of the monetary exigencies and the discursive formations of contemporary society become apparent. Don Quixote, who spends some time with the newlyweds once they return to established society, for example, cautions Basilio that he "stop practicing the skills he knew, for although they brought him fame, they did not bring him money, and [to] attend to acquiring wealth by licit and industrious means . . ." (II:22, 597) ["dejase . . . de ejercitar las habilidades que sabe, que aunque le daban fama, no le daban dineros, y que atendiese a granjear hacienda por medios lícitos e industriosos" (809)]. He also reminds Basilio of the restrictions that regulate this honor-code society. Now that he is married, he must keep in mind the fragility of Quiteria's honor.

Similar realities are alluded to when we return to established society from the privileged space of Barataria. The issue of money, as Carroll Johnson has shown, is again salient, this time in separating Old Christians like Sancho from those who, like Ricote, lack the proper ancestry or "purity of blood" ["pureza de sangre"]. Not only are the latter's possessions confiscated by the Spanish government, but Old Christians, like Sancho, reminded of Pedro Aznar Cardona's sanctions, are forbidden to help Moriscos to recover the wealth they have left behind in Spain ("Ortodoxia" 285–96). The text also betrays the cavalier manner with which Christian principles could be applied in the contemporary period. Despite the statutes of *pureza de sangre*, religious orthodoxy proved to be difficult to implement in Spain as ecclesiastics bemoaned the lack of religious "purity" among Christians. Referring to the old Christians of the Alpujarras, for example, they discovered that even those who had "not a drop of impure blood in their veins . . . hardly retain[ed] a few vestiges of the Christian religion" (Lynch, *Spain 1516–1598* 318).

Traces of this ideological tension are present in Barataria. Don Quixote had assured Sancho that virtue, not blood, was the foundation for correct behavior: "blood is inherited," he reminded him, "and virtue is acquired" (II:42, 731) ["la sangre se hereda, y la virtud se aquista" (970–71)]. Sancho proceeds to follow this advice by using both his "Christian" principles and his practical "street smarts" in order to resolve the eight tests, or *burlas*, imposed upon him by his "betters." He assures everyone that he knows he will be a good governor for "it's enough for me to have the *Christus* in my memory" (II:42, 729) ["tener el Christus en la memoria" (968)], for him to reward the virtuous (774), to rid Barataria of "vagrants, idlers, sluggards" (774), to treat everyone well by protecting the laborers, respecting the hidalgos, and holding fast to Christian ethics, "and, above all, respect religion and the honor of the clergy" (II:42, 774) ["y sobre todo, tener respeto a la religión y a la honra de los religiosos" (1025)]. Those who are there to mock Sancho use these very principles to humiliate him. They take him to the town cathedral and "con algunas ridículas ceremonias" (II:45, 992) declare him governor. The text does not fail to highlight the irony. The credentials of the trickster from Miguel Turra are legitimized because he is married "with the blessing and consent of the Holy Roman Catholic Church" (II:47, 762) ["en paz y en haz de la santa Iglesia Católica Romana" (1010)].

A more conflicting code, which the altered real has elided in the text's privileged spaces, calls attention to the real contemporary period from which the text emerges. It is produced upon Sancho's leaving Barataria. In the *ínsula,* Sancho had successfully resolved the dilemma of the man who must cross the bridge to get to the gallows on the other side. Faced with a decision which pitted justice and law against mercy, Sancho had implemented Don Quixote's Christian advice that "when the law is in doubt, I should favor and embrace mercy" (II:51, 792) ["que cuando la justicia estuviese en duda, me decantase y acogiese a la misericordia" (1047)]. Upon leaving the liminal space of Barataria and re-entering established society, the arbitrariness in the application of the principle is disclosed. Sancho comes face to face, in the person of Ricote, with the lack of mercy and the grave injustice perpetrated on the Moriscos in Spain. The text puts in doubt the privileging of the Christian principle of mercy over justice in contemporary government, and accentuates the disparity between the illiterate peasant's practice and its violation by His Most Catholic Majesty.[5] Under the ideological banner of "good cause" ["justa razón"], the discourse of what we now call "ethnic cleansing" is justified, and left to us to read as irony or as endorsement. The Morisco Ricote explains: "it was just and reasonable for us to be chastised with the punishment of exile: lenient and mild, according to some, but for us it was the most terrible one we could have received" (II:54, 813) ["con justa razón fuimos castigados con la pena del destierro, blanda y suave al parecer de algunos, pero al nuestro la más terrible que se nos podía dar" (1072)].

The process by which racial and classist discourses are organized, produced, and maintained under the transparent mask of the always already, can again be textually isolated as Sancho leaves the *ínsula*. In Barataria, Sancho's gubernatorial behavior has been admirable. He has literally actualized Don Quixote's suspicion that Sancho, as governor, "will turn the whole ínsula upside down" (II:43, 736) ["que has de dar con toda la ínsula patas arriba" (978)]—but in a positive way as "deceptions became the truth and deceivers find themselves deceived" (II:44, 774) ["las burlas se vuelven en versa y los burladores se hallan burlados" (1025)]. The real Barataria citizens, who are unaware of the *burlas,* as well as those who come expressly to mock him, are amazed that this short, fat, illiterate peasant could have issued such thoughtful, prudent, and humane judgements. The steward, one of the *burladores,* admits to Sancho, "I'm amazed to see a man as unlettered as your grace . . . saying so many things full of wisdom and good counsel, far beyond what was expected of your grace's intelligence by those who sent us here and by those who came here with you" (II:49, 774) ["estoy admirado de ver que un hombre tan sin letras . . . diga tales y tantas cosas llenas de sentencias y de avisos, tan fuera de todo aquello que del ingenio de vuesa merced esperaban los que nos enviaron y los que aquí venimos" (1025)]. Sancho himself knows, upon leaving the island, that he has governed "like

---

5. The proponents of the expulsion, and notably King Philip III himself, had no doubt about the justice of it.

an angel" (II:53, 809) ["como un ángel" (1067)], has done everything well, and has been admired by all, to the point of leaving a constitution in his name. Yet he must return, once he steps into the established order, to what he always was—a poor illiterate laborer: "Naked I was born, and I'm naked now: I haven't lost or gained a thing" (II:57, 828) ["Desnudo nací, desnudo me hallo: ni pierdo ni gano" (1090)]. Under the discursive formation of "know thyself," perpetuated by a regime of elite classical representations posited as normative, and therefore desirable, cultural capital is made safe.

The upstart peasant who aspired to share in the dominant class's patrimony is made to realize his place in a hegemonic order that is safeguarded. Sancho has lived the apparent materialization of his utopian dream. His rule as governor now terminated by the staged invasion of a hostile army, he writes to Don Quixote that he prays that God will "take me from this governorship safe and sound" (II:51, 797) ["me saque con bien y en paz deste gobierno" (1052)]. He confesses his inadequacy as he hugs his beloved donkey, regrets that he "climbed the towers of ambition and pride" (807), and is now made aware that "I was not born to be a governor" (II:53, 807–8) ["me subí sobre las torres de la ambición y de la soberbia," . . . Yo no nací para ser gobernador" (1064–65)]. In language reminiscent of Plato's myth of the metals in the *Republic*, and made memorable by Cellorigo in the century, Sancho accepts his "rightful" place in a divinely ordained social order where "each man is fine doing work *he was born for.* I'm better off with a scythe in my hand than a governor's scepter . . ." (II:53, 808: emphasis added) ["bien se está cada uno usando el oficio *para que fue nacido.* Mejor me está a mi una hoz en la mano que un cetro de gobernador" (1065)]. His momentary and dangerous "lapse" (with respect to the social order) in aspiring to rise above his status has been neutralized, first through humor as he chooses a piece of the sky over an earthly governorship in the Duke's palace (II:42, 578), and later through violence as he is expelled from Barataria. Both effect their desired results. Sancho "humbly" accepts the hierarchical order whose rank he never should have aspired to break.[6] Even here, the resistances in the text call attention to a reality unsuccessfully passed

---

6. As Roger Chartier has presciently put it, a work "inscribes within its forms and its themes a relationship with the manner in which, in a given moment and place, modes of exercising power [and] social configurations . . . are organized" (*The Order* p. x).

over and which we have pointed to before: Sancho's continuing nostalgia for the power he once wielded. And so the narrator tells us that Sancho, "although he had despised being governor . . . still wished to give orders and be obeyed, for command, even mock command, brings this misfortune with it" (II:63, 875) ["aunque aborrecía el ser gobernador . . . todavía deseaba volver a mandar y a ser obedecido, que esta mala ventura trae consigo el mando, aunque sea de burlas" (1146)].[7]

---

7. Such resistances are simply ignored by critics who transfer the text's safeguarding of the hegemonic order to the character's alleged self-knowledge, humility, or maturity in relinquishing his governorship. Thus for Williamson: "it makes perfect sense to represent his [Sancho's] giving it [the governorship] up as a release from illusion and an acceptance of actual social realities . . . . the peasant's self-knowledge will inevitably enhance his status as a more mature character" (184).

9

Don Quixote's Utopia

Just as the ducal pair shape the *ínsula* according to Sancho's desires after they have read *Don Quixote* Part I, so they will implement the fantasies of Don Quixote. The knight arrives at their country palace at the moment of deepest dejection. From the beginning of Part II, with his failure to pay homage to his lady Dulcinea and to seek her blessing, his quest seems doomed. His failure in this, a knight's basic obligation, can be read as a sign that he may not be worthy—either of his lady or of his utopian project. His dreams of knightly glory and of restoring justice to a fallen world seem to reach their bleakest moment in chapter 29, as he woefully rehearses his familiar defense mechanism: "the entire world is nothing but tricks and deceptions opposing one another. I can do no more" (II:29, 652) ["todo este mundo es máquinas y trazas, contrarias unas de otras. Yo no puedo más" (874)].

Don Quixote's long sojourn in the country palace (II:30–57) will launch him towards a necessary crisis in his utopian enterprise, not because of the cruel pranks of the ducal pair, but because his fantasy of finally being *recognized* as a knight-errant will be realized. The reception accorded him by the Duke and Duchess convinces him that he truly is the paladin that he has believed himself to be: "this was the first day he really knew and believed he was a true knight errant and not a fantastic one, for he saw himself treated in th same manner in which, he had read, knights were treated in past ages" (II:31, 658) ["y aquél fue el primer día que de todo en todo conoció y creyó ser caballero andante verdadero, y no fantástico, viéndose tratar del mesmo modo que él había leído se trataban los tales caballeros en los pasados siglos" (880)]. Sansón Carrasco had earlier made Quixote aware of his status as a celebrity (II:3, 375;

Rico 647–48). But that status, the result of the many translations of Part I, was attained through the medium of print, not the exercise of arms, as *letras* literally displaced *armas* in the production of his fame.[8] It is the Duke's and Duchess's elaborate chivalric *burlas* that convince him that he is more than a mere literary creation, a real knight-errant who is being regaled in a great castle.

The fantasy that Don Quixote had voiced aloud in two earlier monologues (I:21 and I:50), and Sancho's vision of his island, seem actualized as the result of ducal phantasmagoria. For Don Quixote, the indispensable element of chivalric fantasy, the beautiful maiden who falls in love with the knight, is parodically performed by a flighty maidservant of the Duchess under the romantic name of Altisidora. He has been addressed, in a campy charade, by no less a personage than Merlin the magician; he has been offered (at Sancho's expense) the means of disenchanting his lady Dulcinea; and he and Sancho have ridden the magical wooden horse Clavileño (II:40–41). In defending the honor of the daughter of Doña Rodríguez, he has fulfilled his knightly duty to succor widows and defenseless maidens.

It is necessary to keep in mind, then, that the cruel pranks and hoaxes in the ducal palace that distress some readers are the means by which knight and squire are enabled to believe their fantasies have been realized. Don Quixote believes he has achieved what he aspired to, namely, recognition and fame as a knight-errant. Sancho has been installed as governor, and of an "island" Don Quixote himself had promised him as reward for his loyalty. When Don Quixote decides to leave "the extreme idleness in which he had been living in the castle" (II:57, 828) ["tanta ociosidad como la que en aquel castillo tenía" (1089)], it is not because he is disillusioned in his dream, but because the experience has renewed and strengthened his conviction that the world still has need of him. With his revived self-confidence

> . . . he imagined it would be a great mistake for him to remain confined and inactive among the infinite luxuries and pleasures offered to him as a knight errant by the duke and duchess, and he thought he would have

---

8. There is ironic aptness here in that, were it not for the printing press, Don Quixote would not have even known of the exemplary deeds of his paragons Amadís, Belianís, Reinaldos, or Orlando.

to give a strict accounting to heaven with regard to this confinement and inactivity. (II:57, 828)

[. . . se imaginaba ser grande la falta que su persona hacía en dejarse estar encerrado y perezoso entre los infinitos regalos y deleites que como a caballero andante aquellos señores le hacían y parecíale que había de dar cuenta estrecha al cielo de aquella ociosidad y encerramiento. (1089)]

Don Quixote's long sojourn in the company of the Duke, then, appears to signal the culmination of his aspiration not simply to be a knight, but to be recognized as one. It marks a divide in his public career and also initiates a reorientation of the novel's social thrust. The aristocratic establishment represents the first of a series of powerful institutions in which he will find himself engaged on terms not of his making, and by which he will be dwarfed and overwhelmed.

We recall that the world of Part I had gone no further than the villages and deserted places of La Mancha: Argamasilla, Quintanar de la Orden, Puerto Lápice, El Toboso. These sparsely populated spaces, far from the centers of power, wealth, and influence, were scarcely the place to be if Quixote wished to change the world, but they offered little resistance and allowed his fantasy to roam somewhat unchecked. The few challenges were supplied by individuals who were no match for his unshakable conviction, his crazy logic, and his superior mastery of chivalric texts.

In Part II, he is no longer in La Mancha, and he comes face to face with genuine sources and engines of power: the Duke and Duchess, whose elaborate mockery he takes for respect and admiration; the clan warfare in Catalonia; and the great city of Barcelona's turbulent port and naval base, with its mighty ships and military discipline. Among the crowds, the relentless, unceasing deployment of men, of machines, armies, and fleets in this commercial metropolis, his dream is impossible to realize. We cannot guess how Cervantes would have ended his story had Alonso Fernández de Avellaneda not published his spurious continuation *El ingenioso hidalgo Don Quixote de la Mancha* (1614), which came to Cervantes's notice while he was composing his *Segunda Parte*. What we do know, however, is that the events that flow from the decision to have Don Quixote go to Barcelona rather than Saragossa take a new trajectory with respect to Quixote's utopian vision, testing it with the contingency and dynamism of "real" history.

Diminished, dwarfed, and overshadowed as he is in Part II, where his "adventures" do not get primary attention, Don Quixote is thrust violently into this history. His former freedom of action and movement is taken away in a manner quite different from his being transported in a cage at the end of Part I. His body was then confined but his mind was free to pursue its thought, even to dispute intelligently with the canon of Toledo. On the way to Barcelona, on the other hand, he is made captive by men who speak a strange language, and his path is determined by Roque Guinart, whose "guest" he is, as they travel "using abandoned roads, shortcuts and hidden paths" (II:61, 861) ["por caminos desusados, por atajos y sendas encubiertas" (1130)].

Don Quixote's position in the foreground of the narrative is continually compromised now, as he is overshadowed by the vast natural forces and the human constructions that tower over him. In Barcelona, knight and squire experience an overpowering sight for which they are at a loss to find adequate comparison: the sea. It is "much larger than the lakes of Ruidera that they had seen in La Mancha" (!) (II:61, 862) ["harto más grande que las lagunas de Ruidera que en La Mancha habían visto" (1130)]. Acts of violence now occur, unprecedented in their ferocity and their massive scale. In rural Catalonia, blood is shed, individuals are killed. In Barcelona the galleys of the royal fleet are at action stations. Their violence is not sporadic and personal. It is organized by the State, which commands large forces that are kept under fierce discipline. The men who work the ships that protect the coasts and pursue the Turkish pirates are not free agents, as knights are. They are comrades of those convicts whom Don Quixote liberated as they were being led to serve their sentence in the galleys (I:22). Their officers are under the command of a general who is answerable to a viceroy who is appointed from Madrid. Don Quixote, the singular knight, has no place in this hierarchy. In this massively armed and many-limbed monster that is the modern State he is more of an anachronism than he ever was in La Mancha.

Long before his defeat at the hands of the Knight of the White Moon, then, we see that Quixote has ceased to be the protagonist in the redemptive enterprise that he had invented for himself. His utopian dream, now tested by historical contingency, as was Sancho's, becomes more and more difficult to sustain. It is thus, however, as Gervereau points out, with all utopias, because "[b]y severing itself from the idea of transformation and invention, utopia uses narratives and images to construct static and sealed societies . . . [b]y seeking to bring history to a standstill, [the utopian vision] denies the future. Its laws are sealed . . ." (366).

It is the encounter with the ducal pair—the longest single episode in the book—that initiates a reorientation of the novel's social thrust. In this encounter, the world's response to what Don Quixote represents will be one of amused condescension or dismissal. In the encounter with Roque Guinart, which we will examine shortly, Don Quixote's chivalric vision seems to be actualized in an unexpected, violent and a thoroughly contemporary modulation. But first we note the radical change in the hierarchical relation of master to servant, a form of social violence according to the mentality of the time, which produces real physical violence, and which serves as a prelude to the lawless violence of Roque Guinart.

Whatever the original plan for Quixote's itinerary to Saragossa may have been, the journey through Catalan territory continues a process already marked by the increasing prominence and self-confidence of the squire as well. This process, which began with Sancho's "enchantment" of Dulcinea, continues in his private conversation with the Duchess, his account of the flight on the wooden horse Clavileño, and his shrewd performance as governor of Barataria. The sentence passed on him by the sham Merlin in the Duke's pantomime—that he is to give himself 3,300 lashes in order to restore Dulcinea to her original condition (II:35)—disturbs the amicable relation between master and servant. But the text discloses something more disturbing than the results of other peoples' pranks on the two protagonists. It is traces of the coercive relations and feudal hierarchy concealed behind the romantic façade of chivalry that Don Quixote espouses, the real power that lies behind the knight's and squire's reciprocal dependency. When Sancho is unwilling to flog himself, we recall, Quixote attempts to seize him while he sleeps and to apply the lashes (II:59); when Sancho wrestles his master to the ground, Don Quixote cries: "What, you traitor? You dare to raise your hand against your natural lord and master? You presume to defy the person who gives you your bread? (II:60, 851) ["¿Cómo traidor? ¿Contra tu amo y señor natural te desmandas? ¿Con quien te da su pan te atreves?" (1117)]. This is the "natural" authority Don Quixote upholds: "it is necessary," he tells Sancho, "to distinguish between mas-

ter and minion, gentleman and servant, knight and squire" (I:20, 151)
["es menester hacer diferencia de amo a mozo, de señor a criado y de
caballero a escudero" (221)]. And the text exposes the same arbitrary,
conventional, and "naturalized" result of the *ius gentium,* namely, the
primal usurpation of power bemoaned by the peasant in the *Disputa.*
Sancho's action has forced Quixote's awareness of the realities of his
contemporary world where power is less and less mediated by the sym-
bols and ceremony that have founded Don Quixote's chivalric identity. The act of insubordination signals what is to come: a sequence of
dislocations of Quixote's central position in the narrative. Continuing
dislocations between fantasy and the overwhelming scale of contemporary social forces refracted in the utopian discourse subject to doubt the
tenability of Quixote's utopian dream.

Liminal spaces had formerly protected knight and squire from the
exigencies of the established order. Now even in those spaces, spending
a night sleeping out in the woods, for example, they are subjected to a
violence and lawlessness that is beyond their control: here is where Sancho renders the former hierarchical relation between knight and squire
untenable as he throws his master to the ground; here Don Quixote is
caught unprepared, surprised by live bandits while unhorsed, unarmed,
and unprotected as no genuine knight should be; and here Don Quixote
and Sancho discover the corpses of bandits who have been caught and
executed. For Quixote, this becomes an obvious sign "which leads me
to think I must be close to Barcelona" (II:60, 851) ["por donde me
doy a entender que debo estar cerca de Barcelona" (1118)]. And it is
in the company of the historical bandit chieftain Perot Roca Guinarda
(Cervantes's Roque Guinart) and his gang of thieves, that Quixote and
Sancho will be forced to live a rough life, sleeping outdoors, in perpetual alarm, in a parodically distant mimicry of the behavior he lauded
in his fictional chivalric models—but now "for real."

The scale and seriousness of violence also change abruptly now.
Violence in Quixote's and Sancho's careers had been mostly kept on a
knockabout level: some bruises, the loss of some teeth (I:18) and part of
an ear (I:9) for Quixote; the blanket tossing for Sancho (I:17) which he
will not allow Quixote to forget. But now death is real, not play-acting
as it was in Basilio's performance at the wedding of Camacho (II:21).
When Claudia Jerónima kills her lover (II:60), death is no longer a
trope in the rhetoric of love, but the violent outcome of unfounded jeal-

ousy. Quixote and Sancho, reduced to silent witnesses, will see Roque split open the head of one of his own men who mutters—not quietly enough—a comment on the chief's method of dividing the spoils (II:60, 684 [1128]).

Through the incident with Roque Guinart, the text continues to underline the arbitrariness of concepts. Words that have but one meaning in the knight's lexicon of chivalric values are identical here but their meanings are worlds apart. Roque Guinart tells Quixote that he became an outlaw because of a dispute over a matter of honor (858 [1125]), a concept the knight cherishes in its archaic meaning. Quixote has declared more than once that a knight-errant must not only have knowledge of "distributive justice" (*justicia distributiva*) (II:18, 570 [774]), but he must practice it "and give each man what is his" (I:37, 329) ["y dar a cada uno lo que es suyo" (443)]. Now Roque is the one who practices it. When the bandits rob some travelers, Roque redistributes the takings "with so much equity and prudence that he adhered absolutely to distributive justice and gave no one too much or too little" (II:60, 857) ["con tanta legalidad y prudencia, que no pasó un punto ni defraudó nada de la justicia distributiva" (1124)].[9] But Roque's motivation measures the distance between the two men. It is simple expediency rather than principle that informs his actions, Guinart explains, for were he not so scrupulous in his just dealings, it would be impossible to live with his men (857) ["si no se guardase esta puntualidad con estos, no se podría vivir con ellos" (1125)].

In performing decisive acts of justice, Roque also shows himself capable of doing what Quixote only speaks of doing. In his treatment of Claudia Jerónima and of the captive travelers, for example, there is a powerful contrast between his competence and Quixote's bungling and self-congratulation in the "adventure" of Andrés and the rich farmer Juan Haldudo (I:4). Quixote sees so much of his ideal self in this "generous" and "courteous" man, who succors the damsel in distress Claudia Jerónima, who controls a communitarian society with his fellow bandits, and who actualizes the ideal of distributive justice, that he invites him to "come with me, and I shall teach you how to be a

9. In fact, Roque's justice is both distributive and commutative. He distributes equal shares among his men, and in dealing with his captives he shares in proportion to need and status (see Lorente-Murphy and Frank).

knight errant" (II.60, 858) [véngase conmigo, que yo le enseñaré a ser caballero andante" (1126)]. The text's representation of the qualities the two men share, their generosity and courtesy, serves to heighten the contrast between them. Roque is no more a righter of wrongs than is Don Quixote, nor is he a hero except to his own faction. But then, is Don Quixote either to anyone else except Sancho—and even for him only temporarily?

Thus Roque Guinart becomes an important figure upon whom the text focuses in showing how the utopian discourse is made systematically to subject the utopian fantasy to doubt. When waylaid by Roque and his private army of bandits on the road to Barcelona, Quixote is immobilized, marginalized, and no longer the initiator of action. The narrator's attention is focused instead upon Roque, who ignores Quixote's interjections (II:60, 854 [1122]; 858 [1126]). Quixote himself is not unaware of his captor's fame, as he shows by his apostrophe: "O valorous Roque, whose fame reaches far beyond the borders of your land . . ." (853) ["¡oh valeroso Roque, cuya fama no hay límites en la tierra que la encierren!" (1120)]. But the analogy between the fictional Roque Guinart's career and Quixote's can also be interpreted as the text's deliberate emphasis on their meaningful differences. In order to pursue this argument, we must locate the contemporary "Robin Hood" within the historical formation of brigandage in sixteenth- and seventeenth-century Catalonia.

Roque Guinart is not a figure of passing anecdotal interest as Cardenio was in Part I. He is a real historical figure (Perot Rocaguinarda or Roca Guinarda, 1582–163?) whose notoriety spread far beyond his theatre of operations in the Barcelona hinterland above Vich. Long before *Don Quixote* appeared in print, Roque Guinart had become legendary throughout Spain. News of his daring raids had spread far and wide. His part in the long-running feud between the party of the *nyerros*, to which he belonged, and the rival *cadells*; his vendetta against Francesc Torrents dels Prats, the captain of the Uniò de Vich militia, whom he eventually killed (Riquer 73); and his insolent defiance of the viceroy, the Duque de Monteleón: all of this was well known. We may compare the contemporary reception of Roque Guinart's presentation in *Don Quixote* with that of the Captive's in Part I (I:39–41). The latter story with its details of life in the prison camps of Algiers and the power play among Arabs and Turks would surely have touched many readers through personal knowledge or contact with the hundreds of ransomed prisoners or their families and neighbors (Friedman ch. 1). Likewise, the state of affairs in Catalonia was well known to sixteenth- and seventeenth-century readers.

Since the sea route to Genoa had become too dangerous because of the continuous presence of Turkish and Barbary pirates, silver was exported there over land and via Barcelona under heavy escort. Even so, in an assault that may be compared to the Great Train Robbery, the consignment of 111 boxes of silver was seized by the gang of Pere Barba (alias *Barbeta*) in transit to Barcelona in December 1613 (Riquer 65–66). The situation was not unknown to travelers who had long been writing about the dangers of travel in Catalonia. For example, Francesco Guicciardini wrote in his *Diario del viaggio* (1511) of the hazards of travel between Perpignan and Barcelona (Vilar 579). In 1567 the Florentine diplomat Antonio Tièpolo wrote in his *Relación de España* that in Castile the justice imposed by Philip II was so powerful that "anyone could travel by night through all parts in complete safety" ["a tal punto que cada uno puede con toda seguridad caminar de noche por todos los lugares"]. But, he insisted, "where his Majesty does not enjoy absolute power, the most atrocious crimes are committed." That is, in Aragon, Valencia, or Catalonia, "it is true to say that travelers are not safe at any time, because these regions are infested with bandits" ["en donde su magestad no tiene el poder absoluto, se cometen los crímenes más atroces, y puede afirmarse que allí los viajeros no encuentran seguridad en ningún tiempo, porque esas comarcas están infestadas de bandidos . . ." (García Mercadal 1153).

Of course there were bandits everywhere in Europe. As Fernand Braudel tells it, "[w]hen the Sultan's army marched along the road to Niš, Belgrade, and on into Hungary, it left behind along the roadside scores of hanged brigands whom it had disturbed in their lairs" (Braudel vol. II, 744); and "[i]n Portugal, Valencia, even in Venice, throughout Italy and in every corner of the Ottoman Empire, robber bands, states in miniature with the great advantage of mobility could pass unobtrusively from the Catalan Pyrenees to Granada, or from Albania to the Black Sea" (Braudel vol. II, 744–45). The causes were complex and bear describing if we are to appreciate the figure of Roque Guinart from a perspective other than the quixotic angle from which he is represented in the novel.

The Catalan *bandolers*, like bandits elsewhere, have been seen by recent commentators as an expression of the social malaise that arises from rural poverty.

> The poverty and discontent that cause rebellions and riots also produced the crime and banditry that plagued some regions of Europe in the six-teenth- and seventeenth- centuries. Recruited from the vagrants and the downtrodden, bandits are an inevitable product of social crisis, economic disarray, poverty and resentment.

> [La miseria y el descontento, origen de levantamientos y motines, daban también lugar a la delincuencia y el bandolerismo, auténticas plagas de algunas comarcas europeas durante los siglos XVI y XVII. El bandolero, reclutado entre vagabundos y gentes abatidas, suele ser un producto inevi-table de la crisis social, el desorden económico, la penuria y el resentimiento (Salazar Rincón 33).]

Pierre Vilar gives a more inclusive image. "The greater part, made up of poor people of course, include, as far as one can judge, just as many depraved city dwellers, soldiers on the loose, and foreign refugees as there were country people in revolt." ["[L]a masse, faite bien entendue de pauvres gens, compte, pour autant qu'on puisse en juger, autant de citadins dévoyés, de soldats sans maître, de réfugiés étrangers, que de ruraux en révolte"] (Vilar 581). Such a description accounts for the rank and file of the gangs. But by no means were all the bandits com-mon highway robbers. Their leaders appear to have had other agendas. Among them were "noblemen (but not of the high nobility), who par-ticipate in or protect brigandage" ["Il y a des seigneurs (non toutefois de grands seigneurs) qui rejoignent ou protègent le banditisme"], as well as those who did so for a variety of motives such as personal vendettas. The Portuguese Francisco Manuel de Melo gives us an indication of this. He characterizes the Catalans as:

> deeply resentful of insults and . . . therefore quick to take revenge . . . The roughness of the terrain is helpful to them and encourages their vengeful minds to commit terrible deeds at the least provocation. Men with a grudge or who have suffered a slight will leave their villages to live in the forest, where they harass the roads with continual assaults. Others follow them for no other motive than their own insolence. All of them make a living from

their offenses . . . they don't consider their actions to be dishonorable; on the contrary, their friends and relatives always help them.

[. . . en las injurias muestran gran sentimiento, y por eso son inclinados a venganza . . . La tierra, abundante de asperezas, ayuda y dispone su ánimo vengativo a terribles efectos con pequeña ocasión; el quejoso o agraviado deja los pueblos y se entra a vivir en los bosques, donde en continuos asaltos fatigan los caminos; otros, sin más ocasión que su propia insolencia siguen a estotros; estos y aquellos se mantienen por la industria de sus insultos . . . no es acción entre ellos reputada por afrentosa, antes al ofendido ayudan siempre sus deudos y amigos (60–61).]

Not only does Roque Guinart validate Melo's statement by becoming an outlaw in pursuit of a matter of honor, but he is named in Melo's list of famous bandits alongside Pedraza, and the notorious Pedro de Santa Cilia y Paz, known for having killed 325 persons in a 25-year rampage to avenge the death of a brother (62). By the time of Melo's writing, and Cervantes's chapters on Guinart, both Santa Cilia and Roque Guinart had been pardoned. Guinart was no longer in Catalonia, and had not only been pardoned by King Philip III in 1611, but had been made captain of a regiment of infantry in Naples (where the Conde de Lemos, Cervantes's patron, was Viceroy), serving in His Majesty's imperial army.[10]

Don Quixote romanticizes and softens Roque Guinart's lifestyle, then, and it is not alone in so doing. Guinart may possibly have been less brutal and more chivalrous than the generality of Catalan bandits, as some contemporaries claimed. According to an anonymous diarist: "Roque Guinart was the most courteous bandit of any there have been for many years past: he didn't make deals, or dishonor anyone, or desecrate churches, and God helped him" [Aquest Rocha Guinart és estat lo bandoler més cortès que quants n'i ha aguts de molts anys en aquesta part: no composave ni desonrave ni tocave les iglésies, y Deu li ajudà" (Riquer 78).] That Roque Guinart is consistently labeled "courteous" is of course open to question. Not robbing a person of his last penny, or sparing the life of a defenseless person who offers no threat, can easily

---

10. Cervantes had probably been in Barcelona in 1610, when Roca Guinarda was at the height of his power and depredations. See Soler y Teròl 55–56; Riquer 91–108.

be attributed to generosity among thieves. It is farfetched to claim, as Fernand Braudel does of similar robber bands, however, that "[l]ike the guerrilla forces of the modern popular wars, they invariably had the people on their side" (745). An anonymous soldier's letter proffers another version. It describes how these bands of more than fifty heavily armed men, all crack shots, raided the countryside in broad daylight, "and no-one dared say anything to them" ["sin que ombre les osase hablar"]; how people were not safe from them in their own houses; how they had "the people of this Principality so cowed that they could not leave their homes to work" ["la gente de este Prinçipado tan oprimida que no podían salir de sus casas a hazer sus labores"]; and how protected these bandits were by the local nobility (Riquer 65). The "people," who according to Braudel supposedly sided with them, were actually farmers living in fortified stone houses who were terrorized into sheltering and supplying them (see Soler y Teròl for witnesses' stories and depositions). Consequently, we must concur with Javier Salazar Rincón that "in spite of his unquestionable historical accuracy, there is an obvious dose of idealization in Cervantes's portrait of Perot Rocaguinarda." ["A pesar de su indiscutible historicidad, hay una evidente dosis de idealización en el retrato cervantino de Perot Rocaguinarda" (35)].

Even if we give some credence to the argument that brigandage in Catalonia flourished because of poverty and the economic disruption caused by inflation (Vilar 583), we must wonder why, if Tièpolo is to be believed, similar economic hardship did not produce the same social violence in Castile?[11] The difference between Castile and the territories of the kingdom of Aragon is that the latter had never allowed themselves to be subjected to the centralizing policies of the Habsburg monarchy. In Barcelona, the viceroy appointed from Madrid was continually thwarted by the Council of One Hundred [Consell de Cent] and by unruly nobles in their fiefdoms. The banditry of the early seventeenth

---

11. The standard explanations of brigandage—the age-old assault of mountain people against the plainsmen, and economic and demographic crisis—have been shown to be invalid (see García Cárcel). Both population and production, agrarian and urban, rose in Catalonia in this period. See also Contreras: "the most up-to-date historiography reminds us that there is no special relation between the manifestation of the problem and social and economic conditions" ["hoy la historiografía más avanzada nos recuerda que no hay una especial relación entre la manifestación del problema y las condiciones sociales y económicas" (55)].

century, epitomized in the figure of Roque Guinart, had deep roots not only in existing social discontents but also in the history of local rivalries. Feuding nobles had supported their warring factions generation after generation and, to quote Ferrán Soldevila, "[b]anditry in Catalonia had its roots in the tradition of feudal conflict" ["El banderolismo catalán tenía sus raíces en la tradición de las luchas feudales" (126)]. By the time of Cervantes, as Roque Guinart explains, the bandits, and their sponsors, were divided into two factions, the *nyerros* and the *cadells*. They were in a state of continual vendetta and had split the society from top to bottom. The feuding parties even included the clergy: the abbot and canons of Ripoll were *nyerros* and friends of Rocaguinarda (Soler y Teròl 177–78), and so were the *familiares* of the Holy Office (the Inquisition) and the Knights of the Order of Saint John of Jerusalem. These would later ally themselves with the notorious bandits Tallaferro and Serrallonga, who also were *nyerros*. On the side of the *cadells* were the Conseller en Cap of Barcelona, Julià de Navel, and the bishop of Vich, Francesc de Robuster i Sala, whose episcopal palace served as the gangs' base of operations (Reglà 93). Indeed, Rocaguinarda became an active *nyerro* fighter in response to having been shot by the bishop's hit men in November 1602 (Soler y Teròl 37–39).

It is into this turbulent political Catalonia, with its feuding nobility, its endemic violence, and its lack of an effective, independent central authority, that Don Quixote is introduced in Part II. Whether intentional or not, the text presents a simulacrum of the decadent past ages which follow upon the pre-historic Golden Age of Don Quixote's oration, and which, to his mind, the order of chivalry was instituted to ameliorate.[12] Here, surely, the Age of Iron presents itself with demonic energy. To take up arms in the peaceful region of New Castile, regulated by the Habsburg monarchy, was one thing. To implement Don Quixote's medieval chivalric vision in the violence-ridden Principality of Barcelona, and among ruthless men armed to the teeth with fire-

---

12. "During the viceregency of the Marquis of Almazán (1611–1615) the crisis in Catalonia reached a peak. Banditry was now feeding voraciously on the country. Bandits had their protectors, chiefly among the rural nobility, who took a commission for their services; they had their enemies, in rival bands; and neutrals were bribed or terrorized into silence. A mafia-type regime prevailed in parts of Catalonia, sustained by violence and extortion" (Lynch, *The Hispanic World 1598–1700* 72).

arms, was quite another. And in this "age of iron," it is the "courteous" bandit, Roque Guinart, and not Don Quixote, the knight, who appears capable of dealing with such violent conditions. He is, after all, product and re-producer of them. Ironically, Roque Guinart constitutes the modern flesh-and-blood counterpart of Don Quixote's fictive exemplar Amadís.

In discussing the quixotic character of Roque Guinart, we must not lose sight of the Roque-like character of the choleric Don Quixote, so often rendered harmless by such romanticized representations as *Man of La Mancha*. In a short space, the Don Quixote of Part I, emulating the paladins whom he takes as his exemplars, attacks a swineherd, windmills, sheep, friars, the Basque, and the barber who wears the basin. He violently frees the convicts from their chains, and so, like Roque, becomes an outlaw sought by the Hermandad (I:45, 394–96; Rico 527–28). Again, like Roque, he is vengeful, swearing to avenge himself for the destruction of his helmet (I:10, 72–73; Rico 115–16), and declaring that if he had not been immobilized by enchantment at Sancho's blanket tossing, he would have avenged him, "*even though by so doing I should have contravened the laws of chivalry* (I:18, 124: emphasis added) ["aunque en ello supiera contravenir las leyes de la caballería" (186)]. In his admiration for Reinaldos de Montalbán, Don Quixote reveals another trait that makes Roque his modern-day exemplar, that of banditry. The narrator tells us that "more than any of the others, he admired Reinaldos de Montalbán above all when he saw him emerge from his castle and rob anyone he met, and when he crossed the sea and stole the idol of Mohammed made all of gold, as recounted in his history" (I:1 21) ["sobre todos, estaba bien con Reinaldos de Montalbán, y más cuando le veía salir de su castillo y robar cuantos topaba, y cuando en allende robó aquel ídolo de Mahoma que era todo de oro, según dice su historia" (40)]. The Cura reminds Don Quixote (and the reader) of who the chivalric Reinaldos "really" was: "There you'll find Reinaldos de Montalbán and his friends and companions, greater thieves than Cacus" (I:6, 48) ["Ahí anda el señor Reinaldos de Montalbán con sus amigos y compañeros, más ladrones que Caco" (80)]. Eventually, Don Quixote himself, in a saner moment, admits the truth of the Cura's assessment: "With respect to Reinaldos . . . I dare say . . . his temperament [was] excessively punctilious and choleric, and that he was a friend of thieves and other dissolute people" (II:1, 467) ["De Reinaldos . . . me atrevo a decir que era . . . puntoso y colérico en demasía, amigo de ladrones y de gente perdida" (637)]. Nonetheless, Quixote sets him up as an exemplar. And it is the violent Reinaldos whom Quixote imitates in attacking the barber, that is, the Reinaldos who in *Orlando Furioso*, canto 1, stanza 28, kills Mambrino in order to take his famous helmet.[13] The text discloses, then, not only how much of Quixote there is in Roque, but how much of a potential Roque exists in Quixote. And it is one that has been legitimized by the violent behavior of Don Quixote's exemplars in the books of chivalry. When Don Quixote imagines aloud his future knightly triumph, for example, and his reception by a grateful king (I:21), he also foresees his reward of a beautiful princess. And, he adds, if the king refuses to give him his daughter, due to the knight's lowly birth, Don Quixote will simply act as knights have done before him: "that's when I seize her and carry her off wherever I feel like taking her" (our translation) ["aquí entra el roballa y llevalla donde más gusto me diere" (233)].

As concepts of honor, generosity, community, and justice disclose their ironic semantic ambiguity in the "real" world encounter with Roque Guinart, so does Don Quixote's cherished concept of *armas*. Don Quixote, the literary creation of Part I, had always chosen *armas* over *letras* as his destiny. Within the historical context of the Roque Guinart episode in Part II, *armas* take on a new meaning for him. Thrust into a world where the absurdity of his idealized views is underlined by their total irrelevance, Don Quixote sees in Roque what he himself has aspired to become, a decisive man of *armas*. In the encounter between the two men, "Cervantes achieves a wonderful contrast between this terrifyingly practical man and Quixote whose adventures are always dreamed up" ["y resulta admirable lo contrast que Cervantes se complau en fer, èntre aquèst hòme terriblement práctic y'l Don Quijote de les aventures sempre somiades" (Soler y Teròl 252)].

The encounter in Catalonia with Roque Guinart, then, takes on a significance that, to our knowledge, has been overlooked.[14] As Sancho

---

13. Higuera 71–72.

14. Since this chapter was written, David Quint's *Cervantes's Novel of Modern Times* has appeared. He, too, notes that in Roque, Quixote "seems to be meeting a version of a former possible self" (103), and "a modern version of the chivalric career that Don Quijote professes" (128). We do not agree with Quint, however,

sees his "people's utopia" problematized in the mock *ínsula* of Barataria, so Don Quixote sees in Roque Guinart the incarnation in a modern exemplar—and similarly problematic—of the feudal qualities of the knights he has admired in his chivalric narratives. The text could have pitted the knight against bandits in the Sierra Morena in Part I, since bandits operated there (Guillaume-Alonso 13), and, like Roque, they figure in some of the fiction of the period (Rey Hazas). But the bandits of Sierra Morena were mere highway robbers, of no political importance, and in the new direction taken by Part II, they would have had no significance. The utopian discourse provides, instead, a legendary figure who could stand in a critical and parodic relation to Quixote's utopian fantasy of communitarianism, of equity, of justice and of courtesy. Catalonia, where banditry was institutionalized and intricately linked to legitimate authority, not La Mancha, becomes the most fitting place. And the historical "Roque Guinart [who] *had supporters among the learned men of the Royal Council,* who were divided between nyerros and cadells" ["En Roca Guinarda *tenia partidaris èntre'els doctors del reyal Consell*; los quals estaven dividits en nyèrros y cadells"] (Soler y Teròl, 263: emphasis added), and not Amadís, becomes the exemplar on the political plane. The text must have elicited an ironic reception by the contemporary readers in this regard. Aware of Roque Guinart's terrorist practices, they must have stifled a knowing smile at Don Quixote's naive description of Roque's hands, which "are more compassionate than severe" (II:60, 852) ["manos . . . que tienen más de compasivas que de rigurosas" (1119)].

The view we take here of the historical Roque Guinart as a living demonstration of the ruthlessness necessary to redress injustices in everyday existence is not universally shared. John Elliott palliates the image, affirming that such "bandits could count on the sympathy of many of their countrymen, who perhaps saw them as protectors of the poor against the rich, or as their champion against some royal official who had made himself hated throughout the region" (*Revolt* 104). Others are more skeptical. Jorge Aladro interprets the respect shown in *Don Quixote* for the bandit as being a tongue-in-cheek representation on the part of Cervantes at best, and an implicit condemnation of the historical

---

when he says that "Roque is marginal to Cervantes's novel itself" (131). As our argument makes clear, we think him essential.

figure of Roque Guinart, and of contemporary society, at worst: "The praise and respect for the figure of the bandit implies the condemnation of sixteenth-century Spanish society" ["La exaltación y respeto por la figura del bandolero lleva implícita la condena de la sociedad española del siglo XVI" (136)]. García Cárcel concurs with Aladro's assessment: that "the romantic image of the generous bandit is hardly credible. The redistribution of booty only rarely touched ordinary people." ["La realidad es que la romántica imagen del bandolero pródigo es poco creíble. La redistribución de los botines no incidiría más que ocasionalmente sobre el pueblo" (47)].

The incident with the fictional Roque Guinart for our purposes, then, is essential in two ways. First, it demonstrates the fundamental paradox of utopia that we discussed in chapter 2, namely, its "tyrannical unanimity" (Jameson 17). The iron discipline that Roque Guinart imposes by violent means, the absolute authority he wields, remind us, in Isaiah Berlin's words, that the success of utopia lies in "coercing others for their own sake" (204), in treating them "as objects without wills of their own, and therefore to degrade them" (209). Second, it confirms Raymond Williams's view, which we applied to Sancho Panza's situation, that the dominant order always circumscribes alternate or oppositional forms of resistance. The text must have created ambiguous resonances for the seventeenth-century readers. They lived through both the violent resistance of the historical Roca Guinarda to established authority, as well as his ultimate submission to imperial authority. In the end, the real Roca Guinarda, unlike the fictive Roque Guinart, is resorbed into the status quo, which also offers a suggestive parallel to Don Quixote's final recantation.

As we look back from the end of the novel, we can appreciate how Part II loops back to the foundational myth of chivalric inspiration in order both to test the utopian construct against contingent reality and to test utopian theory against practical relevance. The text is no longer concerned with the chivalric games of Don Quixote, but with the process by which he realizes his cherished ideal to be recognized as a chivalric knight. Don Quixote is able to believe in Part II that this has taken place. He has been recognized as a knight in the Duke's and Duchess's palace of illusion, and he has encountered, in a "communitarian" society, an alter ego—Roque Guinart—who has espoused precisely his lofty ideals of honor and of distributive justice.

In Don Quixote's confrontation with Roque Guinart, the text finally presents the knight with what it takes, in the early modern world, to actualize "chivalric" ideals. And so the book ends as the mad knight, made by authorial and historical compromise to become suddenly sane, and just as suddenly to die, utters the necessary confession and remorse that is expected of him. Like the eponymous hero most admired in *Don Quixote* itself, *Tirant lo Blanc*, the paragon of those knights who "sleep and die in their beds, and make a will before they die, and do everything else that all the other books of this sort leave out" (I:6, 50) ["duermen y mueren en sus camas, y hacen testamento antes de su muerte, con estas cosas de que todos los demás libros deste género carecen" (83)], Don Quixote too awakens only to make his will and to die.

The novel's end is narrated in the same light vein in which its story has been told. The narrator tells us that the knight is now "stretched out full length" (our translation) ["yace tendido de largo a largo" (II:74, 1223)], that he must be allowed to lie with his "weary, and already rotting bones" in the grave (our translation) [con sus] "cansados y ya podridos huesos" (1223)], and that after Don Quixote's death life simply goes on as usual. So the narrator tells us that "the niece ate, the housekeeper drank, and Sancho Panza was content, for the fact of inheriting something wipes away or tempers in the heir the memory of the grief that is reasonably felt for the deceased" (II:74, 938) ["comía la sobrina, brindaba el ama y se regocijaba Sancho Panza, que esto del heredar algo borra o templa en el heredero la memoria de la pena que es razón que deje el muerto" (1221)].

The final narratorial disparagement of the chivalric novel is, however, rendered questionable by its author's ironic twist. We recall that in the Prologue it is not an implied author but a "friend" who surmises the "purpose" for which the novel has been written. It is he who makes the qualifying and dismissive judgment against books of chivalry: " . . . if I understand it correctly, this book of yours . . . is an invective against books of chivalry" (8) ["si bien caigo en la cuenta, este vuestro libro . . . es una invectiva contra los libros de caballerías" (17)]. At the novel's close, as the fictitious Arabic "narrator" Cide Hamete takes his leave and hangs up his pen, it is the pen that is made to repeat the "friend's" disparaging judgment. It affirms that "my only desire has been to have people reject and despise the false and nonsensical histories of the books of chivalry" (II:74, 940) ["no ha sido otro mi deseo que poner en aborrecimiento de los hombres las fingidas y disparatadas historias de los libros de caballerías" (1223)]. But Cide Hamete goes further; now it is he who adds a crucial qualification as he addresses his pen. He assures it that the (other) novels of chivalry "are already stumbling over my true Don Quixote, and will undoubtedly fall to the ground" (940) ["por las de mi verdadero don Quijote van ya tropezando y han de caer del todo sin duda alguna (1223)"]. Neither in the Prologue, nor in the final farewell, does Cervantes speak in his own voice.

In the 123 chapters that precede the end, *Don Quixote* has succeeded in what the "friend" in the Prologue urged its author to strive for: to "move the melancholy to laughter, increase the joy of the cheerful, not irritate the simple, fill the clever with admiration for its invention, not give the serious reason to scorn it, and allow the prudent to praise it" (Prologue, 8) ["Procurad que . . . el melancólico se mueva a risa, el risueño la acreciente, el simple no se enfade, el discreto se admire de la invención, el grave no la desprecie, ni el prudente deje de alabarla" (18)]. But that is not all. As Mario Vargas Llosa remarked long ago, Cervantes has also made his own novel render "a superb homage to the novel of chivalry, taking what was best in it and adapting its mythology, its rituals, its characters and its values to his time, using the only means possible—an ironic perspective" ["un soberbio homenaje . . . [a la novela de caballerías] aprovechando lo mejor que había en ella, y adaptando a su tiempo, de la única manera en que era posible—mediante una perspectiva irónica—su mitología, sus ritos, sus personajes, sus valores" (12–13)]. Cide Hamete's pen, then, can be confidently laid down at the end of *Don Quixote*, for the "nonsensical books" of chivalry that had preceded Cervantes's novel were, as a result, "already stumbling over the history of [the] true Don Quixote" (940). Cervantes, the master ironist, has the final word.

Works Cited and Consulted

Aladro, Jorge. "Entre Roque Guinart y Don Quijote, o el desdoblamiento de Cervantes." *Anales Cervantinos* 30 (1992): 129–37.

Alemán, Mateo. *Guzmán de Alfarache.* Edited by José María Micó. 3d ed. Madrid: Cátedra, 1997.

Amador de los Ríos, José. *Historia crítica de la literatura española.* Vol. 7. Madrid: Rodriguez, 1865. Facsimile reprint, Madrid: Gredos, 1969.

Anghiera, Pietro Martire d.' *Décadas del nuevo mundo: Por Pedro Mártir de Anglería, primer cronista de Indias.* 2 vols. Mexico: J. Porrúa, 1964–65.

Asensio, Eugenio. *Itinerario del entremés desde Lope de Rueda a Quiñones de Benavente con cinco entremeses de Francisco de Quevedo.* 2d rev. ed. Madrid: Gredos, 1971.

Augustine, Saint. *The City of God.* An Abridged Version from the translation by Gerald G. Walsh et al. Edited by Vernon J. Bourke. New York: Image Books, 1958.

Avalle-Arce, Juan Bautista. *La novela pastoril española.* 2d ed. Madrid: Istmo, 1974.

Averintsev, Sergei S. "Bakhtin and the Russian Attitude to Laughter." In *Bakhtin*, 13–19.

Aznar Cardona, Pedro. *Espulsion iustificada de los Moriscos Espanoles, y suma de las excelencias Christianas de nuestro Rey Don Felipe el Catholico Tercero deste nombre. Dividida en dos partes.* Huesca: Pedro Cabarte, 1612.

Bacon, Francis. *The Advancement of Learning and New Atlantis.* Edited by Arthur Johnston. Oxford: Clarendon, 1974.

Baker, Edward. *La biblioteca de Don Quijote.* Madrid: Marcial Pons, 1997.

Bakhtin, Mikhail M. *Rabelais and His World.* Translated by Helene Iswolsky. Cambridge: MIT Press, 1968.

———. *The Dialogic Imagination: Four Essays.* Edited by Michael Holquist.

Translated by Caryl Emerson and Michael Holquist. Austin: University of Texas Press, 1981.

Baring-Gould, Sabine. "The Fortunate Isles." In *Curious Myths of the Middle Ages.* Second Series, 259–95. Philadelphia: Lippincott, 1868.

Bartra, Roger. *El salvaje en el espejo.* Mexico: UNAM (Universidad Autónoma de México), 1992.

—————. *El salvaje artificial.* Mexico: UNAM-ERA, 1997.

Bataillon, Marcel. *Erasmo y España: Estudios sobre la historia espiritual del siglo xvi.* 2d ed. Mexico: Fondo de Cultura Económica, 1966.

Beauchamp, Gorman. "The Dream of Cockaigne: Some Motives for the Utopias of Escape." *Centennial Review* 24 (Fall 1981): 345–62.

Benassar, Bartolomé. *Valladolid au siècle d'or.* Paris: Mouton, 1967

Bennett, J. A.W. *Middle English Literature.* Oxford: Clarendon, 1986.

Berlin, Isaiah. *The Proper Study of Mankind: An Anthology of Essays.* Edited by Henry Hardy and Roger Hausheer. Foreword by Noel Annan. Introduction by Roger Hausheer. New York: Farrar, Straus and Giroux, 1997. 191–242.

Bhabha, Homi K. *The Location of Culture.* London: Routledge, 1994.

Biasin, Gian-Paolo. *The Flavors of Modernity: Food and the Novel.* Princeton: Princeton University Press, 1993.

Bible. Revised Standard Version.

Blanco Aguinaga, Carlos, Julio Rodríguez-Puértolas, and Iris Zabala. *Historia social de la literatura española.* 3 vols. Madrid: Castalia, 1975–1978.

Bloch, Ernst. *The Principle of Hope.* Translated by Neville Plaice et al. 3 vols. Cambridge: MIT Press, 1986.

Bloch, Marc. *Feudal Society.* Translated by L.A. Manyon. London: Routledge Kegan Paul, 1961.

Boas, George. *Primitivism and Related Ideas in the Middle Ages.* Baltimore: The Johns Hopkins University Press, [1948] 1997.

Bossert, Rex. "Godzilla in Cloudcuckooland: Or, Literary Theory Comes to Utopia." *Utopian Studies* 1 (1987): 138–46.

Bourdieu, Pierre. *Distinction: A Social Critique of the Judgement of Taste.* Translated by Richard Nice. Cambridge: Harvard University Press, 1985.

—————. "The Economics of Linguistic Exchanges." *Social Science Information* 26 (December, 1977): 645–68.

—————. *Language and Symbolic Power.* Edited with an introduction by John B. Thompson. Translated by Gino Raymond and Matthew Adamson. Reprint, Cambridge: Harvard University Press, 1994.

Brandon, William. *New Worlds for Old.* Athens, Ohio: Ohio University Press, 1986.

Braudel, Fernand. *The Mediterranean and the Mediterranean World in the Age of Philip II*. Translated by Siân Reynolds. 2 vols. New York: Harper and Row, 1972.

Bullough, Geoffrey. "The Later History of Cockaigne." In *Festschrift Prof. Dr. Herbert Koziol zum Siebzigsten Geburtstag* (Wiener Beiträge zur englischen Philologie 75). Edited by Gero Bauer, Franz K. Stanzel, and Franz Zaic, 22–35. Stüttgart: Wilhelm Baraunmüller, 1973.

Burke, Peter. *Popular Culture in Early Modern Europe*. New York: New York University Press, 1978.

————. *Varieties of Cultural History*. Ithaca, N.Y.: Cornell University Press, 1997.

Calmo, Andrea. *Le lettere di Messer Andrea Calmo*. Edited by Vittorio Rossi. Torino: Loescher, 1888.

Caluwé-Dor, Juliette de. "L'anti-Paradis du *Pays de Cocagne*." In *Marche Romane: Mélanges de Philologie et de Littératures Romanes Offerts a Jeanne Wathelet-Willem*, 103–23. Liège: Cahiers de l'A. R. U., 1978.

Calvin, Jean. *Treatises against the Anabaptists and against the Libertines*. Edited and translated by Benjamin W. Farley. Grand Rapids, Mich.: Baker Book House, 1982.

Calvino, Italo. *Under the Jaguar Sun*. Translated by William Weaver. London: Jonathan Cape, 1992.

Campanella, Tomasso. *La città del sole: diàlogo poetico* [*The City of the Sun: A Poetical Dialogue*]. Translated by Daniel J. Donno. Berkeley: University of California Press, 1981.

Campbell, Mary B. *The Witness and the Other World: Exotic European Travel Writing, 400–1600*. Ithaca, N.Y.: Cornell University Press, 1988.

Camporesi, Piero. *Bread of Dreams: Food and Fantasy in Early Modern Europe*. Translated by David Gentilcore. Chicago: University of Chicago Press, 1989.

Campos y Fernández de Sevilla, Francisco Javier. "El Campo de Montiel en la época de Cervantes." *Anales Cervantinos* 35 (1999), 37–73.

Caro Baroja, Julio. *El carnaval*. 2d ed. Madrid: Taurus, 1979.

————. *Ensayo sobre la literatura de cordel*. Madrid: Revista de Occidente, 1969.

Carpintero Benítez, Francisco. *Del derecho natural medieval al derecho natural moderno: Fernando Vázquez de Menchaca*. Salamanca: Acta Salmaticensia, 1977.

Castrillo, Alonso de. *Tractado de República. Con otras hystorias y antigüedades*. Madrid: Instituto de Estudios Políticos, [1521] 1958.

Cavillac, Michel. *Pícaros y mercaderes en el "Guzmán de Alfarache."* Granada: Universidad de Granada, 1994.

Caxa de Leruela, Miguel. *Restauración de la abundancia de España*. Edited by

Jean-Paul Le Flem. Madrid: Ministerio de Hacienda, Instituto de Estudios Fiscales, [1631] 1975.

Certeau, Michel de. *The Mystic Fable: The Sixteenth and Seventeenth Centuries.* Translated by Michael B. Smith. Chicago: University of Chicago Press, 1992.

Cervantes Saavedra, Miguel de. *El ingenioso hidalgo Don Quijote de la Mancha.* Edited by Francisco Rico and Joaquin Foradellas. 2 vols. Barcelona: Crítica, 1998.

—————. *Don Quixote.* Translated by Edith Grossman. New York: Harper Collins, 2003.

—————. *Teatro completo.* Edited by Florencio Sevilla Arroyo and Antonio Rey Hazas. Madrid: Planeta, 1987.

—————. *Novelas ejemplares.* Edited by Harry Sieber. 2 vols. Madrid: Cátedra, 1986.

Chartier, Roger. *The Order of Books: Readers, Authors, and Libraries in Europe between the Fourteenth and Eighteenth Centuries.* Translated by Lydia G. Cochrane. Stanford: Stanford University Press, 1994.

—————. *On the Edge of the Cliff: History, Language, and Practices.* Translated by Lydia G. Cochrane. Baltimore: The Johns Hopkins University Press, 1997.

Cicero, Marcus Tullius. *De Officiis.* With a translation by Walter Miller. Cambridge: Harvard University Press, The Loeb Classical Library, 1913.

—————. *De re publica, De legibus*, with an English translation by Clinton Walker Keyes. London: Heineman; New York: G.P. Putnam's Sons, The Loeb Classical Library, 1928.

Cioranescu, Alexandre. *L'avenir du passé: Utopie et littérature.* Paris: Gallimard, 1972.

—————. "Utopie: Cocagne et âge d'or." *Diogène* 75 (1971): 86–123.

Cocchiara, Giuseppe. *Il paese di Cuccagna e altri studi di folklore.* Torino: Einaudi, 1956.

Cohn, Norman. *The Pursuit of the Millenium.* London: Heinemann, Mercury Books, 1962.

Colmenares, Diego de. *Historia de la insigne ciudad de Segovia y compendio de las Historias de Castilla.* 2 vols. Segovia: Academia de Historia y Arte San Quirce, [1636] 1982, 1984.

Contreras, Jaime. "Bandolerismo y fueros: El Pirineo a finales del Siglo XVI." In *El bandolerismo y su imagen en el Siglo de Oro [Le bandit et son image au Siècle d'Or]*, edited by Juan Antonio Martínez Comeche, 55–78. Paris: PU de la Sorbonne, 1991.

Cornejo Polar, Antonio. "Mestizaje, Transculturación, Heterogeneidad." In *Asedios a la Heterogeneidad Cultural: libro de homenaje a Antonio Cornejo*

Polar, 54–56. Philadelphia: International Association of Peruvianists, 1996.

Covarrubias, Sebastián de. *Tesoro de la lengua castellana o española*. Edited by Martín de Riquer. Barcelona: Horta, 1943.

Cruz, Anne J. *Discourse of Poverty: Social Reform and the Picaresque Novel in Early Modern Spain*. Toronto: University of Toronto Press, 1999.

Delumeau, Jean. *History of Paradise: The Garden of Eden in Myth and Tradition*. Translated by Matthew O'Connell. New York: Continuum, 1995.

————. *La mort des pays de cocagne*. Paris: Publications de la Sorbonne, Série "Études" tome 12, 1976.

Demerson, Guy. "Cocagne: utopie populaire?" *Revue belge de philologie et d'histoire* 59 (1981): 529–53.

D'Entrèves, A. P. [Passerin d'Entrèves, Alessandro]. *Natural Law: An Introduction to Legal Philosophy*. London: Hutchinson, 1951.

Domínguez Ortiz, Antonio. *La sociedad española en el siglo XVII*. Madrid: CSIC, Instituto Balmes de Sociología, 1963.

Doody, Margaret Anne. *The True Story of the Novel*. New Brunswick, N.J.: Rutgers University Press, 1996.

Durán, Agustín, ed. *Romancero General*. Biblioteca de Autores Españoles 16. Madrid: Rivadeneira, 1851.

Durán, Manuel. "El *Quijote* a través del prisma de Mikhail Bakhtine: carnaval, disfraces, escatología y locura." In *Cervantes and the Renaissance*, 71–86.

Eisenberg, Daniel. "Who Read the Romances of Chivalry?" *Kentucky Romance Quarterly* 20, no. 2 (1973): 209–33.

Eisenstein, Elizabeth. *The Printing Press as an Agent of Change*. 2 vols. Cambridge, England: Cambridge University Press, 1979.

Endress, Heinz-Peter. *Los ideales de Don Quijote en el cambio de valores desde la Edad Media hasta el Barroco: La utopía restaurativa de la Edad de Oro*. Pamplona: EUNSA, 2000.

Ettinghausen, Henry. "De edad de oro a edad de hierro: cabreros, caballeros, cautivos y cortesanos en el *Quijote*." In *Edad de Oro XV*. Madrid: Ediciones de la Universidad Autónoma de Madrid, 1996.

Elliott, John H. *Imperial Spain, 1469–1716*. London: Edward Arnold, 1963.

————. *The Revolt of the Catalans: a Study of the Decline of Spain, 1598–1640*. Cambridge, England: Cambridge University Press, 1963.

Farrington, Benjamin. "Francis Bacon after His Fall." *Studies in the Literary Imagination* 4 (April 1971): 143–58.

Fernández Alvarez, Manuel. *La sociedad española del Renacimiento*. Salamanca: Anaya, 1970.

Fernández-Armesto, Felipe. *Columbus*. New York: Oxford University Press, 1991.

Fernández Navarrete, Pedro. *Conservación de monarquías*. Madrid: Imprenta Real, 1626.

Finello, Dominick. *Pastoral Themes and Forms in Cervantes's Fiction*. Lewisburg, Pa.: Bucknell University Press, 1994.

Flint, Valerie I.J. *The Imaginative Landscape of Christopher Columbus*. Princeton: Princeton University Press, 1992.

Foucault, Michel. *The Order of Things. An Archeology of the Human Sciences*. London: Tavistock, 1970.

Friedman, Ellen G. *Spanish Captives in North Africa in the Early Modern Age*. Madison: University of Wisconsin Press, 1983.

Froissart, Sir John. *The Chronicles of England, France and Spain*. New York: Dutton, 1961.

García Cárcel, Rodrigo. "El bandolerismo catalán en el Siglo XVII." In *El bandolerismo y su imagen en el Siglo de Oro/Le bandit et son image au Siècle d'Or*, edited by Juan Antonio Martínez Comeche, 43–54. Paris: PU de la Sorbonne, 1991.

García Mercadal, Juan, ed. *Viajes de extranjeros por España y Portugal*. Madrid: Aguilar, 1952.

García Santo-Tomás, Enrique. "Aventura fingida y aventura verdadera: Roque Guinart frente a Don Quijote." *Anales Cervantinos* 31 (1993): 215–28.

Gardiner, Michael. "Bakhtin's Carnival: Utopia as Critique." In *Bakhtin*, 21–47.

Génin, François. "Pays de Cocagne." In *Recréations Philologiques*, 2 vols., vol. 2: 89–97. Paris: Chamerot, 1856.

Gervereau, Laurent. "Symbolic Collapse: Utopia Challenged by Its Representations." In *Utopia*, 357–67.

Gewirth, Alan. *Marsilius of Padua: The Defender of Peace*. Vol. 1: *Marsilius of Padua and Medieval Political Philosophy*. New York: Columbia University Press, 1951.

Gierke, Otto. *Natural Law and the Theory of Society 1500 to 1800*. Translated by Ernest Barker. Cambridge, England: Cambridge University Press, 1950.

———. *Political Theories of the Middle Age*. Translated by Frederic William Maitland. 1900. Reprint, Cambridge, England: Cambridge University Press:1987.

Giginta, Miguel. *Tratado de remedio de pobres*. Coimbra, 1579.

Ginzburg, Carlo. *The Cheese and the Worms: The Cosmos of a Sixteenth-Century Miller*. Translated by John and Anne Tedeschi. New York: Dorset, 1989.

González de Amezúa, Agustín. "Cómo se hacía un libro en nuestro siglo de oro." In *Opúsculos histórico-literarios*, vol. 1: 348–59. Madrid: CSIC, 1951.

González de Cellorigo, Martín. *Memorial de la política necesaria y útil restau-*

ración a la república de España y estados de ella y del desempeño universal de estos reinos. Edited by José L. Pérez de Ayala. Madrid: Instituto de Estudios Fiscales, [1600] 1991.

Graf, Arturo. *Miti, leggende e superstizioni del Medio Evo.* Torino: Loescher, 1892.

Grafton, Anthony et al. *New Worlds, Ancient Texts: The Power of Tradition and the Shock of Discovery.* Cambridge: Harvard University Press, 1992.

Gramsci, Antonio. *Selections from Cultural Writings.* Edited by David Forgacs and David Nowell-Smith. Cambridge: Harvard University Press, 1985.

Graus, F. "Social Utopias in the Middle Ages." *Past and Present* 38 (1967): 3–19.

Greene, Roland. *Unrequited Conquests: Love and Empire in the Colonial Americas.* Chicago: University of Chicago Press, 1999.

Grice-Hutchinson, Marjorie. *Early Economic Thought in Spain, 1177–1740.* London: Allen and Unwin, 1978.

Guevara, Antonio de. *Las Obras del Illustre Señor don Antonio de Guevara, Obispo de Mondoñedo, predicador y chronista del consejo de su Magestad.* n.p. 1515.

———. *[Relox de príncipes.* Vol. 2 of *Obras completas.* 5 vols. Madrid: Turner, 1994.

———. *El villano del Danubio y otros fragmentos.* Introduction by Américo Castro. Princeton: Princeton University Press, 1945.

Guillaume-Alonso, Araceli. "Le brigand castillan du Siècle d'Or vu à travers les archives des Santas Hermandades viejas: Essai de typologie." In *El bandolerismo y su imagen en el Siglo de Oro/Le bandit et son image au Siècle d'Or,* edited by Juan Antonio Martínez Comeche, 11–19. Paris: PU de la Sorbonne, 1991.

Gundersheimer, Werner L. "Patronage in the Renaissance: An Exploratory Approach." In *Patronage in the Renaissance,* edited by Guy Fitch Lytle and Stephen Orgel, 3–23. Princeton: Princeton University Press, 1981.

Güntert, Georges. *Cervantes: Novelar el mundo desintegrado.* Barcelona: Puvill, 1993.

Guzman, Gregory G. "Reports of Mongol Cannibalism in Thirteenth Century Latin Sources." In *Discovering New Worlds: Essays on Medieval Exploration and Imagination,* edited by Scott D. Westrem, 31–68. New York: Garland, 1991.

Habermas, Jürgen. *Knowledge and Human Interests.* Translated by Jeremy J. Shapiro. Boston: Beacon Press, 1971

Hall, Joseph. *The Discovery of a New World [Mundus alter et idem]* (ca. 1609) Translated by John Healey. Edited by Huntington Brown. Cambridge: Harvard University Press, 1937.

Hamilton, Bernice. *Political Thought in Sixteenth-Century Spain.* Oxford: Clarendon, 1963.

Hampton, Timothy. *Writing from History: The Rhetoric of Exemplarity in Renaissance Literature.* Ithaca, N.Y.: Cornell University Press, 1990.

Hanke, Lewis. *Aristotle and the American Indians.* Bloomington: Indiana University Press, 1957.

————. *The Spanish Struggle for Justice in the Conquest of America.* Philadelphia: University of Pennsylvania Press, 1949.

Hendrix, W. S. "Sancho Panza and the Comic Types of the Sixteenth Century." In *Homenaje a Don Ramón Menéndez Pidal.* vol. II. Madrid, 1925. 485–94.

Hexter, J.H. *More's Utopia: The Biography of an Idea.* New York: Harper, 1965.

Higuera, Henry. *Eros and Empire. Politics and Christianity in "Don Quixote."* Lanham, Md.: Rowman and Littlefield, 1995.

Hinrichs, Hans. *The Glutton's Paradise, being a pleasant dissertation on Hans Sachs's "Schlaraffenland" and some similar Utopias.* Mount Vernon, N.Y.: Peter Pauper, 1955.

Historiadores de sucesos particulares, I. Edited by Cayetano Rosell. Biblioteca de Autores Españoles, vol. 21. 1852.

Hurtado de Mendoza, Diego. *Algunas cartas de Don Diego Hurtado de Mendoza escritas 1538–1552. Edited by* Alberto Vázquez and R. Selden Rose. New Haven: Yale University Press, Yale Romanic Studies X, 1935.

Huxley, Aldous. *Brave New World.* London: Chatto & Windus, 1934.

Iffland, James. "*Don Quijote* dentro de la 'Galaxia Gutenberg' (Reflexiones sobre Cervantes y la cultura tipográfica)." *Journal of Hispanic Philology* 14, no. 1 (Autumn, 1989): 23–41.

Jameson, Fredric. "Of Islands and Trenches: Neutralization and the Production of Utopian Discourse." *Diacritics* (Summer 1977), 2–21. Reprinted in *The Ideologies of Theory: Essays 1971–1986.* Theory and History of Literature 48–49. 2 vols. Vol. 2: 75–101 Minneapolis: University of Minnesota Press, 1988.

————. *The Political Unconscious: Narrative as a Socially Symbolic Act.* Ithaca, N.Y.: Cornell University Press, 1981.

Jáuregui, Carlos. *Querella de los indios en las* Cortes de la Muerte *(1557) de Michael de Carvajal.* Mexico: UNAM, 2002.

Joannou, Maroula. *Contemporary Women's Writing: From "The Golden Notebook" to "The Color Purple."* Manchester, England: Manchester University Press, 2000.

Johnson, Carroll B. "Ortodoxia y anticapitalismo en el siglo XVII: El caso del morisco Ricote." In *Hispanic Studies in Honor of Joseph H. Silverman,* edited by Joseph V. Ricapito, 285–96. Newark, Del.: Juan de la Cuesta, 1988.

————. *Cervantes and the Material World*. Urbana: University of Illinois Press, 2000.

Justinian (Emperor). *The Digest of Justinian*. Edited by Theodore Mommsen and Paul Krueger. Translated and edited by Alan Watson. 2 vols. Latin text. Philadelphia: University of Pennsylvania Press, 1985.

————. *Justinian's Institutes*. Latin text of Paul Krueger. Translation and introduction by Peter Birks and Grant McLeod. Ithaca, N.Y.: Cornell University Press, 1987.

Kaiser, Walter. *Praisers of Folly: Erasmus, Rabelais, Shakespeare*. London: Victor Gollancz, 1964.

King, P.D. "The Barbarian Kingdoms." In *Cambridge History of Medieval Political Thought c350-c1450*, edited by J.H.Burns, 123–53. Cambridge, England: Cambridge University Press, 1988.

Kumar, Krishan. *Utopia and Anti-Utopia in Modern Times*. Oxford: Blackwell, 1987.

Lacan, Jacques. *Écrits: A Selection*. Translated by Alan Sheridan. New York: Norton, 1977.

Lapeyre, Henri. *Une famille de marchands: les Ruiz*. Paris: Colin, 1955.

Lecoq, Danielle and Roland Schaer. "Ancient, Biblical, and Medieval Traditions." In *Utopia*, 35–82.

Leslie, Marina. *Renaissance Utopias and the Problem of History*. Ithaca, N.Y.: Cornell University Press, 1998.

Levin, Harry. *The Myth of the Golden Age in the Renaissance*. Bloomington: Indiana University Press, 1967.

Levinas, Emmanuel. "Reality and its Shadow." In *The Levinas Reader*, edited by Sean Hand. Translated by Alphonso Lingis. Oxford: Blackwell, 1989.

Levitas, Ruth. *The Concept of Utopia*. Syracuse, N.Y.: Syracuse University Press, 1990.

López Madera, Gregorio. *Excelencias de la monarchia y reyno de España*. Valladolid: Diego Fernández de Córdoba, 1597.

Lorente-Murphy, Silvia and Roslyn M. Frank. "Roque Guinard y la justicia distributiva en el *Quijote*." *Anales Cervantinos* 20 (1982): 103–11.

Lovejoy, Arthur O. and George Boas. *Primitivism and Related Ideas in Antiquity*. Baltimore: The Johns Hopkins University Press, [1935] 1997.

Lovett, A.W. *Early Habsburg Spain 1517–1598*. New York: Oxford University Press, 1986.

Lucian of Samosata. *Satirical Sketches*. Translated by Paul Turner. Bloomington: Indiana University Press, 1990.

Lynch, John. *Spain 1516–1598: From Nation State to World Empire.* Oxford: Blackwell, 1992.

———. *The Hispanic World in Crisis and Change, 1598–1700.* Oxford: Blackwell, 1992.

Macherey, Pierre. *A Theory of Literary Production.* Translated by Geoffrey Wall. London: Routledge, 1985.

Machiavelli, Niccolò. *The Prince.* Translated with an introduction by Harvey Mansfield. 2d ed. Chicago: University of Chicago Press, 1998.

Mandeville, Sir John. *Libro d'las maravillas del mundo y d'l viage dela tierra sancta.* Valencia: Jorge Castilla, 1531.

———. *The Travels of Sir John Mandeville.* Translated by C. W. R. D. Moseley. New York: Penguin, 1983.

Mannheim, Karl. *Ideology and Utopia.* Translated by Louis Wirth and Edward Shils. New York: Harcourt, Brace, 1936.

Manuel, Frank E. and Fritzie Manuel. *Utopian Thought in the Western World.* Cambridge: Harvard University Press, 1979.

Maravall, José Antonio. *Carlos V y el pensamiento político del Renacimiento.* Madrid: Instituto de Estudios Políticos, 1960.

———. *Estado moderno y mentalidad social. Siglos XV a XVII.* 2 vols. Madrid: Revista de Occidente, 1972.

———. *El humanismo de las armas en "Don Quijote."* Madrid: Instituto de Estudios Políticos, 1948.

———. "Réformisme socio-agraire pendant la crise du XVIIe siècle: terre, travail et salaire d'après Pedro de Valencia." *Bulletin Hispanique* 72 (1970): 5-55.

———. *Teatro y literatura en la sociedad barroca.* Madrid: Seminarios y Ediciones, 1972.

———. *Utopía y contrautopía en el "Quijote."* Santiago de Compostela: Pico Sacro, 1976.

———. *Utopia and Counterutopia in the "Quixote."* Translated by Robert W. Felkel. Detroit: Wayne State University Press, 1991.

Marin, Louis. *Food for Thought.* Translated with an afterword by Mette Hjort. Baltimore: The Johns Hopkins University Press, 1989.

———. "Interview." *Diacritics* (Summer 1977): 44–53.

———. "Les corps utopiques Rabelaisiens." *Littérature* 21 (1976): 35–51.

———. "Texts/Contexts. Puss-In Boots: Power of Signs—Signs of Power." *Diacritics* (Summer 1977): 54–63.

———. *Utopics: Spatial Play.* Translated by Robert Vollrath. Atlantic Highlands, N.J.: Humanities, 1984.

Mariscal, George. *Contradictory Subjects: Quevedo, Cervantes, and seventeenth-century Spanish culture.* Ithaca: Cornell University Press, 1991.

Márquez Villanueva, Francisco. *Fuentes literarias Cervantinas.* Madrid: Gredos, 1973.

Martial [M. Valerius Martialis]. *Epigrams.* With English translation by W. C. A. Ker. 2 vols. Cambridge: Harvard University Press, 1919.

Martyr, Peter. See Anghiera, Pietro Martire d'

Martz, Linda. *Poverty and Welfare in Habsburg Spain: The Example of Toledo.* New York: Cambridge University Press, 1983.

McGaha, Michael D., ed. *Cervantes and the Renaissance.* Easton, Pa.: Juan de la Cuesta, 1980.

McIlwain, Charles H. *The Growth of Political Thought in the West from the Greeks to the End of the Middle Ages.* New York: Macmillan, 1932.

Megías Quirós, José J. *La teoría política entre la Edad Media y la Edad Moderna: Alonso de Castrillo.* Cádiz: Universidad, Servicio de Publicaciones, 1992.

Melo, Francisco Manuel de. *Historia de los Movimientos, Separación y Guerra de Cataluña.* Madrid: Editorial Ibero-Africano-Americana, n.d.

Metzger, Ernest, ed. *Companion to Justinian's Institutes.* London: Duckworth, 1998.

Migne, Jacques-Paul. *Patrologiae cursus completa. Series Latina.* Paris: Garnier (reprint) 1925.

Milhou, Alain. "*Mundus novus et renovatio mundi*: Messianic and utopian currents in the Indies of Castille." In *Utopia,* 140–60.

Molho, Maurice. *Cervantes: Raíces folklóricas.* Madrid: Gredos, 1976.

Moner, Michel and Michel Lafon, eds. "Texte/Paratexte: *Don Quichotte.*" In *Le livre et l'édition dans le monde hispanique, XVIe-XXe siècles. Pratiques et discours paratextuels,* 95–100. Grenoble: Université Stendhal, 1992.

Montemayor, Jorge de. *Los siete libros de la Diana.* Edited by Francisco López Estrada. 4th ed. Madrid: Espasa, 1967.

Montesquieu, Charles de Secondat, baron de. *Oeuvres complètes.* Edited by Roger Caillois. Paris: Gallimard, 1951.

More, Thomas. *Utopia.* Latin Text and English Translation. Edited by George M. Logan, Robert M. Adams, and Clarence H. Miller. Cambridge, England: Cambridge University Press, 1995.

Morison, Samuel Eliot. *Admiral of the Ocean Sea. A Life of Christopher Columbus.* Boston: Little, Brown, 1942.

—————. *The European Discovery of the New World. The Southern Voyages.* New York: Oxford University Press, 1974.

Morton, A. L. *The English Utopia.* London: Lawrence and Wishart, 1952.

Mullett, Michael A. *Popular Culture and Popular Protest in Late Medieval and Early Modern Europe.* London: Croom Helm, 1987.

Mumford, Lewis. *The Story of Utopias.* New York: Boni and Liveright, 1932.

Murillo, Luis A. *The Golden Dial: Temporal Configuration in "Don Quijote."* Oxford: Dolphin Book Co., 1975.

—————. *"Don Quijote* as Renaissance Epic." In *Cervantes and the Renaissance*, 51–70.

Nalle, Sara. "Literacy and Culture in Early Modern Castile." *Past and Present* 125 (1989): 65–96.

Nerlich, Michael. *Ideology of Adventure.* Vol. 1. Minneapolis: University of Minnesota Press, 1987.

Novati, Francesco. Review of *Storia di Campriano contadino*, by A. Zenatti. In *Giornale Storico della Letteratura Italiana* 5 (1885): 258–69.

Ortega y Gasset, José. *Meditations on Quixote.* Translated by Evelyn Rugg and Diego Marín. New York: Norton, 1961.

Ortega y Medina, Juan. "El indio absuelto y las Indias condenadas en las *Cortes de la Muerte.*" *Historia Mexicana* 4, no. 2 (1954–1955): 480–482.

Ovid. *The Metamorphoses.* Translated by Mary M. Innes. Harmondsworth: Penguin, 1955.

Pacheco Pereira, Duarte. *Esmeraldo de situ orbis.* Translated by George H. T. Kimble. London: Hakluyt Society, 1937.

Pagden, Anthony. "Dispossessing the barbarian: the language of Spanish Thomism and the debate over the property rights of the American Indians." In *The Languages of Political Theory in Early Modern Europe*, edited by Anthony Pagden, 79–98. Cambridge, England: Cambridge University Press, 1983.

—————. *The Fall of Natural Man: The American Indian and the Origins of Comparative Ethnology.* Cambridge, England: Cambridge University Press, 1982.

—————. *Lords of all the World: Ideologies of Empire in Spain, Britain, and France, c.1500-c.1800.* New Haven: Yale University Press, 1995.

—————. *Spanish Imperialism and the Political Imagination.* New Haven: Yale University Press, 1990.

Parker, Geoffrey. *Europe in Crisis 1598–1648.* Ithaca, N.Y.: Cornell University Press, 1980.

Parker, Patricia. "Deferral, Dilation, Différance: Shakespeare, Cervantes, Jonson." In *Literary Theory/Renaissance Texts*, edited by Patricia Parker and David Quint, 182–209. Baltimore: The Johns Hopkins University Press, 1986.

Pennington, Kenneth. "Law, Legislative Authority, and Theories of Government, 1150–1300." In *The Cambridge History of Medieval Political Thought c350-c1450*, edited by J. H. Burns, 424–53. Cambridge, England: Cambridge University Press, 1987.

Pérez de Herrera, Cristóbal. *Discursos del amparo de los legítimos pobres y reducción de los fingidos.* Edited by Michel Cavillac. Madrid: Espasa, 1975.

Pike, Ruth. *Aristocrats and Traders. Sevillian Society in the Sixteenth Century.* Ithaca, N.Y.: Cornell University Press, 1972.

Pirenne, Jacqueline. *La Légende du Prêtre Jean.* Strasbourg: Presses Universitaires de Strasbourg, 1992.

Pleij, Herman. *Dreaming of Cockaigne: Medieval Fantasies of the Perfect Life.* Translated by Diane Webb. New York: Columbia University Press, 2001.

Poggioli, Renato. *The Oaten Flute.* Cambridge: Harvard University Press, 1975.

Pragmatica y Provision Real de su Magestad, sobre el precio del pan, en que se declara la Pragmatica del año de cincuenta y ocho . . . Y la instrucion y orden que cerca dello se da a las justicias. Madrid: Alonso Gómez, 1571.

Quint, David. *Cervantes's Novel of Modern Times: A New Reading of Don Quijote.* Princeton: Princeton University Press, 2003.

Redondo, Augustin. "Acercamiento al *Quijote* desde una perspectiva histórico-social." In *Cervantes,* edited by Anthony Close et al. Alcalá de Henares: Centro de Estudios Cervantinos, 1995.

—————. "Tradición carnavalesca y creación literaria del personaje de Sancho Panza al episodio de la Insula Barataria en el *Quijote.*" *Bulletin Hispanique* 80 (1978): 39–70. Reprinted in *Otra manera de leer el "Quijote."* Madrid: Castalia, 1997.

Reglà, Joan. *El bandolerisme català. Vol. I. La història.* Barcelona: Aymà, 1962.

Rey Hazas, Antonio. "Introducción a la novela del Siglo de Oro, I: Formas de narrativa idealista." In *Edad de Oro,* vol. 1: 65–105. Madrid: Depto. de Lit. Española, Univ. Autónoma de Madrid. 1982–1983.

Ricoeur, Paul. *Lectures on Ideology and Utopia.* Edited by George H. Taylor. New York: Columbia University Press, 1986.

Riquer, Martín de. *Cervantes en Barcelona.* Barcelona: Sirmio, 1989.

Rivers, Elias L. "Don Quixote's Fatherly Advice, and Olivares's." *Cervantes* 18, no. 2 (1998): 74–84.

Robles (or Medina), Fr. Juan de. *De la orden que en algunos pueblos de España se ha puesto en la limosna para remedio de los verdaderos pobres.* Salamanca: Juan de Junta, 1545.

Rodríguez-Moñino, Antonio. *Construcción crítica y realidad histórica en la poesía española de los siglos xvi y xvii.* Madrid: Castalia, 1968.

Rogers, Francis. M. *Travels of the Infante Dom Pedro of Portugal.* Cambridge: Harvard University Press, 1961.

Roig, Adrien. "L'aventure catalane de Don Quichotte." In *Hommage à Robert Jammes,* edited by Francis Cerdan, vol. 3: 995–1003. Toulouse: Presses Universitaires du Mirail, 1994.

Romm, James S. *The Edges of the Earth in Ancient Thought: Geography, Exploration, and Fiction.* Princeton: Princeton University Press, 1992.

Rueda, Lope de. *Pasos completos.* Edited by F. García Pavón. Madrid: Taurus, 1970.

―――――. *Pasos completos.* Edited by Juan María Marín Martínez. Madrid: Espasa, 1990.

Ruiz Ramón, Francisco. *América en el teatro clásico español: estudio y textos.* Pamplona: Universidad de Navarra, 1993.

Russell, Peter. "*Don Quixote* as a Funny Book." *Modern Language Review,* 64 (1969): 312–26.

Sabine, George H. *A history of Political Theory.* London: Harrap, 1937.

Sachs, Hans. *Sämtliche Fabeln und Schwänke.* Edited by E. Goetze. Halle: Niemeyer, 1993.

Salazar Rincón, Javier. *El mundo social del "Quijote."* Madrid: Gredos, 1986.

Salomon, Noël. *La campagne de la Nouvelle Castille à la fin du XVIe siècle.* Paris: S.E.V.P.E.N., 1964.

―――――. *Sobre el tipo del "labrador rico" en el "Quijote."* Talence: Institut d'études ibériques et ibéro-americaines de l'Université de Bordeaux, 1968.

―――――. *La vida rural castellana en tiempos de Felipe II.* Barcelona: Ariel, 1982.

Sargent, Lyman Tower. "The Three Faces of Utopianism Revisited." *Utopian Studies* 5, no.1 (1994): 1–37.

Savater, Fernando. *La tarea del héroe: elementos para una ética trágica.* Barcelona: Destino, 1992.

Schaer, Roland, Gregory Claeys, and Lyman Tower Sargent, eds. *Utopia: The search for the Ideal in the Western World.* New York Public Library/Oxford University Press, 2000.

Seneca, Lucius Annaeus. *Epistles.* Translated by Richard M. Gummere. Loeb Classical Library. Cambridge: Harvard University Press, 1990.

Seymour, M. C. *Sir John Mandeville.* Authors of the Middle Ages, vol. 1. Aldershot, England: Variorum, 1993.

Las Siete Partidas del Sabio Rey Alonso el nono [sic] nueuamente glosadas por el Licenciado Gregorio López. Salamanca: Andrea de Portonariis, 1555.

Shepherd, David, ed. *Bakhtin: Carnival and Other Subjects.* Selected Papers from the Fifth International Bakhtin Conference, University of Manchester, July 1991. Amsterdam: Rodopi, 1993.

Simmel, Georg. *The Sociology of Georg Simmel.* Translated and edited by Kurt H. Wolff. Glencoe, Ill.: Free Press, 1950.

Skinner, Quentin. "Sir Thomas More's *Utopia* and the language of Renaissance humanism." In Pagden, *The Languages of Political Theory,* 123–58.

Socrate, Mario. *Prologhi al "Don Chisciotte."* Venezia: Marsilio, 1974.

Soldevila, Ferrán. *Historia de España*, vol. 4. Barcelona: Ariel, 1955.

Soler y Teròl, Lluis Maria. *Perot Roca Guinarda: Història d'aquèst bandoler.* Manresa: Impremta de San Josep, 1909.

Soriano, Marc. *Les Contes de Perrault. Culture savante et traditions populaires.* Paris: Gallimard, 1977.

Spivakovsky, Erika. *Son of the Alhambra: Diego Hurtado de Mendoza, 1504–1575.* Austin: University of Texas Press, 1970.

Stagg, Geoffrey. "*Illo tempore*: Don Quixote's discourse on the Golden Age and its antecedents." In *La Galatea de Cervantes, 400 años después*, edited by Juan Bautista Avalle-Arce, 71–90. Newark, Del.: Juan de la Cuesta, 1986.

Stallybrass, Peter, and Allon White. *The Politics and Poetics of Transgression.* Ithaca, N.Y.: Cornell University Press, 1986.

Stein, Peter. *Roman Law in European History.* Cambridge, England: Cambridge University Press, 1999.

Suárez, Francisco. *Selections From Three Works of Francisco Suárez, S.J.* Edited by James Brown Scott. Vol 2., *The Classics of International Law.* Publications of the Carnegie Endowment for International Peace, Washington. London: Oxford University Press, 1944.

Tierney, Brian. "Public Expediency and Natural Law: A Fourteenth-Century Discussion on the Origins of Government and Property." In *Authority and Power: Studies on Medieval Law and Government Presented to Walter Ullmann*, edited by Peter Linehan and Brian Tierney, 167–82. Cambridge, England: Cambridge University Press, 1980.

Todorov, Tzvetan. *The Conquest of America: The Question of the Other.* New York: Harper, 1984.

Torquemada, Juan de. *Jardín de flores curiosas.* Edited by Giovanni Allegra. Madrid: Castalia, 1982.

Troeltsch, Ernst. "The Ideas of Natural Law and Humanity in World Politics." In Gierke, *Natural Law*, 201–22.

Tuck, Richard. *Natural Rights Theories.* Cambridge, England: Cambridge University Press, 1979.

Väänänen, Veikko, ed. "Le *fabliau* de Cocagne." *Neuphilologische Mitteilungen* 48 (1947): 3–36.

Valencia, Pedro de. *Escritos sociales I: Escritos económicos.* Edited by Rafael González Cañal. Vol. 4, pt. 1 of *Obras completas.* General editor Gaspar Morocho Gayo. León, Spain: Universidad de León, 1993-2002.

———. *Escritos sociales.* Edited by Carmelo Viñas y Mey. Biblioteca de Clásicos Sociales Españoles, vol. 2. Madrid: Escuela Social de Madrid, 1945.

Vargas Llosa, Mario. "Presentación" [Introduction to] Edwin Williamson. In *El Quijote y los libros de caballerías* [Spanish translation of *The Half-Way House of Fiction*], 11–17. Madrid: Taurus, 1991.

Vassberg, David E. *Land and Society in Golden Age Castile.* Cambridge, England: Cambridge University Press, 1984.

Vázquez de Menchaca, Fernando. *Controversiarum illustrium aliarumque usu frequentium libri tres* [*Controversias fundamentales y otras de más frecuente uso.*] Edited and translated by Fidel Rodríguez Alcalde. 3 vols. Valladolid: Juan de la Cuesta, [1599]1931–33.

Vega Garcilaso de la, El Inca. *Royal Commentaries of the Incas and General History of Peru.* Translated by H.V. Livermore. Austin: University of Texas Press, 1966.

———. *Comentarios reales de los Incas.* Edited by Aurelio Miró Quesada. Caracas: Biblioteca Ayacucho, 1991.

Vilar, Pierre. *La Catalogne dans L'Espagne Moderne.* Paris: S.E.V.P.E.N., 1962.

Vilar Berrogain, Jean. *Literatura y economía: La figura satírica del arbitrista en el Siglo de Oro.* Madrid: Revista de Occidente, 1973.

Viñas y Mey, Carmelo. *El problema de la tierra en la España de los siglos XVI-XVII.* Madrid: Consejo Superior de Investigaciones Científicas, 1941.

Vitoria, Francisco de. *Political writings.* Edited by Anthony Pagden and Jeremy Lawrance. Cambridge, England: Cambridge University Press, 1991.

Waters, E. G. R., ed. *The Anglo-Norman Voyage of St Brendan.* Oxford: Clarendon, 1928.

Welsh, Alexander. *Reflections on the Hero as Quixote.* Princeton: Princeton University Press, 1981.

White, Thomas I. "*Festivitas, utilitas, et opes:* The concluding irony and philosophical purpose of Thomas More's *Utopia.*" *Albion* 10 (1978): 135–50.

Whitebook, Joel. *Perversion and Utopia: A Study in Psychoanalysis and Critical Theory.* Cambridge: MIT Press, 1996.

Williams, Lynn F. "Everyone Belongs to Everyone Else: Marriage and the Family in Recent American Utopias 1965–1985." *Utopian Studies* 1 (1987): 123–36.

Williams, Raymond. *The Country and the City.* New York: Oxford University Press, 1973.

———. *Marxism and Literature.* Oxford: Oxford University Press, 1977.

———. *Problems in Materialism and Culture.* London: Verso, 1980.

Williamson, Edwin. *The Half-Way House of Fiction: Don Quixote and Arthurian Romance.* Oxford: Clarendon, 1984.

Willis, Susan. "I Shop Therefore I Am: Is There a Place for Afro-American Culture in Commodity Culture?" In *Changing Our Own Words: Essays on*

Criticism, Theory and Writing by Black Women, edited by Cheryl A. Wall, 173–95. London: Routledge, 1989.

Wilson, Diana de Armas. *Cervantes, the Novel, and the New World.* Oxford: Oxford University Press, 2000.

Zenatti, Albino. *Storia di Campriano Contadino* [with *Capitolo di Cuccagna* and *Trionfo de' Poltroni*]. In *Scelta di curiosità letterarie inedite o rare dal secolo XIII al XIX,* vol. 69. Reprint, Bologna: Commissione Per I Testi di Lingua, 1968.

Zumthor, Paul. *Histoire littéraire de la France médiévale (VIe-XIVe siècles).* Paris: PUF, 1954.

Index